Cultural Diversity, Heritage and Human Rights

Cultural Diversity, Heritage and Human Rights investigates the problematic linkages between conserving cultural heritage, maintaining cultural diversity, defining and establishing cultural citizenship and enforcing human rights.

Heritage, both tangible and intangible, provides the basis of humanity's rich cultural diversity. Yet conflicts over cultural heritage and cultural identity around the world are the subject of media scrutiny and academic scholarship, from local disputes through to ethnic cleansing over larger regions and to Huntington's grand clash of civilizations. This volume outlines the ways in which the protection and preservation of cultural heritage is especially linked to 'cultural rights' as a form of human rights.

While there is a considerable literature dealing separately with cultural diversity, cultural heritage and human rights, this book is distinctive and has contemporary relevance in focusing on the intersection between the three concepts. *Cultural Diversity, Heritage and Human Rights* establishes a fresh approach that will interest students and practitioners alike and on which future work in the heritage field might proceed.

Michele Langfield is Associate Head (Research) in the School of History, Heritage and Society, Deakin University. She has published widely in the fields of migration, ethnicity, identity and cultural heritage. Her most recent books include *Testifying to the Holocaust* (joint editor, 2008) and *Welsh Patagonians: the Australian Connection* (co-author, 2005).

William Logan is UNESCO Professor of Heritage and Urbanism, and Director, Cultural Heritage Centre for Asia and the Pacific, Deakin University. His research interests include world heritage, Asian heritage, heritage and human rights and heritage theory. His books include: *Hanoi: Biography of a City* (2000), *The Disappearing Asian City* (2003), *Vientiane: Transformation of a Lao Landscape* (2007, co-author) and *Places of Pain and Shame* (2009, co-editor).

Máiréad Nic Craith is Professor of European Culture and Society, University of Ulster, Northern Ireland. Her research focuses primarily on the conceptual understanding of contemporary political–linguistic debates in Ireland and across Europe. She served on the European Studies sub-panel in the recent UK research assessment exercise and was elected to the Royal Irish Academy in 2009.

**Bishop McGuinness High
School Library**
1725 Highway 66 South
Kernersville, NC 27284

Key issues in cultural heritage

Series Editors: William Logan and Laurajane Smith

Also in the series:

Intangible Heritage
Laurajane Smith and Natsuko Akagawa

Places of Pain and Shame
William Logan and Keir Reeves

Cultural Diversity, Heritage and Human Rights

Intersections in theory and practice

Edited by
Michele Langfield, William Logan and
Máiréad Nic Craith

**Bishop McGuinness High
School Library**
1725 Highway 66 South
Kernersville, NC 27284

 Routledge
Taylor & Francis Group

LONDON AND NEW YORK

First published 2010
by Routledge
2 Park Square, Milton Park, Abingdon, Oxon OX14 4RN

Simultaneously published in the USA and Canada
by Routledge
270 Madison Ave, New York, NY 10016

Routledge is an imprint of the Taylor & Francis Group, an informa business

© 2010 Selection and editorial matter, Michele Langfield, William
Logan and Máiréad Nic Craith; individual chapters, their
contributors

Typeset in Garamond by Wearset Ltd, Boldon, Tyne and Wear
Printed and bound in Great Britain by TJ International, Padstow, Cornwall

All rights reserved. No part of this book may be reprinted or
reproduced or utilized in any form or by any electronic,
mechanical, or other means, now known or hereafter invented,
including photocopying and recording, or in any information
storage or retrieval system, without permission in writing from
the publishers.

British Library Cataloguing in Publication Data
A catalogue record for this book is available from the British
Library

Library of Congress Cataloging in Publication Data
Cultural diversity, heritage, and human rights: intersections in
theory and practice/edited by Michele Langfield, William Logan,
and Máiréad Nic Craith.
p. cm.
Includes index.
1. Human rights. 2. Multiculturalism. 3. Indigenous peoples' civil
rights. 4. Cultural property. 5. Culture conflict. I. Langfield,
Michele. II. Logan, William, 1948– III. Nic Craith, Máiréad.
JC571.C76 2009
323.01–dc22   2009025091

ISBN10: 0-415-56366-6 (hbk)
ISBN10: 0-415-56367-4 (pbk)
ISBN10: 0-203-86301-1 (ebk)

ISBN13: 978-0-415-56366-6 (hbk)
ISBN13: 978-0-415-56367-3 (pbk)
ISBN13: 978-0-203-86301-5 (ebk)

Contents

Part II
National versus local rights

Part III
Rights in conflict

Illustrations

Contributors

Susan Balderstone is an Australian conservation architect and Adjunct Professor in Cultural Heritage at Deakin University, Melbourne, Australia. She has worked on Australian Aid funded conservation and research projects in China and Vietnam and archaeological projects in the Middle East.

Dr Graeme Bristol teaches architecture at King Mongkut's University of Technology Thonburi in Thailand. He is the Executive Director of the Centre for Architecture and Human Rights, a Canadian foundation advancing a rights-based approach to development in the practice of architecture, engineering and planning.

Professor Hilary Charlesworth is Director of the Centre for International Governance and Justice, and Professor of International Law and Human Rights in the Faculty of Law, Australian National University. In 2005, she was awarded a Federation Fellowship by the Australian Research Council for a project on building democracy and justice after conflict.

Dr Ian Fairweather teaches social anthropology at the University of Manchester, UK. He has conducted fieldwork in North-Central Namibia on the heritage industry and the construction of national and ethnic identities. He is currently working with the North West Museums Hub on a collaborative project involving cultural diversity, social inclusion and cultural citizenship.

Professor Jérémie Gilbert is a Senior Lecturer at Middlesex University in London. He researches and publishes in the fields of minority and indigenous peoples' rights, especially on territorial rights for indigenous peoples. His latest publication is *Indigenous Peoples' Land Rights under International Law* (Transnational Publishers, November 2006).

Yuuki Hasegawa was born in Yamanashi, Japan, with Ainu and Japanese heritage. She is especially interested in Ainu culture and indigenous human rights, indigenous peoples' heritage management and indigenous exhibitions. Yuuki has an MA in International Relations from Waseda University and a Master of Cultural Heritage from Deakin University, and currently holds a research position in the Centre for Ainu and Indigenous Studies at Hokkaido University, Japan.

Associate Professor Michele Langfield is Associate Head (Research) in the School of History, Heritage and Society, Deakin University. She has published widely in the fields of migration, ethnicity, identity and cultural heritage. Her most recent books include *Testifying to the Holocaust* (joint editor, 2008) and *Welsh Patagonians: the Australian Connection* (co-author, 2005).

William Logan is UNESCO Professor of Heritage and Urbanism, and Director, Cultural Heritage Centre for Asia and the Pacific, Deakin University. His research interests include world heritage, Asian heritage, heritage and human rights, and heritage theory. His books include: *Hanoi: Biography of a City* (2000), *The Disappearing Asian City* (2003), *Vientiane: Transformation of a Lao Landscape* (2007, co-author) and *Places of Pain and Shame* (2009, co-author).

Dr Fiona Magowan is a Senior Lecturer in Social Anthropology at Queen's University Belfast. Among her books are *Melodies of Mourning: Music and Emotion in Northern Australia* (2007), *Landscapes of Indigenous Performance* (co-edited 2005) and *Telling Stories: Indigenous History and Memory in Australia and New Zealand* (co-edited 2001).

Dr Judith Nagata is Professor Emerita of Social Anthropology, York University, Canada, and Senior Research Fellow, York Centre for Asian Research. Her research relates to the politics of identity, notably ethnic and religious relations, in Southeast Asia, Taiwan and France. Recently she has focused on historical and contemporary revivals in Islam, and their transnational networks.

Máiréad Nic Craith is Professor of European Culture and Society, University of Ulster, Northern Ireland. Her research focuses primarily on the conceptual understanding of contemporary political–linguistic debates in Ireland and across Europe. She served on the European Studies sub-panel in the recent UK research assessment exercise and was elected to the Royal Irish Academy in 2009.

Dr Shalini Panjabi is an independent researcher based in Bangalore, India. Her research interests include private education in India, as well as orality, literacy and development. Her field sites have been in Kashmir and Rajasthan. In Kashmir, her research focus has been on the complex interface between development, tourism and heritage conservation in a post-conflict era.

Dr Janette Philp is a Cultural Geographer, currently employed in Research and Consultancy Services at Bond University, Queensland, Australia. Her research interests are broadly in cultural politics and the appropriation of cultural heritage by the military regime in Burma, and more specifically in the Theravada Buddhist dimensions of Burmese culture.

Dr Ana Filipa Vrdoljak is Marie Curie Fellow, Law Department, European University Institute, Florence, currently working on a European Union funded book project entitled *Law and Cultural Heritage in Europe.* She is also Senior Lecturer, Faculty of Law, University of Western Australia, Perth, and author of *International Law, Museums and the Return of Cultural Objects* (2006).

Dr Tim Winter is based at the University of Sydney. He is author of *Post-conflict Heritage, Postcolonial Tourism: culture, politics and development at Angkor* (2007), and editor of *Expressions of Cambodia: the politics of tradition, identity and change* (2006) and *Asia on Tour: exploring the rise of Asian tourism* (2008). He is also editor of the journal *Historic Environment*.

Acknowledgements

The editors wish to thank to thank Matthew Gibbons at Routledge for his good advice and support during the preparation of this volume. Most of the authors' chapters were trialled at two research workshops, the first held as part of the Australia ICOMOS National Conference on 'Extreme Heritage' at James Cook University of Northern Queensland in July 2007 and the second co-hosted by Deakin University and the University of Ulster's Academy for Irish Cultural Heritages, at Londonderry/Derry, Northern Ireland, in December 2007. Most of the figures in the volume are photographs taken by the chapter authors, but others are published courtesy of *The New Light of Myanmar* (Figures 6.1–6.3), Aaron Corn (Figure 10.1), UNESCO Hanoi Office (Figures 12.1, 12.2) and Makiko Ui (Figures 13.1–13.3).

Series general co-editors' foreword

The interdisciplinary field of Heritage Studies is now well established in many parts of the world. It differs from earlier scholarly and professional activities that focused narrowly on the architectural or archaeological preservation of monuments and sites. Such activities remain important, especially as modernization and globalization lead to new developments that threaten natural environments, archaeological sites, traditional buildings and arts and crafts. But they are subsumed within the new field that sees 'heritage' as a social and political construct encompassing all those places, artefacts and cultural expressions inherited from the past which, because they are seen to reflect and validate our identity as nations, communities, families and even individuals, are worthy of some form of respect and protection.

Heritage results from a selection process, often government-initiated and supported by official regulation; it is not the same as history, although this, too, has its own elements of selectivity. Heritage can be used in positive ways to give a sense of community to disparate groups and individuals or to create jobs on the basis of cultural tourism. It can be actively used by governments and communities to foster respect for cultural and social diversity, and to challenge prejudice and misrecognition. But it can also be used by governments in less benign ways, to reshape public attitudes in line with undemocratic political agendas or even to rally people against their neighbours in civil and international wars, ethnic cleansing and genocide. In this way there is a real connection between heritage and human rights.

This is time for a new and unique series of books canvassing the key issues dealt with in the new Heritage Studies. The series seeks to address the deficiency facing the field identified by the Smithsonian in 2005 – that it is 'vastly under-theorized'. It is time to look again at the contestation that inevitably surrounds the identification and evaluation of heritage and to find new ways to elucidate the many layers of meaning that heritage places and intangible cultural expressions have acquired. Heritage conservation and safeguarding in such circumstances can only be understood as a form of cultural politics and this needs to be reflected in heritage practice, be that in educational institutions or in the field.

It is time, too, to recognize more fully that heritage protection does not depend alone on top-down interventions by governments or the expert actions of heritage industry professionals, but must involve local communities and communities of interest. It is critical that the values and practices of communities, together with traditional management systems where such exist, are understood, respected and incorporated in management plans and policy documents of heritage resources so that communities feel a sense of 'ownership' of their heritage and take a leading role in sustaining it into the future.

This series of books aims then to identify interdisciplinary debates within Heritage Studies and to explore how they impact on the practices not only of heritage management and conservation, but also the processes of production, consumption and engagement with heritage in its many and varied forms.

William S. Logan
Laurajane Smith

Part I

Setting agendas

Chapter 1

Intersecting concepts and practices

*William Logan, Michele Langfield and
Máiréad Nic Craith*

This volume in the Key Issues in Cultural Heritage series investigates the linkages between conserving cultural heritage, maintaining cultural diversity and enforcing human rights. The three concepts of cultural diversity, heritage and human rights have been researched widely over the past 60 years since the United Nations Organization (1945) and the United Nations Educational Scientific and Cultural Organization (UNESCO 1946) were formed and the *Universal Declaration of Human Rights* (*UDHR*) was adopted (1948). In the scholarly world, however, the concepts have tended to be studied separately, with the various disciplines focusing more on one concept than the others, whereas, in fact, the concepts developed alongside each other and are inextricably linked. Recognition of these linkages influences the way in which the purpose of heritage conservation is seen and heritage protection work is carried out.

These linkages are enshrined today in much of the agenda and discourse of the UN and its associated global bodies, such as UNESCO, as well as in some nation states and local governments and their agencies. The linkages appear to be well understood in the international committees and secretariats of the global heritage bodies. In 2008 the International Council on Monuments and Sites (ICOMOS), for instance, ranked human rights issues associated with heritage, both natural and cultural, as one of seven 'new and complex global pressures' impacting negatively on conservation outcomes (ICOMOS 2008: 5). But the linkages remain poorly understood by the heritage conservation profession in many countries, where too often heritage work is seen as merely technical. It is essential for those engaged in heritage conservation projects to understand the broader economic, political and social context of their work and to recognize that official heritage interventions can have many motives, be used to achieve political aims, and, at their worst, can undermine rather than strengthen community identity, cultural diversity and human rights.

Setting agendas

Globalization is a buzz word of our time and, driven by electronic information technologies and reflected in global movements of capital, resources and workers, its impact on the heritage field is proving to be enormous. Indeed, another volume in the Key Issues in Cultural Heritage series – *Heritage and Globalization* (Labadi and Long, in press) has been devoted to this specifically. But the trend towards uniting all parts of the globe and all of the world's people into a single economic system has a long history going back at least to the great explorations of the fifteenth century and including the subsequent formation of colonial empires. In the mid-twentieth century, during the last stage of the Second World War, another significant chapter in the history of globalization flowed from a series of meetings held in the Bretton Woods in the United States. At these meetings representatives of nations fighting on the Allied side of the war strove to find ways to prevent another such global catastrophe and to facilitate post-war recovery and development. Out of these meetings grew the United Nations and the 'specialized agencies' associated with but independent of it, such as the World Health Organization, Food and Agricultural Organization, UNICEF and International Labour Organization, as well as the International Monetary Fund, the World Bank and, in the heritage field, UNESCO.

Many commentators see these organizations as key agencies of both economic and cultural globalization. Their various resolutions and charters seek to enforce on the member states a common set of principles governing political, economic, social and cultural attitudes and behaviour. The formation of these organizations reflected the spirit of goodwill and optimism that infused twentieth-century modernism (Logan 2002). The goals reflected the key interlocking elements in the modernist outlook – universalism, utopianism and belief in humanity's steady progress towards better things, usually defined in terms of the material conditions of life. It was an optimistic and idealistic outlook that led architects, planners, economists, sociologists, development workers and others to cut away from tradition and to embrace new 'modern' ideas and practices that could be applied around the world regardless of differences in local cultures. This immediately set up an ongoing global/national tension within the efforts to achieve one of the chief purposes of the United Nations Organization, which was to encourage co-operation between nation states in solving international economic, social, cultural and humanitarian problems.

Development of the cultural aspects was relatively slow on the whole but, although the UN does not play a direct role in cultural heritage conservation, some of its activities have come to have an effect on heritage, especially through the promotion of cultural diversity and human rights. The concept and discourse of human rights has been described as a unique product of modernity, a new invention of modern times, with so-called 'first generation' human rights – civil and political rights – emerging in the Age of Enlightenment of the seventeenth and eighteenth centuries in 'response to the might of the modern state in which immense power of coercion and violence had been concentrated' (Chen 2006: 487, 506). It was only after the Holocaust, according to Geoffrey Robertson (1999: xiv), that individual agents of the state were deemed to be answerable before the law for 'crimes against humanity', which led to new attempts to create universal standards such as the UN's 1948 *UDHR*. However, when Article 22 of the *UDHR* insists that '[e]veryone ... is entitled to the realization, through national efforts and international co-operation..., of the economic, social and cultural rights indispensable for his dignity and the free development of his personality', the emphasis on individual rather than group or community rights is clear, and the tension between collective and individual rights continues to haunt theory and practice today, a point returned to later in this chapter and in the case study chapters that follow.

Indeed, 'second generation' human rights – that is social and economic rights, especially directed towards the group – did not emerge until later, in the 1960s, in response to the new forms of social and economic inequality produced by capitalism and industrialization (Chen 2006: 506) and in the context of the Cold War and decolonization (Yusuf 2005). The UN's *International Covenant on Civil and Political Rights 1966 (ICCPR)* and the *International Covenant on Economic, Social and Cultural Rights 1966* are increasingly recognized to have relevance to the management of cultural heritage. While not specifically mentioning cultural heritage, Article 15 of the latter instrument affirms that States party to the Covenant 'recognize the right of everyone ... to take part in cultural life'. In the same year, 1966, UNESCO's General Conference went further, adopting a *Declaration on the Principles of International Cultural Cooperation* that asserted more clearly the link between human rights, human dignity and culture: 'Each culture has a dignity and value which must be respected and preserved', 'Every people has the right and duty to develop its culture' and 'In their rich variety and diversity,... all cultures form part of the common heritage belonging to all mankind.'

It was during the immediate post-Second World War years and in the optimistic, modernist spirit that UNESCO and the other global organizations specifically focused on cultural heritage – the International Council on Museums (ICOM), the International Centre for the Study of the Preservation and Restoration of Cultural Property (ICCROM) and ICOMOS – were established. While official programmes of heritage protection had been around since at least the fifth century AD (Jokilehto 1999: 6), the distinctive new chapter that the twentieth century brought to cultural heritage protection was the establishment of a globalized effort over and above although still very much dependent on the work of nation states (Logan 2002). This led to a new cultural heritage bureaucracy at the international level, the development of new sets of standards for the world to follow, and a new set of places deemed to be of world heritage significance.

UNESCO was founded in 1946 with its headquarters in Paris, the result of a French recommendation at the first UN conference in 1945 that the governments should meet at another conference to draw up the statute of an international organization focusing on cultural cooperation (Valderrama 1995: 21). UNESCO's Constitution makes clear the organization's ambitions and clearly connects the trilogy of concepts which this volume is exploring. Adopted in London in November 1945, it starts with the key sentence 'That since wars begin in the minds of men, it is in the minds of men that the defences of peace must be constructed.' These words have remained even though the Constitution has been amended at least 17 times. They reflect the Second World War context but hold a greater socio-psychological truth: that when meeting peoples with cultures strange to us, we react too easily with hostility, rather than seeking to understand, accommodate, negotiate and compromise. Cultural diversity is, therefore, often the cause of conflict – or at least the excuse for it. International normative statements insist, however, that humans have the right to maintain their diversity, their own or their group's identity, their cultural heritage. This is a process essentially of intercultural dialogue and understanding, a process that the UNESCO Constitution from 1946 onwards has seen as being fundamental if greater tolerance and, ultimately, peace are to be achieved.

UNESCO's operations were initially divided into the three sectors signalled in its name, although today the natural sciences and the social and human sciences are dealt with in separate sectors and a fifth sector has been added to focus on communications and information technology. The remit of the Culture Sector has grown over 60 years and especially since the World Conference on Cultural Policies, Mexico City, 1982 when the notion of 'culture' was broadened from a narrow, high art definition to be seen in its widest sense, as the whole complex of distinctive spiritual, material, intellectual and emotional features that characterize a society and social group. It includes not only the arts and letters, but also modes of life, the fundamental rights of the human being, value systems, traditions and beliefs (*Mexico Declaration on Cultural Policies 1982*).

It was this shift that ultimately made possible the expansion of UNESCO's heritage conservation activities from the tangible – heritage places under the *World Heritage Convention 1972* and heritage artefacts through its work relating to collections management, libraries, archives and museums – to intangible cultural heritage (practices, representations, expressions, knowledge, skills, such as language, oral history, song, dance, music, as well as intellectual property) under the 2003 *Convention for the Safeguarding of Intangible Heritage*. Again, another volume in this Key Issues series focuses specifically on intangible heritage, its emergence as a global concern and the efforts to safeguard it (see Smith and Akagawa 2009).

It was during the 1990s that the diversity theme, and especially the protection of diversity, began to emerge as a major focus of UNESCO activities, in large part due to fears that globalization was threatening the survival of the world's cultural diversity (Logan 2007a: 36). The UN's 'Decade for Cultural Development' (1988–1997), which had cultural diversity as a key theme, ended with the World Commission on Culture and Development presenting its final report under the title *Our Creative Diversity* (UN 1995). By 2000, the UNESCO Director-General, Koïchiro Matsuura, had put in place a scheme called 'Proclamation of Master Pieces of the Oral and Intangible Heritage of Humanity', which was to be the advance guard of the 2003 *Convention for the Safeguarding of Intangible Heritage*. The intention was to recognize and protect embodied cultural heritage in societies where perhaps the built heritage was less significant. The push to protect intangible as well as tangible heritage can be seen, therefore, as a further step in recognizing cultural diversity, and the 2003 *Intangible CH Convention* and the 2005 *International Convention on the Protection of the Diversity of Cultural Contents and Artistic Expressions* seek to engage states in binding legal instruments representing a commitment to cultural diversity.

In October 2000, UNESCO's Executive Board invited the Director-General to prepare a declaration aimed at 'promoting cultural diversity in the context of globalization'. The resulting instrument was the *Universal Declaration on Cultural Diversity*, adopted by UNESCO's General Conference in 2001. The UNESCO web site refers to it as the founding act of a new ethic for the twenty-first century, providing the international community, for the first time, with a 'wide-ranging standard-setting instrument to underpin its conviction that respect for cultural diversity and intercultural dialogue is one of the surest guarantees of development and peace'. This was followed by the Johannesburg World Summit on Sustainable Development in September 2002, which adopted a Declaration that recognizes cultural diversity as a collective force that must be promoted to ensure sustainable development.

Meanwhile, indeed since the 1960s, human rights have come to include specifically the maintenance of one's culture within the concept of 'cultural rights'. Even though many human rights scholars have argued that cultural rights are a particularly neglected category of human rights (O'Keefe 1999: 187; Logan 2007a, 2008), the position taken in the *ICCPR* of 1966 is now well accepted in international discourse and the programmes of global organizations; that is,

> In those States in which ethnic, religious or linguistic minorities exist persons belonging to such minorities shall not be denied the right, in community with other members of their group, to enjoy their own culture, to profess their own religion, or to use their own language.

It was this agenda set by the *ICCPR* that UNESCO sought to extend with its own normative statements, notably the 2001 *Universal Declaration on Cultural Diversity*, which declares in Article 5 that:

Cultural rights are an integral part of human rights, which are universal, indivisible and interdependent. The flourishing of creative diversity requires the full implementation of cultural rights.... All persons have therefore the right to express themselves and to create and disseminate their work in the language of their choice, and particularly in their mother tongue; all persons are entitled to quality education and training that fully respect their cultural identity; and all persons have the right to participate in the cultural life of their choice and conduct their own cultural practices, subject to respect for human rights and fundamental freedoms.

Gaps, inconsistencies and lack of commitment

In this volume, Hilary Charlesworth outlines the linkage between human rights and one of the UNESCO programmes that receives relatively little attention in the heritage literature – the Memory of the World Programme. She argues that, while the areas of cultural heritage and human rights have developed in quite separate ways and with different emphases and purposes, there is room for much more engagement and dialogue between these two fields. Indeed, they have much to learn from each other. She also suggests that human rights should itself be understood as heritage.

Looking at the extensive UNESCO's flagship programme, World Heritage, on the other hand, it is also true that human rights has not assumed as great a presence as it might have done; indeed, it is perhaps even surprising that human rights features so little as a key universal value and reason for the inscription of historic sites. Certainly Robben Island is inscribed for its link with Nelson Mandela, leader of the South African democracy movement, and the fight against apartheid. But where are sites reminding the world of the democratic and/or independence struggles of racial and ethnic groups elsewhere? Some groups, like the Kurds, are split between several states and exist as ethnic minorities in each, whereas together they have more people than the majority of states in the UN. Denied statehood, their culture is under challenge in often hostile 'host states'. Gorée in Senegal is inscribed for its link to the infamous New World slave trade that ended in the nineteenth century, but what about sites to commemorate the end of colonialism? Auschwitz-Birkenau and Hiroshima's Genbaku Dome are symbols of technological warfare and provide moral lessons to us all, but what about other genocides and massacres?

Much of the difficulty lies in the nature of UNESCO as an intergovernmental organization. How can difficult sites become listed if this is likely to offend or be opposed by a Member State? Olwen Beazley (in press) reveals the intense international politics that were played out behind the nomination and inscription of the Genbaku Dome and attempts by the US to derail the process. How would France react to a Vietnamese nomination of the cultural landscape of Dien Bien Phu, the site of one of the greatest battles in history (Stanley Karnow, quoted in Simpson 1994: xi) where not only the French troops were routed but European colonialism in Asia effectively came to an end?

Clearly the implementation of conservation programmes based on the interlocking concepts of cultural diversity, heritage and human rights is far from simple or easy. Part of the problem lies in the contradictions and inconsistencies in the way the concepts themselves are conceived and used. Paradoxically, some attempts to protect cultural diversity represent threats to other human rights. While cultural heritage can be a unifying force, emphasizing a nation's shared identity, non-democratic governments, especially in multi-ethnic states, can also use it in negative ways to encourage community involvement in wars, for ethnic cleansing or even genocide. Often this means forcing groups to adopt the dominant culture and can lead to the destruction of cultural identity.

However, Albro and Bauer, editors of a 2005 issue of *Human Rights Dialogue* focusing on 'cultural rights', note that while cultural rights claims are being recognized as an 'important means for the recuperation of identity and as an essential basis for advancing social justice, there is still weak political commitment to cultural rights by national governments' (2005: 2–3). Indeed, it is lack of action by governments that is probably the largest threat to cultural diversity, cultural heritage and cultural rights. In some countries with neo-liberal governments the focus of 'human rights' has been shifted towards protection of individual property rights. In the wake of the 11 September 2001 destruction of the New York Trade Center, there has also been a focus on 'national security' and the 'war on terror'. In Australia, for instance, critics argue that there has been a reduction in civil liberties in the pursuit of 'national security' on the one hand, but, on the other hand, an emphasis on the 'human right' of individuals to do what one wants with property (Logan 2007b: 218). In some other countries, regimes seem to support cultural heritage but this is part of a strategy of legitimizing their own position of power.

The global heritage organizations quietly resist the misuse of heritage at the national government level where they can, through the development of policy statements and the promotion of professional practice. It has also moved to engage the local communities in heritage identification and management. The notion of 'World Heritage' is based on the idea of 'outstanding universal value' but may not always coincide with local ideals. UNESCO used the 'Linking Universal and Local Values' conference held in Amsterdam in 2003 (published in 2004 as *World Heritage Papers 13*) to promote the view that heritage protection does not depend alone on top-down interventions by governments or the expert actions of heritage industry professionals, but must involve local communities.

This is especially important where indigenous minorities and cultures are concerned. Jérémie Gilbert's chapter in this volume argues that for indigenous communities a particular way of life – their culture – is normally associated intimately with the use of their lands. Even though the notion of heritage encompasses traditional practices in a broad sense, including for example language, art, music, dance, song, sacred sites and ancestral human remains, in the case of indigenous peoples, the preservation of heritage is deeply embedded in and linked to the protection of traditional territories. Gilbert notes that, although the notion of cultural heritage does not appear as such in the *UDHR*, the *ICCPR* protects the right of minorities to enjoy their own culture and that, under such protection, the Human Rights Committee has developed a specific protection for indigenous peoples' land rights. Gilbert's chapter shows the complexities involved when this jurisprudence establishes a 'cultural test' that examines the connection between tradition and modernity in its effort to establish a link between cultural rights and land rights for indigenous peoples.

In her chapter, Máiréad Nic Craith considers the concept of indigeneity within contemporary Europe and political–legal frameworks that imbue it with significance as a pre-requisite for ethnic minority recognition and identity maintenance. By exploring in particular the notion of 'linguistic human rights', she reveals the precarious position of migrant linguistic heritage in the region because states, for a variety of conceptual and practical reasons, are reluctant to afford official recognition to intangible cultural heritages of migrants. The debates on the management of linguistic diversity are evolving, however, and with specific reference to the European Charter for Regional and Minority Languages, the chapter charts the gradual emergence of migrant linguistic heritage onto the European agenda.

National versus local heritage

The first part of this volume focuses on agenda setting at the global and, in the case of Nic Craith's chapter, regional levels and highlights the tensions at play between global institutions and nation states in terms of, first, notions of cultural identity, heritage and human rights and, second, responsibility for managing these aspects of the life of communities and individuals. In Part II of the volume, the chapters focus primarily on tensions between national and local values and the conflicts that arise where an official version of heritage is promoted by nation states, usually as part of a strategy to achieve social cohesion and political unity, to the exclusion of minority group views.

From a state perspective, heritage has been an important tool in engendering a homogeneous 'national' identity (Crooke 2000; Nic Craith 2008). Heritage is a way 'in which the nation slowly constructs for itself a sort of collective social memory'. The emergence of nationalism coincided with a particular representation of the past which was designated as 'national heritage' (Graham *et al.* 2004: 27). States began selectively 'binding their chosen high points and memorable achievements into an unfolding "national story"'

(Hall 2005: 25). Nation states developed a concept of a particular national heritage to consolidate a sense of national identity and to assimilate or dispense with competing regional or minority groups. Many nations established museums and folklore societies, which played a formative role in the nation-building process (Crooke 2000; Nic Craith 2008; Shannan Peckham 2003). Museums became a tool whereby nation states represented themselves at local, national and international levels. Moreover, these national institutions endorsed and served to legitimize the state version of heritage. Museums anchored official memory. 'Ironically the process involves both remembering and forgetting, inclusion and exclusion' (Davidson 2004: 186).

In the past 50 years, many of the international charters have reinforced the value of a national heritage (Ahmad 2006: 296). The *Venice Charter* of 1964 highlighted the need to formulate specific national principles (Congress of Architects and Technicians of Historic Monuments 1964). It advocated that principles for the preservation and restoration of ancient buildings should be agreed on an international basis, 'with each country being responsible for applying the plan within the framework of its own culture and traditions'. On the European continent, the Council of Europe designed and adopted many charters that dealt specifically with the national context of European countries. Consider, for example, the Council's *European Cultural Convention* (1954) which encouraged contracting parties to 'take appropriate measures to safeguard and to encourage the development of its national contribution to the common cultural heritage of Europe'.

Graham *et al.* (2004) suggest that the flexibility of the concept of heritage has made it a very adaptable tool for nation-building. 'We create the heritage that we require and manage it for a range of purposes defined by the needs and demands of our present societies' (Graham 2002: 1004). The flexibility of the concept is both a strength and a weakness. Loulanski (2006: 210) suggests that its most typical features are 'dynamism and elasticity'. 'The definition of what makes up heritage is said to be "elastic" at its broadest, including "anything inherited from the past," and at its narrowest comprised of items of historic or cultural significance, as judged by heritage experts and professionals.' In this volume, Judith Nagata argues that the elastic banner of heritage has become increasingly aligned with other non-governmental and activist causes and has stretched to include human rights issues. In her case study of Malaysia, she indicates that the notion of human rights has been merged with unique local interpretations of 'Asian values'. The final outcome is highly dependent on economic interests and political will at a national level.

The concept of nation state as it emerged in eighteenth- and nineteenth-century Europe in particular, moulded notions of shared heritage in order to emphasize a common political destiny for a 'national family'. The 'family members' shared a mutual ethnicity, a unique history and a particular heritage. Moreover, this 'national family' had its attachment to particular locales within state territories. Specific forms of heritage were anchored to particular territories or cultural landscapes. In Europe, for example, the true spirit of the Irish nation was located primarily in the Irish-speaking regions on the west coast. In Finland, the spiritual home was in Karelia. In Austria, it was located in the mountains of Tyrol (Nic Craith 2008). However, the promotion of national heritages did not include the full range of cultural diversity within state boundaries and the notion of family unity did not augur well for minorities. Ana Vrodljak's contribution, for example, illustrates the centrifugal and centripetal forces at work within Iraq. On the one hand, there is a range of ethnic, religious and linguistic minorities within the territorial boundaries. On the other, the concept of a rich cultural, national heritage has been emphasized to give a sense of unity and nationality to these disparate groups.

The process of identification of 'national heritage' did not necessarily involve negotiation and consent from all family members. In the past, dominant strands of society claimed ownership of the national heritage. The elite determined which elements of heritage were worthy of affirmation or preservation in the public space at the national level. Frequently, the more powerful groups ignored diversity in favour of a one-dimensional narrative. They had the authority and the means to locate fixed representations of heritage in specific sites (Atkinson 2005). This can be aligned with the notion of 'cultural capital' as developed by Pierre Bourdieu (1977). Bourdieu pointed to the capacity of the ruling elite to exercise power in the process of selecting and determining dominant ideologies. In her case study, Janette Philp highlights the politicization of Burma's cultural heritage under the military rule of the State Peace and Development Council. In order to assimilate Burma's diverse ethnic and religious cultures into a national identity that is ethnically Burman and Buddhist, the State promoted 'Myanmar' traditional cultural values that are historically connected with the monarchy, thereby legitimizing its own political authority. This process of selection has ignored the cultural heritage of other ethnic and religious minority groups. As a result, the 'national' cultural heritage hardly reflects the community's own sense of identity and history.

In the late twentieth and early twenty-first centuries, there has been a radical change in the conceptualization of nation states as homogeneous units. The acknowledgement of cultural diversity within state boundaries has served as the catalyst for a more inclusive review of 'national' heritages in some instances. In Britain, for example, Black History Month is held every October with the aim of promoting knowledge of Black History and experience (Nic Craith 2007). It also endeavours to 'disseminate information on positive Black contributions to British society and heighten the confidence and awareness of Black people in their cultural history'. Ultimately, the Black History Month aims to restore some inclusivity to British history and to challenge conventional national narratives (Constantine-Simms 2005: 12).

One of the big questions is the extent to which societies are required to accommodate and recognize all cultural differences and languages – or whether any such recognition should be confined to indigenous groups (Nic Craith 2006: 159). It is reasonable for a state to suggest that it would be impossible to give parity of esteem to each and every potential group claiming distinctiveness. Moreover, issues of recognition appear to rely on the categorization of some cultural groups as 'more entitled' to recognition than others. A typology of minorities has been constructed by several sociologists (cf. Eriksen 1993; Kymlicka 1995; Fenton 1999; May 2001). Such taxonomies usually prioritize indigenous rather than migrant groups in a state. This principle is reflected in the Council of Europe's *Framework Convention for the Protection of National Minorities* which was opened for signature in February 1995. Although there is no definition of 'national minorities' in this Convention, the very title suggests priority is given to natives.

Several chapters in this volume focus on the recognition of indigenous peoples (or lack of it) shown by various national governments. Michele Langfield argues that the rights of indigenous peoples in Australia do not have adequate safeguards. Her chapter explores the heritage rights of different cultural groups in the British Commonwealth, before presenting a case for a different framework of human rights for indigenous Australians, who clearly distinguish themselves from other minorities. Fiona Magowan focuses on the intangible cultural heritage of Australian Aboriginal groups and the pressures on them to share their cultural knowledge with outsiders in arenas such as cultural tourism and government development projects.

These chapters explore tensions between indigenous groups and settler groups in the development of a national narrative. While settled groups may encourage minorities to co-exist, they generally do not support the agenda of self-determination. The national heritage is greater than any local – even indigenous – narrative. Settler groups reject the notion of differentiated citizenship, favouring instead the principle of universal individual rights – which runs counter to the indigenous people's aspiration for shared sovereignty and collective rights (Havemann 1999: 332). Settler groups may endeavour to rewrite the indigenous culture to fit the 'national story'. In doing so, they create what Magowan suggests is an external politics of authorization that does not always converge with indigenous expectations.

Tensions between indigenous peoples and settler groups also spill into the arena of tradition versus modernity. To what extent must traditional ways be sacrificed in order to achieve progress? In a case study of urban planning and human rights in Bangkok, Graeme Bristol explores the Rattanakosin Master Plan designed to beautify the royal and monumental Rattanakosin district. Here, city planners, rushing to modernize the region and desperate to gain some economic benefits from tourism, are rendering local, vibrant, vernacular histories invisible. Different visions of the city, of the past, and of human rights are colliding in the struggle to modernize and capitalize.

Ian Fairweather's contribution points to a more successful reconciliation of the traditional and the modern in heritage performances in Namibia.

He explores the extent to which indigenous groups are expected to remain 'traditional' for the economic benefit of the nation. To what extent are such groups expected to pander to the expectations of tourists who come in search of an authentic, traditional past. Although heritage is performed in a traditional way by the locals, such performances can actually subvert or even contest expectations. Performers combine the traditional and the modern by locating themselves in modern cosmopolitan collectivities, while remaining distinctively local.

Rights in conflict

Human rights are often evoked when claims in favour of cultural diversity and heritage (particularly intangible) are at stake, but such claims are fraught with contradictions and inconsistencies. For instance, often groups claim a cultural practice as a human right, even though others may claim that the practice contravenes laws and/or human rights instruments. Also some forms of heritage contravene the individual's right to take an independent line and to choose his or her own lifestyle. Indeed, as the Academy of European Law (2005) has noted:

> Cultural rights are torn between two different but linked meanings: first, as a sub-category of human rights, cultural rights are endowed with universal character, which is a major characteristic and postulate of human rights as a whole; second, cultural rights are clearly related to cultural diversity and cultural diversity is an obvious challenge to the very idea of universal human rights.

Although recognized as human rights since the 1948 *UDHR*, the understanding and application of the notion of cultural rights has been complicated by ongoing international debates over the principle of universalism, over *whose* rights should be given precedence in cases of contestation, and over the primacy of individual or collective/group rights, the latter often involving claims of self-determination.

A major issue that has arisen as a result of recent UNESCO Declarations (for example, its *Universal Declaration on Cultural Diversity* 2001) and Conventions (specifically the *Convention for the Safeguarding of the Intangible Cultural Heritage* 2003, and the *International Convention on the Protection of the Diversity of Cultural Contents and Artistic Expressions* 2005) is that, in practice, some cultural rights and values still practised in religious or ethnic minority groups contravene individual human rights, particularly in relation to the less powerful in society, such as women and children, stateless persons and the weak or destitute. Cultural practices such as child sacrifice, arranged marriages and genital mutilation are cases in point. The 2003 Convention, which came into force in 2006, has led to major concerns over such human rights abuses (Kurin 2004; Logan 2007a: 37, 43; Logan 2008: 446; Smith and Akagawa 2009: 2). Those who framed the Convention sought to mini-mize such abuses with the statement in Article 2 that:

> For the purposes of this Convention, consideration will be given solely to such intangible cultural heritage as is compatible with existing human rights instruments, as well as with the requirements of mutual respect among communities, groups and individuals, and of sustainable development.

For many, however, the concern remains. Valentine Moghadam and Manilee Bagheritari, for instance, look at the cultural rights of women in their 2007 article in UNESCO's journal, *Museum International*. They argue that under the Intangible Cultural Heritage Convention women could be 'vulnerable to manipulation or dismissal of women's participation and rights' because of its gender-neutral language and because it fails to refer to the UN's 1979 *Convention on the Elimination of All Forms of Discrimination against Women* (CEDAW) and other women's rights instruments. Their fundamental point is that ' "culture" is not a valid justification for gender inequality' (p. 11). It follows that cultural forms that represent and perpetuate gender inequality should not be safeguarded.

Taking a case study approach, the chapters in Part III of this volume examine various claims for cultural recognition made by diverse groups of people in areas of the world where conflict between different interests has occurred. In two earlier publications, William Logan (2007a, 2008) fore-shadowed some of the global issues of debate mentioned above, setting an agenda for further research at both the national and local levels. Here, Logan uses the example of the Tay Nguyen hill tribes of central Vietnam and recent political and social turbulence involving state-initiated population migra-tions into the central uplands, land tenure and land use changes, and the intervention of Christian sects notably from the United States and of anti-communist overseas Vietnamese, again mostly based in the United States. He argues that in this case claims to the community's right to protect tradi-tional culture, including local religious practices, conflict with the right to religious freedom, especially at the individual level.

Focusing on the inscription of the Tay Nguyen peoples' gong-playing skills onto the UNESCO 'Masterpieces of the Oral and Intangible Heritage of Humanity', Logan canvasses a series of key dilemmas critical to cultural heritage theory and practice. How are the cultural rights of ethnic minority groups best protected? Is the commodification of their cultures through cul-tural tourism a problem that requires a policy response? How do we deal with situations where local communities prefer to achieve higher standards of living by rejecting tradition and modernizing their cultures? How do we deal in practice with situations where cultural heritage is used by powerful actors, both domestic and external, to obtain political goals that are essentially unrelated to heritage conservation? How do we respond as professionals to instances where various claims to cultural practices based on human rights are in conflict with each other?

These issues spill over into other contributions in this volume. Yuuki Hasegawa outlines the rights movement and cultural revitalization of her own people, the Ainu, one of the indigenous peoples of Japan. From the mid-nineteenth century, Ainu cultural practices were forbidden through a forced assimilation policy, and their land and natural resources removed by the Japanese government through dispossession and annexation. These policies caused the Ainu to experience radical cultural, social and economical change, which almost led to the loss of their entire culture. Despite discrimination and marginalization over a long period, the 1960s marked the rise of the Ainu rights movement with the specific aim of regaining collective rights as indigenous peoples, rather than simply the rights of an ethnic minority. Over the next three decades, the rights movement improved the overall situation of Ainu within Japanese society and contributed to the revival of their cultural heritage and identity. Eventually, in June 2008 the Japanese Diet unanimously passed a resolution recognizing Ainu as an indigenous people of Japan who have their own language, culture and religion (*Japan Times*, 7 June 2008). Despite this, the Ainu still face significant social and economic hardship with a high proportion of the population living in situations of extreme poverty. The continued reinvigoration of their culture will depend on securing the most basic of human rights – their daily survival needs.

As well as conflicts between local ethnic and indigenous groups and their unsympathetic governments or diasporic populations with different political agendas, ethnic or religious groups in multicultural societies frequently conflict with each other in terms of ownership of heritage spaces and lack respect for each others' cultural identities. Susan Balderstone in her chapter describes the separation of the ethnic communities of Cyprus after the Greece-inspired coup against the Greek Cypriot President of Cyprus in 1974 and the Turkish invasion. Greek Cypriots fled to the south while Turkish Cypriots moved to the north. Both left heritage places and cultural connections in the zones they had vacated. The Turkish military continues to occupy the northern third of the island, creating human rights issues related to missing persons, property rights and access. Continuing efforts to solve the Cyprus problem have yet to deal with the underlying difficulties of cultural and ethnic identities and how they could combine in a culturally diverse, reunified Cyprus Republic. The failure of each community to recognize the sensibilities of the other in relation to cultural heritage conservation does not assist the process.

Bi-communal, cultural heritage conservation projects funded by the European Union have, however, begun to highlight issues of identity and human rights in relation to social and intangible heritage, particularly religion. The projects require cooperation between mutually distrustful, fearful and disdainful communities for the sake of common objectives – social and economic well-being. Cyprus has apparently opted for conflict management rather than resolution, with both sides focused on achieving prosperity. But there is an opportunity for participants in cultural heritage projects to contribute to reunification by developing a genuine understanding and respect in relation to each community's cultural identity, and demonstrating this in the way the cultural heritage of Cyprus is conserved and presented.

In unstable parts of the world, where fighting occurs over a protracted period, the destruction of cultural heritage can be both deliberate and devastating. The repair and rebuilding of physical heritage, as well as the recovery of less tangible heritage such as community beliefs and traditions is sometimes difficult to achieve. There is, however, a growing acceptance amongst practitioners that cultural heritage policies in post-conflict zones cannot proceed in isolation but must be incorporated within the broader objectives of redevelopment and recovery, including the accommodation of cultural diversity and human rights. The contribution by Tim Winter and Shalini Panjabi investigates these issues in the context of Srinagar, the capital city of Indian-administered Kashmir and a city well known for its pre-modern urban landscapes but one which has suffered over 15 years of conflict and extensive damage. At the same time, politically and culturally, it remains the centre of a wider collective identity within the Kashmir Valley. A holistic approach, as suggested above, to the restoration of the built environment and the socio-cultural and economic needs of the population can only be achieved when wider goals of cultural sovereignty, multiculturalism and security are also addressed.

Heritage conservation as cultural practice

It is now 60 years since the *Universal Declaration of Human Rights* was adopted by the United Nations as a key instrument in its programme to reduce conflicts between peoples of different cultures. Despite this, human rights issues feature little in the literature of the interdisciplinary field of cultural heritage studies. This is no doubt part of a more general problem referred to by the Smithsonian Institute (2005) as the field's under-theorized state. Conferences, workshops and their associated reports and proceedings sometimes see the need to protect minority cultures as part of a more inclusive, even democratic approach to heritage conservation but do not refer directly to the link with cultural rights or human rights, even where such events flag cultural diversity as a key component of their overall theme.

Heritage industry professionals in the past have commonly seen cultural heritage protection as either a technical or a management matter – a matter of applying the best or latest scientific solution or the appropriate management strategy to preserve or restore an artefact, monument or site (Logan 2008: 439; Garcìa Canclini 1995: 108). This was never true: heritage

protection has always been about resource management and resource alloca-
tion, and therefore always had a powerful political dimension. With the
focus shifting towards intangible forms of heritage – 'living heritage embodied in people' efforts to protect heritage are more likely to run up against
what many people consider to be infringements of human rights. The paradigm has shifted so that cultural heritage in both its formation and protection is now best seen as cultural practice.

As heritage professionals we engage in seemingly innocuous heritage conservation projects but we need to be aware of the wider socio-political
context and consider the likely impact of our work. We need to find ways –
as practitioners, policy-makers, researchers and educators – to learn to work
within this new paradigm, to deal with the many disjunctures between conservation and human rights principles, and to engage more fully with the
public whose cultural heritage we are seeking to conserve.

Bibliography

Academy of European Law (2005) *Cultural Rights as Human Rights*. Available at
www.iue.it/AEL/Projects/Cultural Rights.shtml, accessed 13 December 2005.
Ahmad, Y. (2006) 'The Scope and Definitions of Heritage: From Tangible to Intan-
gible,' *International Journal of Heritage Studies* 12 (3): 292–300.
Albro, R. and Bauer, J. (2005) 'Introduction,' *Human Rights Dialogue: An Interna-
tional Forum for Debating Human Rights* (series 2) 12: 2–3.
Atkinson, D. (2005) 'Heritage,' in D. Atkinson, P. Jackson, D. Sibley and N. Wash-
bourne (eds) *Cultural Geography: A Critical Dictionary of Key Concepts*, London, New
York: I. B. Tauris.
Beazley, O. (in press) 'Politics, Power and Representation: The Hiroshima Peace
Memorial (Genbaku Dome) as World Heritage,' in S. Labadi and C. Long (eds)
Heritage and Globalization, London: Routledge.
Bourdieu, P. (1977) *Outline of a Theory of Practice*, Cambridge: Cambridge University
Press.
Chen, A. H. Y. (2006) 'Conclusion: Comparative Reflections on Human Rights in
Asia,' in R. Peerenboom, C. J. Petersen and A. H. Y. Chen (eds) *Human Rights in
Asia: A Comparative Legal Study of Twelve Asian Jurisdictions, France and the USA*,
London: Routledge, 487–516.
Congress of Architects and Technicians of Historic Monuments (CATHM) (1964) *The
International Charter for the Conservation and Restoration of Monuments and Sites*, Venice
(the *Venice Charter 1964*). Available at www.icomos.org/venice_charter.html.
Constantine-Simms, D. (2005) 'Black History in Britain: the African British Experi-
ence,' *Black Heritage Today*, October/November: 12–14.
Council of Europe (1954) *European Cultural Convention*, Paris. Available at http://
conventions.coe.int/Treaty/EN/Treaties/Html/018.htm.
Council of Europe (1995) *Framework Convention for the Protection of National Minori-
ties*. Available at http://conventions.coe.int/Treaty/EN/Treaties/Html/157.htm.
Crooke, E. (2000) *Politics, Archaeology and the Creation of a National Museum in
Ireland: An Expression of National Life*, Dublin: Irish Academic Press.

Davidson, P. (2004) 'Museums and the Re-shaping of Memory,' in G. Corsane (ed.) *Heritage, Museums and Galleries: an Introductory Reader*, London and New York: Routledge.

Eriksen, T. (1993) *Ethnicity and Nationalism: Anthropological Perspectives*, London: Pluto Press.

Fenton, S. (1999) *Ethnicity: Racism, Class and Culture*, Basingstoke, New York: Basingstoke: Macmillan.

Garcìa Canclini, N. (1995) *Hybrid Cultures: Strategies for Entering and Leaving Modernity*, Minneapolis: University of Minnesota Press.

Graham, B. (2002) 'Heritage as Knowledge: Capital or Culture?' *Urban Studies* 39 (5–6): 1003–17.

Graham, B., Gregory, G. and Ashworth, J. (2004) 'The Uses and Abuses of Heritage,' in G. Corsane (ed.) *Heritage, Museums and Galleries: an Introductory Reader*, London and New York: Routledge.

Hall, S. (2005) 'Whose Heritage? Un-settling "the Heritage", Re-Imaging the Post-Nation,' in J. Littler and R. Naidoo (eds) *The Politics of Heritage: the Legacies of 'Race'*, London and New York: Routledge.

Havemann, P. (ed.) (1999) *Indigenous Peoples' Rights in Australia, Canada and New Zealand*, Auckland: Oxford University Press.

ICOMOS (2008) *Submission by ICOMOS {to the} Reflection Workshop on the Future of the World Heritage Convention*, Paris: ICOMOS, 17 October.

Japan Times, 7 June 2008, Japan Times Online. Available at http://search.japantimes.co.jp/mail/nn20080607al.html, accessed 8 June 2008.

Jokilehto, J. (1999) *A History of Architectural Conservation*, Oxford: Butterworth-Heinemann.

Kurin, R. (2004) 'Safeguarding Intangible Cultural Heritage in the 2003 UNESCO Convention: A Critical Appraisal,' *Museum International* 56 (1–2): 66–76.

Kymlicka, W. (ed.) (1995) *The Rights of Minority Cultures*, Oxford: Oxford University Press.

Labadi, S. and Long, C. (eds) (in press) *Heritage and Globalization*, London: Routledge.

Logan, W. S. (2002) 'Globalizing Heritage: World Heritage as a Manifestation of Modernism, and Challenges from the Periphery,' in D. Jones (ed.) *Twentieth Century Heritage: Our Recent Cultural Legacy: Proceedings of the Australia ICOMOS National Conference 2001, 28 November–1 December 2001, University of Adelaide, Adelaide, Australia*, Adelaide: University of Adelaide and Australia ICOMOS: 51–7.

Logan, W. S. (2007a) 'Closing Pandora's Box: Human Rights Conundrums in Cultural Heritage Protection,' in H. Silverman and D. F. Ruggles (eds) *Cultural Heritage and Human Rights*, New York: Springer.

Logan, W. S. (2007b) 'Reshaping the "Sunburned Country": Heritage and Cultural Politics in Contemporary Australia,' in R. Jones and B. J. Shaw (eds) *Loving a Sunburned Country? Geographies of Australian Heritages*, Aldershot, UK: Ashgate Publishing Ltd, 207–23.

Logan, W. S. (2008) 'Cultural Diversity, Heritage and Human Rights,' in B. Graham and P. Howard (eds) *The Ashgate Research Companion to Heritage and Identity*, Aldershot, UK: Ashgate.

Loulanski, T. (2006) 'Revising the Concept for Cultural Heritage: the Argument for a Functional Approach,' *International Journal of Cultural Property* 3: 207–33.

May, S. (2001) *Language and Minority Rights: Ethnicity, Nationalism and the Politics of Language*, Harlow: Longman.

Moghadam, V. and Bagheritari, M. (2007) 'Cultures, Conventions, and the Human Rights of Women: Examining the Convention for Safeguarding Intangible Cultural Heritage, and the Declaration on Cultural Diversity,' *Museum International* 59 (4): 9–18.

Nic Craith, M. (2006) *Europe and the Politics of Language: Citizens, Migrants, Outsiders*, Basingstoke and New York: Macmillan.

Nic Craith, M. (2007) 'Cultural Heritages: Process, Power, Commodification,' in U. Kockel and M. Nic Craith (eds) *Cultural Heritages as Reflexive Traditions*, Basingstoke and New York: Macmillan.

Nic Craith, M. (2008) 'Intangible Cultural Heritages: the Challenges for Europe,' *Anthropological Journal of European Cultures* 17: 54–73.

O'Keefe, Patrick J. (1999) 'Archaeology and Human Rights,' *Public Archaeology* 1: 181–94.

Robertson, G. (1999) *Crimes against Humanity: The Struggle for Global Justice*, London: Allen Lane.

Shannan Peckham, R. (2003) 'The Politics of Heritage and Public Culture,' in R. Shannan Peckham (ed.) *Rethinking Heritage: Cultures and Politics in Europe*, London and New York: I. B. Tauris.

Silverman, H. and Ruggles, D. F. (2007) 'Cultural Heritage and Human Rights,' in H. Silverman and D. F. Ruggles (eds) *Cultural Heritage and Human Rights*, New York: Springer.

Simpson, H. R. (1994) *Dien Bien Phu: The Epic Battle America Forgot*, Washington, DC: Brassey's Inc.

Smith, L. and Akagawa, N. (2009) 'Introduction,' in L. Smith and N. Akagawa (eds) *Intangible Heritage*, London: Routledge.

Smithsonian Center for Folklife and Cultural Heritage (2005) *Theorizing Cultural Heritage*. Available at www.folklife.si.edu/opportunities/fellowships_RF.html, accessed 20 December 2005.

Timothy, D. J. (1997) 'Tourism and the Personal Heritage Experience,' *Annals of Tourism Research* 24 (3): 751–4.

United Nations Organization (UN) (1995) *Our Creative Diversity. Report of World Commission on Culture & Development*, Paris: EGOPRIM.

UNESCO (1972) *Convention Concerning the Protection of the World Cultural and Natural Heritage* (The World Heritage Convention).

UNESCO (2001) *Universal Declaration on Cultural Diversity*.

UNESCO (2003) *Convention for the Safeguarding of the Intangible Cultural Heritage* (The Intangible Heritage Convention).

UNESCO (2004) 'Linking Universal and Local Values,' *World Heritage Papers 13*, World Heritage Centre, Paris.

UNESCO (2005) *International Convention on the Protection of the Diversity of Cultural Contents and Artistic Expressions*.

Valderrama, F. (1995) *A History of UNESCO*, Paris: UNESCO Publishing.

World Conference on Cultural Policies (1982) *Mexico Declaration on Cultural Policies*.

Yusuf, A. A. (2005) *Towards a Convention on Cultural Diversity: Background and Evolution. Presentation to the Third Forum on Human Development*, Paris: UNESCO.

Chapter 2

Human rights and the UNESCO Memory of the World Programme

Hilary Charlesworth

International institutions have a tendency to compartmentalize areas of knowledge and endeavour. Within the United Nations (UN), for example, broad topics such as peace, security, the environment, the global economy, health and human rights are all associated with different parts of the UN system; they have different geographical locations and headquarters, and different systems and sensibilities. There is an inevitable tendency for institutional jealousies to develop over budgets and influence.

The UN has attempted to develop 'cross-cutting' themes in order to break down some of the artificial barriers created between major areas of activity; for example, the idea of gender mainstreaming has been introduced into the UN to ensure that all areas consider the differing impact of policies and programmes on women and men. In 1997 the UN Secretary-General designated human rights as a cross-cutting issue in his reform programme; this has become known as the project of 'human rights mainstreaming'. According to the UN, mainstreaming human rights means integrating human rights into the broad range of UN activities.

However, mainstreaming projects have had, overall, a limited impact on the UN's compartments; this is due to inadequate resources being devoted to the task; lack of time available for experts in one area to become familiar with another set of ideas and vocabulary; and a sense that the mainstreaming project is at heart cosmetic, irrelevant and likely to have little to offer (Charlesworth 2005).

The focus of this chapter is the relationship between the areas of human rights and cultural heritage at the international level. They have developed in quite separate ways, with different emphases and purposes. Human rights scholars have largely ignored the issue of cultural heritage, and, with a few notable exceptions (e.g. Logan 2008), the converse is also true. I want to argue that there is room for much more engagement between these two fields and they have much to learn from each other. This chapter considers a particular aspect of cultural heritage – UNESCO's Memory of the World Programme – and what a greater human rights focus might mean in this context.

The Memory of the World Programme

UNESCO launched its Memory of the World Programme in 1992 in response to the poor state of documentary heritage in many countries. The immediate catalyst was the 1992 destruction of the National Library in Sarajevo by Serbian nationalists (Harvey 2007: 263). Lack of resources devoted to preserving this heritage had been exacerbated by armed conflict and social upheaval; collections of documents had also been broken up, scattered or destroyed through theft and removal. The programme is based on the understanding that the world's documentary heritage belongs to everyone and that it should be preserved and protected. Its goal is to allow free access to this heritage, subject to the rights of custodians, to legislative and other limitations on the accessibility of archives and to cultural sensitivities, such as Indigenous peoples' relationship to their materials.

The programme operates through an International Advisory Committee as well as National and Regional Memory of the World Committees. A Memory of the World Register has been established to record those documents agreed to be part of the world's heritage, ranging from the Bayeux Tapestry, the International Committee of the Red Cross' register of prisoners from the First World War, records of the South African court case against Nelson Mandela which led to his imprisonment, a stone recording the Phoenician alphabet to the papers of the Pakistani independence leader, Jinnah.

The Memory of the World Programme has no explicit links with human rights. Its constitutive documents emphasize the value of making documentary heritage freely accessible, but this is not framed as an individual or communal right. What is the human rights context of such an important cultural heritage programme?

The international human rights system

The international human rights system is an intricate regime that sets human rights standards and creates machinery for implementing them and for monitoring their implementation. The protection of human rights, long considered a matter of purely domestic concern, became a matter of international obligation through the adoption of the UN Charter in 1945. The Charter's preamble and first Article declared the protection of human rights and fundamental freedoms to be a basic purpose of the UN. These general words of commitment were given detailed content in the *Universal Declaration of Human Rights* (*UDHR*) adopted in 1948. The Declaration set out to record the fundamental rights recognized in legal systems across the globe. It included civil and political rights familiar to European and American lawyers, such as rights to life, liberty and property, as well as economic and social rights found in Latin American, Scandinavian and Soviet constitutions, such as the rights to work and to health.

After lengthy negotiations, most provisions of the *UDHR* were given treaty status in the two major human rights covenants, the *International Covenant on Civil and Political Rights* (*ICCPR*) and the *International Covenant on Economic, Social and Cultural Rights* (*ICESCR*), both adopted by the UN General Assembly in 1966. These three documents, the *UDHR* and the two Covenants, are sometimes referred to together as the 'international bill of rights'. They are at the heart of the international human rights system, but it also includes a great range of other treaties and declarations – some relating to particular rights (e.g. the *Convention against Torture* 1984) and some relating to particular groups of people (e.g. the *Convention on the Rights of the Child* 1989). There are also well-developed regional systems for the protection of human rights, which operate in tandem with the UN system. The European system, based on the *European Convention on Human Rights* 1950, has been operating for almost 60 years, and the Inter-American (*Inter-American Convention on Human Rights* 1969) and African (*African Charter of Human and Peoples' Rights* 1982) systems also contribute to the international system.

Although it is not generally considered part of the UN human rights system, UNESCO has long promoted the language of human rights (Logan 2008), and, in 2003 UNESCO adopted a detailed Strategy on Human Rights. All UNESCO's major declarations and treaties on cultural heritage acknowledge the importance of human rights.

International standards and recognition of culture

The relationship of human rights principles to the protection of cultural diversity and heritage is complex. The international human rights system is built on the elaboration of international standards, intended to have global relevance. The move to formulate universal statements of rights in the mid-twentieth century was largely a reaction to the atrocities of the Second World War. The human rights movement set out to contradict the idea that countries were able to treat their people in any way they wanted and asserted instead a generalized, universal notion of human dignity that would provide protection from the actions of national governments. The recognition of specific cultures, on the other hand, is built on the celebration of particularity.

The tension between the universalism of human rights and the particularity of cultural heritage emerged early. In 1947 the American Anthropological Association (AAA) prepared a lengthy critique of the drafting of the *UDHR*, undertaken by a sub-committee of the UN Commission on Human Rights (Glendon 2001: 222). The AAA's major concern was the ethnocentrism of the idea of formulating a statement of universal values. It asked how such a declaration would be applicable to all human beings and not just a statement of Western values. The American anthropologists urged the drafting committee to respect cultural differences. They argued that 'no technique of qualitatively evaluating cultures has been discovered' and that 'standards and values are relative to the culture from which they derive'. Their statement declared that 'what is held to be a human right in one society may be regarded as anti-social by another people, or by the same people in a different period of their history' (American Anthropological Association 1947). The AAA has since changed its relativistic approach to human rights, adopting a *Declaration on Anthropology and Human Rights* in 1999. This Declaration states that: 'the AAA [is] concerned whenever human difference is made the basis for a denial of basic human rights, where "human" is understood in its full range of cultural, social, linguistic, psychological, and biological senses.'[1]

Concerns about cultural specificity influenced debates about the *UDHR* within the UN system. Saudi Arabia, for example, argued that a guarantee of religious freedom, including the right to change one's religion, was inconsistent with Islam, as was the guarantee of equal marriage rights for men and women. It ended up abstaining from the vote on the *UDHR* for this reason. Other abstentions were South Africa (on the basis that the *UDHR* would be used to attack the apartheid system) and the Soviet Bloc countries (on the basis that such a declaration was not needed in a communist society where there was no conflict between the interests of the state and those of the individual). Although few countries would today openly reject the *UDHR*, some traces of the early debates about the possibility of universal human rights standards remain, particularly in the claim that human rights essentially are 'a western construct with limited applicability' (Pollis and Schwab 1979). Various countries, particularly from Asia, have been critical of what they see as Western imperialism in imposing human rights standards (Cerna 1994: 741).

States regularly invoke notions of culture to justify breaches of rights, particularly in the area of women's rights. This can be seen in the terms of the large number of formal reservations made to the *Convention on the Elimination of All Forms of Discrimination against Women* 1979 on the basis of culture and religion, by countries as diverse as the United Kingdom, Israel and the Maldives. A typical reservation asserts that the principle of women's equality with men is not consistent with religious teachings or longstanding cultural practices.

The erosion of human rights standards through extensive assertions of culture has created controversy. For example, Article 2 of the *Intangible Heritage Convention* restricts its coverage to those aspects of culture that are 'compatible with existing human rights instruments', suggesting that some aspects of culture are consistent with human rights standards and some are not. But many human rights standards in themselves make allowances for elements of local culture. Thus, the right to freedom of religion or beliefs contained in Article 18 of the *ICCPR* can be limited by laws protecting public safety, order, health or morals. The idea then that we can pit 'human rights norms' against manifestations of 'culture' gives the wrong impression of their relationship, suggesting that it is adversarial. Culture and human rights should rather be understood as having a symbiotic connection.

At the same time, it is important to be wary of assertions of culture as a reason to resist human rights standards and to investigate the politics of the particular cultures that are invoked in this context. For example, dominant public cultures are, among other things, usually constructed from male histories, traditions and experiences (Rao 1995). Arati Rao has proposed a series of questions to assess claims of culture, particularly those used to counter women's claims of rights: first, whose culture is being invoked? Second, what is the status of the interpreter? Third, in whose name is the argument being advanced? Finally, who are the primary beneficiaries of the claim (Rao 1995: 174)? Such an investigation reminds us that the idea of culture is a malleable and political one and that we should scrutinize carefully each invocation of culture in debates about human rights.

The tension between the assertion of universal standards and the particular claims of culture is longstanding. In many ways it is productive, because it underlines the need for the thoughtful translation of universal standards into particular local contexts. In this sense, universalism and particularity are symbiotic, or perhaps indeed part of each other. As Marie-Bénédicte Dembour has written:

> Universalism cannot exist independently of particularism. It is in opposition to practices which appear abhorrent that universal norms are being set, and it is by reference to local particularities that these universal norms are implemented. The reverse is also true: particularism does not exist independently of universalism. As moral beings concerned with ethics, we are not just beings of culture; we [also] respond to ... the call of universalism.
>
> (Dembour 2006: 179)

The *Vienna Declaration on Human Rights*, adopted in 1993 by the international community, attempted to resolve the debate over the clash between universal standards and the arguments of cultural relativism in the following statement:

> All human rights are universal, indivisible and interdependent and interrelated. The international community must treat human rights globally in a fair and equal manner, on the same footing, and with the same emphasis. While the significance of national and regional particularities and various historical, cultural and religious backgrounds must be borne in mind, it is the duty of the State, regardless of their political, economic and cultural systems, to promote and protect all human rights and fundamental freedoms.

The language of the Vienna Declaration suggests that the idea of the universality of human rights prevailed, but it has not stemmed a strong undercurrent of appeals to the particularities of national cultures.

What international human rights standards are relevant to the protection of cultural heritage?

Article 27 (1) of the *UDHR* provides that 'everyone has the right freely to participate in the cultural life of the community, to enjoy the arts and to share in scientific advancement and its benefits'. This provision was included partly because of pressure from UNESCO (Morsink 1999: 218). Article 27 does not, however, endorse the idea of a diversity of cultural traditions; the use of the definite article 'the' implies that the community is co-extensive with the state, that there is a monolithic national culture, and does not explicitly acknowledge the importance of cultural pluralism, or the right of every person to participate in the cultural life of his or her particular community (Morsink 1999: 269).

A proposal to include a provision in the *UDHR* that protected the rights of minorities to their culture, religion and language was ultimately rejected. This was due in part to the hostility of the United States to such a provision, with Eleanor Roosevelt informing the Commission on Human Rights in 1947 that 'in the United States, there was no minority problem' (Morsink 1999: 272). While the Soviet representatives strongly supported the provision, Latin American delegates were also concerned about this recognition of minority rights; Australia's delegate spoke against the provision on the basis that 'Australia had adopted the principle that assimilation of all groups was in the best interests of all in the long run' (Morsink 1999: 274).

Whatever these limitations, Article 27 (1) suggests a type of shared ownership of culture (Morsink 1999: 217). But the second part of the Article refers to a privatized form of ownership of culture: 'everyone has the right to the protection of the moral and material interests resulting from any scientific, literary or artistic production of which he is the author.' There is, then, a tension between collective and individual rights created in the international definition of the right to cultural life, and it has not been resolved. It reappears, for example, in the controversies about the exploitation of traditional knowledge of Indigenous peoples. Whereas the international intellectual property system administered by both the World Trade Organization and the World Intellectual Property Organization is built on individual ownership of intellectual property, it does not deal easily with Indigenous notions of collective ownership of traditional knowledge.

Article 27 of the *UDHR* was translated into the *ICESCR* in Article 15, which states that treaty parties 'recognise the right of everyone: (a) to take part in cultural life'. As its *UDHR* predecessor, it also refers to the right to benefit from intellectual property in scientific, literary and artistic works.

Article 15 goes on to specify that treaty parties have a duty to conserve, develop and disseminate science and culture.

There are other human rights provisions that help define a right to particular cultural heritage. For example, Article 27 of the *ICCPR* provides that:

> In those States in which ethnic, religious or linguistic minorities exist, persons belonging to such minorities shall not be denied the right, in community with the other members of their group, to enjoy their own culture, to profess and practise their own religion, or to use their own language.

This provision has been the basis of successful claims by Indigenous peoples in Sweden and Canada to preserve cultural practices. It has not yet been used in campaigns to preserve documentary cultural heritage, but it is well adapted to this task.

Another fundamental human rights provision, the right to self-determination, contained in Article 1 of the two Covenants, also contributes to the definition of a duty on states to preserve cultural heritage. Common Article 1 provides: 'All peoples have the right of self-determination. By virtue of that right they freely determine their political status and freely pursue their economic, social and cultural development.' So, international human rights standards set out a range of obligations on nation states to protect cultural heritage. The standards are not perfect, but they could be invoked by the cultural heritage community more actively. One way of doing this is by using the various mechanisms to monitor states' implementation of their human rights obligations. States that are parties to the two Covenants, for example, are required to make regular reports to specialist treaty-monitoring committees and to engage in a process of 'constructive dialogue' with them (Alston and Crawford 2000). The Committees rely on information from civil society and NGOs to scrutinize these reports and to pressure governments to observe their obligations. National Memory of the World committees could contribute to this process.

The Optional Protocol to the *ICCPR* provides for a further, optional, monitoring mechanism through a system of individual complaints to its expert committee, the Human Rights Committee. This could be a useful avenue if a state's refusal to protect cultural heritage constituted a breach of Article 27. I should note that not all states' parties to the *ICCPR* recognize the right of individual complaint under the Optional Protocol, but Australia has, as have 109 other countries.

Many other human rights provisions are relevant to questions of the protection of cultural heritage: these include the prohibition on discrimination on the basis of (among other things) race, sex, language, religion, political or other opinion, national or social origin (*ICESCR*, Article 2; *ICCPR*, Articles

2, 26); the right to freedom of thought, conscience and religion (*ICCPR*, Article 18); and the right to freedom of expression, which includes the freedom to seek, receive and impart information and ideas of all kinds in any media (*ICCPR*, Article 19).

International human rights law thus provides a network of standards, a safety net, which supports the rights of all people to have access to their documentary heritage. The destruction of such material either by deliberate human intervention, for example during armed conflict, or by failure or neglect in preserving these documents, is a violation of human rights norms. Moreover, in certain circumstances, the destruction of documentary heritage can constitute a war crime, over which the International Criminal Court has jurisdiction (*ICC Statute*, Article 8.2. iv).

In this sense, the Memory of the World Programme has firm human rights foundations. But a human rights approach to the programme suggests some further, and perhaps uncomfortable, questions for debate. For example, a human rights approach might challenge the focus on documentary sources by the Memory of the World Programme. It would draw attention to the human rights of those people who have been deprived of access to memories or those with an oral tradition. This is a particular problem given the lack of Western states' participation in the *Intangible Cultural Heritage Convention*, which recognizes non-written traditions. Another human rights question that could be raised is whether the Memory of the World nomination and registration processes discriminate, even unintentionally, on the basis of race, sex or political belief? The major criterion employed is that of 'significance', which is an intensely political judgement at both national and international levels (Harvey 2007: 269–70). How responsive is such a system to recording the memories of women who are in many societies excluded from the public sphere and relegated to the private realm of home and family? Are the memories of particular racial groups accorded priority over others? These questions suggest the value of a thorough human rights analysis of the Memory of the World project.

Human rights as heritage

A human rights approach to cultural heritage indicates that human rights themselves should be understood as heritage. This already happens to a certain extent. For example, the Australian Memory of the World Register already lists some important documents in the struggle for recognition of human rights here in Australia: the manuscripts relating to the landmark *Mabo* case, decided by the High Court of Australia in 1992, which recognized Indigenous forms of title over land; and the Sorry Books, which record Australians' reactions to the plight of the Stolen Generations of Indigenous people.

But, there are many other important human rights documents that could be considered from Australia. There is the evidence collected by the Human

Rights and Equal Opportunity Commission's inquiry into the Stolen Generations in 1995–1996 (HREOC 1997); documents relating to the treatment of refugee applicants in Australia; and the community consultations in the Australian Capital Territory and Victoria that led to those two jurisdictions adopting Australia's first bills of rights in 2004 and 2007 respectively. At the international level, the documents relating to the adoption of the *UDHR* are an important part of the world's cultural heritage.

In 2007 the UN Human Rights Council held an informal meeting on the topic of 'Archives and Human Rights' and emphasized the importance of setting up a universal databank of the archives of authoritarian regimes in order to allow prosecutions for crimes. It was suggested that this databank could be hosted by the Memory of the World Programme. Although such a proposal raises significant questions of privacy and criminal procedure, it is a valuable initiative to consider.

I have argued that the human rights and cultural heritage communities should engage more closely with one another and become aware of the connections and dissonances between the two fields. The discourse of human rights is imperfect in many ways, but it offers, at least, in the words of Roberto Unger, 'a protective sphere for vital interests, which people need to persuade them that they may accept vulnerability, run risks, undertake adventures in the world, and operate as citizens and people' (Harvard Human Rights Program 1995: 13). For this reason, human rights can ground, extend and challenge the Memory of the World Programme and reshape the memories that the programme preserves.

Note

1 Available at www.aaanet.org/stmts/humanrts.htm (accessed 29 September 2008). The Declaration goes on to say:

> Thus, the AAA founds its approach on anthropological principles of respect for concrete human differences, both collective and individual, rather than the abstract legal uniformity of Western tradition. In practical terms, however, its working definition builds on the *Universal Declaration of Human Rights (UDHR)*, the *International Covenants on Civil and Political Rights*, and on *Social, Economic, and Cultural Rights*, the *Conventions on Torture, Genocide, and Elimination of All Forms of Discrimination Against Women*, and other treaties which bring basic human rights within the parameters of international written and customary law and practice. The AAA definition thus reflects a commitment to human rights consistent with international principles but not limited by them. Human rights is not a static concept. Our understanding of human rights is constantly evolving as we come to know more about the human condition. It is therefore incumbent on anthropologists to be involved in the debate on enlarging our understanding of human rights on the basis of anthropological knowledge and research.

References

Alston, Philip and Crawford, James (eds) (2000) *The Future of UN Human Rights Treaty Monitoring*, Cambridge: Cambridge University Press.

American Anthropological Association (1947) 'Statement on Human Rights,' *American Anthropologist* 49: 537–43.

Cerna, Christina M. (1994) 'Universality of Human Rights and Cultural Diversity: Implementation of Human Rights in Different Socio-Cultural Contexts,' *Human Rights Quarterly* 16: 740–52.

Charlesworth, Hilary (2005) 'Not Waving but Drowning: Gender Mainstreaming and Human Rights,' *Harvard Human Rights Law Journal* 18: 1–20.

Dembour, Marie-Bénédicte (2006) *Who Believes in Human Rights? Reflections on the European Convention*, Cambridge: Cambridge University Press.

Glendon, Mary Ann (2001) *A World Made New: Eleanor Roosevelt and the Universal Declaration of Human Rights*, New York: Random House.

Harvard Human Rights Program (1995) *Economic and Social Rights and the Right to Health*, Cambridge: Harvard Law School.

Harvey, Ross (2007) 'UNESCO's Memory of the World Programme,' *Library Trends* 56: 259–74.

Human Rights and Equal Opportunity Commission (HREOC) (1997) *Bringing Them Home: Report of the National Inquiry into the Separation of Aboriginal and Torres Strait Islander Children from their Families*, Sydney: Human Rights and Equal Opportunity Commission.

Logan, William (2008) 'Cultural Heritage and Human Rights,' in B. J. Graham and P. Howard (eds) *Ashgate Research Companion to Heritage and Identity*, Aldershot, UK: Ashgate Publishing Ltd, 439–54.

Morsink, Johannes (1999) *The Universal Declaration of Human Rights: Origins, Drafting and Intent*, Philadelphia: University of Pennsylvania Press.

Pollis, Adamantia and Schwab, Peter (1979) 'Human Rights: A Western Construct with Limited Applicability,' in A. Pollis and P. Schwab (eds) *Human Rights: Cultural and Ideological Perspectives*, New York: Praeger, 4–34.

Rao, Arati (1995) 'The Politics of Gender and Culture in International Human Rights Discourse,' in J. Peters and A. Wolper (eds) *Women's Rights, Human Rights: International Feminist Perspectives*, New York: Routledge, 167–75.

Chapter 3

Custodians of the land

Indigenous peoples, human rights and cultural integrity

Jérémie Gilbert

'We, the Indigenous Peoples, walk to the future in the footprints of our ancestors.'

Kari-Oca Declaration, Brazil, 30 May 1992

'Without the land and the knowledge that comes mainly from use of the land, we as Indigenous peoples cannot survive' (Baer 2002: 17). This statement from Lars Anders Baer, a well-renowned Indigenous activist,[1] highlights how land is central to Indigenous peoples' cultures. For Indigenous peoples, territories and lands are the basis not only of economic livelihood but also are the source of spiritual, cultural and social identity. While Indigenous communities certainly represent the world's most diverse population,[2] most Indigenous cultures worldwide share a similar deep-rooted relationship between cultural identity and land. As highlighted by the United Nations Permanent Forum on Indigenous Issues:

> Land is the foundation of the lives and cultures of Indigenous peoples all over the world. (...) Without access to and respect for their rights over their lands, territories and natural resources, the survival of Indigenous peoples' particular distinct culture is threatened.
>
> (UNPFII 2007: 2)

Land rights assume special importance for Indigenous peoples, as without access to their land Indigenous cultures are in danger of extinguishment. As highlighted by Suagee: 'because tribal cultures are rooted in the natural world, protecting the land and its biological communities tends to be a prerequisite for cultural survival' (Suagee 1999: 50). Hence, there is a strong relationship between cultural rights, cultural heritage and land rights for Indigenous peoples. However, throughout the world Indigenous peoples are facing land dispossession (IWGIA 2004). Present-day economic imperatives arising from globalization are putting new strains on Indigenous peoples' rights over their traditional territories (Stewart-Harawira 2005). Driven by the needs of an increasingly globalized economy, activities such as mining and logging are becoming synonymous with violations of Indigenous peoples' land rights. Consequently, Indigenous peoples have approached international legal institutions to protect their rights over their traditional territories.[3] This has resulted in the emergence of a significant body of international human rights law regarding Indigenous peoples' land rights (Gilbert 2006). An important aspect of this emerging body of law is based on the recognition of the cultural value of land rights for Indigenous peoples.

The present chapter examines to what extent human rights law has developed a specific legal approach to the interaction between cultural rights and land rights for Indigenous peoples. The notions of 'cultural diversity' and 'cultural heritage' have been key factors in the development of such a body of laws. The first part of the chapter will examine how the issue of definition itself (i.e. who are Indigenous peoples) has played an important role in acknowledging Indigenous peoples' specific cultural attachment to land (Part 1). The second part of the chapter will explore how, under the banner of 'cultural diversity', human rights law has developed a legal connection between cultural rights for minorities and land rights in the case of Indigenous peoples (Part 2). The third part of the chapter will analyse how the human rights legal discourse on 'cultural heritage' relates to the rights of Indigenous peoples to maintain their cultural territorial connections (Part 3). Finally, in its concluding remark the chapter will examine to what extent these two approaches (cultural diversity and cultural heritage) participate to the emergence of a right to cultural integrity.

Indigenous peoples and land rights: the holistic approach

'Ladies and Gentlemen, our land is our identity and history ... It is our heritage ... our life. Our survival as Indigenous peoples depends on our gaining of land rights over what is justly and rightfully ours' (Magdagasang and Riches 1999: 71). This statement from Likid Magdagasang, Chief of the Mandaya Indigenous group in the Davao Provinces of Mindanao in the Philippines highlights Indigenous peoples' 'holistic' approach to land rights. Indigenous peoples' relationship to their ancestral territories could be referred to as 'holistic' as it includes social, cultural, spiritual and environmental connections. In this holistic approach to land rights, land is seen as a living tradition over which the collectivity holds a communal responsibility and exercises custodianship. From this perspective, the idea of inter-generational transfer by reference to specific lands is extremely important for Indigenous cultures. This idea of the trans-generational importance of land rights has been reflected in a recent landmark decision involving the Tsilhqot'in Indigenous community in Canada in which one of the judges of the Supreme Court of British Columbia stated: 'A tract of land is not just a

hunting blind or a favourite fishing hole ... [these sites are] but a part of the land that has provided "cultural security and continuity" to Tsilhqot'in people for better than two centuries' (Justice Vickers 2007, para.1376).[4] This notion of 'cultural security and continuity' is a central aspect of Indigenous peoples' relationship with their territories. As summarized by members of the former Australian Aboriginal and Torres Strait Islander Commission (ATSIC)[5]:

> the land is the basis for the creation stories, for religion, spirituality, art and culture. It is also the basis for the relationship between people and with earlier and future generations. The loss of land, or damage to land, can cause immense hardship to Indigenous people.
>
> (ATSIC 1997: 5)

The recently adopted *UN Declaration on the Rights of Indigenous Peoples* does recognize Indigenous peoples' holistic approach to land rights. Article 25 of the UN Declaration affirms that:

> Indigenous peoples have the right to maintain and strengthen their distinctive spiritual relationship with their traditionally owned or otherwise occupied and used lands, territories, waters and coastal seas and other resources and to uphold their responsibilities to future generations in this regard.

Hence, based on Indigenous peoples' holistic approach to land rights, the UN Declaration recognizes the cultural inter-generational approach to land rights. The holistic nature of Indigenous peoples' attachment to land is also reflected in the different legal attempts to define who Indigenous peoples are. While there are no agreed international legal definitions on who Indigenous peoples are, the different existing definitions agree on the specific territorial attachment of Indigenous peoples to their lands. The definition proposed by Cobo in his *Study of Discrimination against Indigenous Populations* is usually accepted as authoritative in UN circles.[6] The definition proposed by Cobo states:

> Indigenous communities, peoples and nations are those which, having a historical continuity with pre-invasion and pre-colonial societies that developed on their territories, consider themselves distinct from other sectors of the societies now prevailing in those territories, or parts of them. They form at present non-dominant sectors of society and are determined to preserve, develop and transmit to future generations their ancestral territories, and their ethnic identity, as the basis of their continued existence as peoples, in accordance with their own cultural patterns, social institutions and legal systems.
>
> (Cobo 1983)

**Bishop McGuinness High
School Library**
1725 Highway 66 South
Kernersville, NC 27284

This definition clearly highlights how land is at the centre of Indigenous cultural systems. In this definition one of the central factors is the territorial connection of Indigenous peoples to their territories. There are three temporal levels to this territorial attachment:

1   *Past*: Indigenous peoples have a historical continuity with 'pre-invasion' and 'pre-colonial societies' that developed on their territories;
2   *Present*: Indigenous peoples live on these territories (or part of them);
3   *Future*: Indigenous peoples are determined to transmit to future generations their ancestral territories.

This holistic and trans-generational aspect of land rights for Indigenous peoples is also reflected in the International Labour Organization (ILO) approach to Indigenous peoples' rights. The ILO Convention No. 169 affirms that in applying the convention

> governments shall respect the special importance for the cultures and spiritual values of the peoples concerned of their relationship with the lands or territories, or both as applicable, which they occupy or otherwise use, and in particular the collective aspects of this relationship.
>
> (ILO Convention 169, Article 13)

Likewise, the World Bank, which has adopted special procedures for projects impacting on Indigenous peoples, also 'recognizes that the identities and cultures of Indigenous Peoples are inextricably linked to the lands on which they live and the natural resources on which they depend' (World Bank Operational Policies, 2005). The World Bank policy draws attention to the fact that Indigenous peoples' rights over their traditional territories are linked to their identities and cultures. More recently, the African Commission on Human and Peoples' Rights (ACHPR) has also insisted on the need to acknowledge Indigenous peoples' specific attachment to a territory as an essential marker of identification. One of three criteria used by the ACHPR is 'a special attachment to and use of their traditional land, whereby their ancestral land and territory have a fundamental importance for their collective physical and cultural survival as peoples' (ACHPR, 2007). It is interesting to note that in this definition the ACHPR insists on the importance of recognizing such fundamental attachment to a territory for the survival of Indigenous peoples' cultures.

Overall, while there are no formal internationally accepted legal definitions on who Indigenous peoples are, there is a broad agreement from different international institutions that one of the main parameters in the identification of Indigenous peoples is the acknowledgement of a specific cultural attachment to a territory. This recognition of Indigenous peoples' specific attachment to land recognizes that, for Indigenous peoples, land is not seen as a simple commodity but a space of socio-economic, spiritual and cultural anchorage. As Malezer, an Aboriginal leader from Australia affirmed: 'Our claim to a global identity is based upon our ancient cultures and viable relationships with our territories, in contrast to the modern political identities of nation states and consumer cultures' (Malezer 2005: 67). As this statement highlights, because of Indigenous peoples' specific cultural attachment to their lands, rights over land represent much more than the usual commercial value attached to title to land. While traditionally, rights to property and rights regarding land laws are concerned with deeds, titles and other forms of individual titles, for Indigenous peoples their claims to land rights are much more deeply engrained with cultural values. From this perspective, Indigenous peoples' claim to land rights challenges the traditional individualistic approach to property rights. Property laws are concerned with individualistic title to ownership, a claim which is foreign to Indigenous peoples' communal cultural claim to their land. Accordingly, the protection of Indigenous peoples' land rights fits more into the category of cultural rights rather than the right to property, and human rights law has provided Indigenous peoples with legal avenues for the recognition of their specific cultural attachment to their traditional territories.

Cultural diversity and land rights: the minority rights approach

Generally speaking, the word 'culture' carries many meanings, including: a style of social and artistic expression; the totality of social transmitted behaviour patterns, arts, beliefs, characteristic of a community or population; and the customary beliefs, social forms and material trait of a racial, religious or social group. The flexibility and richness of the notion of culture usually makes lawyers uncomfortable when it comes to discussing rights relating to cultural rights. Nonetheless, the universal system of human rights offers some protection for cultural rights. Under the heading of cultural rights, the *Universal Declaration on Human Rights (UDHR)* focuses on education and the right to participate in 'cultural life'. The *International Covenant on Economic, Social and Cultural Rights (ICESCR)* expressly refers to 'cultural rights' and its Article 15 recognizes 'the right of everyone ... to take part in cultural life'. In this context 'cultural rights' refer to the arts and sciences. Whereas the accent in the *UDHR* and *ICESCR* is put on a right to culture in the sense of arts and sciences, the emphasis in the *International Covenant on Civil and Political Rights (ICCPR)* is on the rights of minorities to enjoy their own culture. Hence, in terms of international law it is generally admitted that there is a dual nature to cultural rights. Cultural rights are considered in the sense of arts and sciences but also in the sense of respect for cultural differences through the rights of minorities to enjoy their own traditional culture. This right of individual members of minority groups to enjoy their own culture comes from Article 27 of the *ICCPR*, which reads:

> In those States in which ethnic, religious or linguistic minorities exist, persons belonging to such minorities shall not be denied the right, in community with the other members of their group, to enjoy their own culture, to profess and practise their own religion, or to use their own language.

This article has been interpreted as involving rights of minorities including the recognition of some of their cultural practices as well as the symbolic recognition and material support for the expression and preservation of their cultural distinctiveness. Based on States' obligation to respect the cultural practices of persons belonging to minority groups, the Human Rights Committee (HRC) has developed a specific protection for Indigenous peoples' land rights. This protection is based on the idea that for Indigenous communities a particular way of life is associated with the use of their lands. In an important statement, the HRC stated:

> With regard to the exercise of the cultural rights protected under article 27, the Committee observes that culture manifests itself in many forms, including a particular way of life associated with the use of land resources, especially in the case of Indigenous peoples. That right may include such traditional activities as fishing or hunting and the right to live in reserves protected by law.
>
> (Human Rights Committee 1994)

From this perspective, the HRC has clearly established a link between cultural protection and land rights for Indigenous peoples. The approach is that where land is of central significance to the sustenance of a culture, the right to enjoy one's culture requires the protection of land. In this context the right to territory is understood as requiring sufficient habitat and space to reproduce culturally as a people.

This affirmation by the HRC of the cultural importance of land rights for Indigenous peoples has been a crucial starting point in terms of access to human rights law for Indigenous peoples. In several cases involving individual complaints from members of Indigenous communities the HRC has established a link between culture and traditional forms of livelihood. Based on this link the HRC has developed a strong jurisprudence regarding Indigenous peoples' land rights. For example, in a case against Canada, the HRC has highlighted that by allowing leases for oil and gas exploration and timber development within the ancestral territory of the Lubicon Lake Band Indigenous community without consulting them, the government had threatened the way of life and culture of the Indigenous community (Human

Rights Committee 1990). In other cases involving Sami communities from Sweden and Finland the HRC has re-affirmed this connection between land rights and Indigenous peoples' cultural rights protected under Article 27 of the *ICCPR*. In these cases the HRC has pointed out that because reindeer husbandry is an essential element of the Sami culture, States have an obligation to protect access for Sami herders to their traditional territories to allow the practice of reindeer husbandry (Human Rights Committee 1988, 1992 and 2005). Hence, while Article 27 of the *ICCPR* does not per se provide protection for Indigenous peoples' rights to land, the HRC has developed a jurisprudence which protects activities that form an essential part of an Indigenous culture, and activities relating to the use of the land have often been recognized as constituting such essential cultural elements.

One of the difficulties for the HRC was to establish what constituted an activity forming an essential element of Indigenous peoples' culture. For example, in the case of reindeer herding for the Sami populations, one of the arguments developed by the government of Sweden was that reindeer herding was more an economic, rather than a purely cultural, activity. On this point the HRC concluded that: 'the regulation of an economic activity is normally a matter for the State alone. However, where that activity is an essential element in the culture of an ethnic community, its application to an individual may fall under Article 27 of the Covenant' (Human Rights Committee 1988). This was later confirmed in other cases in which the HRC re-affirmed that economic activities may come within the ambit of Article 27, if they are an essential element of the culture of an ethnic community. However, in another case involving members of the Rehoboth Baster Community who are descendants of Indigenous Khoi and Afrikaans settlers, the HRC made a distinction between economic activities that are culturally embedded and purely economic activities which are not protected under Article 27. The members of the Rehoboth Baster Community were claiming their right to land based on their traditions of cattle herding. In this case the HRC stated that 'although the link of the Rehoboth community to the lands in question dates back some 125 years, it is not the result of a relationship that would have given rise to a distinctive culture' (Human Rights Committee 2000a). Hence, while an activity which has an economical component (such as reindeer herding, fishing or hunting) can be regarded as a cultural activity protected under Article 27, there are some limitations and the HRC will examine in detail to what extent such activity forms part of a cultural way of life.

Regarding the HRC jurisprudence on cultural activities, another difficulty for the HRC was to appreciate to what extent modern technology could form part of such traditional activities. For example, can the use of a helicopter to practise traditional reindeer herding, or the use of modern technology fishing nets, be regarded as activities constituting an essential element of Indigenous peoples' culture? These questions could be extremely important, for if they do not constitute a culturally traditional activity, the protection of Article 27 would not be granted. On this issue, in a case concerning Sami communities in Finland, the HRC highlighted: 'that the authors may have adapted their methods of reindeer herding over the years and practice it with the help of modern technology does not prevent them from invoking article 27 of the Covenant' (Human Rights Committee 1992). Likewise in a case concerning fisheries in New Zealand, the HRC re-affirmed 'that article 27 does not only protect traditional means of livelihood of minorities, but allows also for adaptation of those means to the modern way of life and ensuing technology' (Human Rights Committee 2000b). Hence, the HRC has clearly stated that the notion of culture in Article 27 is not static. It views Article 27 as being invoked in support of the Indigenous way of life, with historical links to traditional life which may have nevertheless changed over the centuries. The view is that this provision can be invoked to support the Indigenous traditional cultural way of life while having evolved over the centuries. Human rights law is not advocating keeping Indigenous cultures 'frozen in time', but allows Indigenous peoples to develop in their own way and offers protection for their right to enjoy their own traditional culture. As described by the Australian Aboriginal and Torres Strait Islanders Social Justice Commissioner:

> [T]he right to enjoy a culture is not 'frozen' at some point in time when culture was supposedly 'pure' or 'traditional'. The enjoyment of culture should not be falsely restricted as a result of anachronistic notions of the 'authenticity' of the culture.
>
> (Aboriginal and Torres Strait Islander Social Justice
> Commissioner 2000)

Overall, under the minority regime, human rights law promotes and protects the rights of specific groups based on their right to maintain and practise their own different cultural practices and traditions. In the case of Indigenous peoples this right to maintain cultural differences has been connected with the protection of cultural traditions linked with a territory. The rationale for such protection is based on the idea that since Indigenous peoples' land rights are essential to the maintenance of their specific way of life, human rights law ought to provide particular protection for Indigenous peoples. In many ways such rationale is based on a human rights law approach to cultural diversity. It is the recognition that cultural distinctiveness, in this case a specific cultural attachment to a territory, is a contribution to the overall cultural heritage of mankind.

Cultural heritage and Indigenous peoples

In general terms, the notion of cultural heritage is often associated with physical artefacts such as museums, libraries and other institutional aspects of culture. (*Convention Concerning the Protection of the World Cultural and Natural Heritage, 1972*, Article 1). However, more recently the concept has been broadened to refer also to intangible and ethnographic heritage. In the case of Indigenous peoples the notion has to be appreciated in this wider sense. While the notion of heritage encompasses traditional practices in a broad sense, including for example language, art, music, dance, song, sacred sites and ancestral human remains, for Indigenous peoples the preservation of heritage is deeply embedded and linked to the protection of traditional territories. As highlighted earlier, because Indigenous peoples' cultures are deeply rooted in the natural world, the notion of cultural heritage for Indigenous peoples is connected to the notion of territoriality. This has been highlighted by the Inter-American Court of Human Rights in the *Awas Tingni* case, in which the court stated:

> For Indigenous communities, the relationship with the land is not merely one of possession and production, but also a material and spiritual element that they should fully enjoy, as well as a means through which to preserve their cultural heritage and pass it on to future generations.
>
> (Inter-American Court of Human Rights 2001: 149)

This legal approach based on the recognition that cultural heritage is associated with protection of land rights has also been highlighted in a study undertaken by the former UN Sub-Commission on Prevention of Discrimination and Protection of Minorities on the protection of the heritage of Indigenous peoples. The Sub-Commission Special Rapporteur on the protection of the heritage of Indigenous people, Mrs Erica-Irene Daes, highlighted that:

> the protection of cultural and intellectual property is connected fundamentally with the realization of the territorial rights and self-determination of Indigenous peoples. Traditional knowledge of values, autonomy or self-government, social organization, managing ecosystems, maintaining harmony among peoples and respecting the land is embedded in the arts, songs, poetry and literature which must be learned and renewed by each succeeding generation of Indigenous children.
>
> (Daes 1993: 4)

Moreover, as noted by the UN Special Rapporteur, while:

> [i]ndustrialized societies tend to distinguish between art and science, or between creative inspiration and logical analysis, Indigenous peoples regard all products of the human mind and heart as interrelated, and as

flowing from the same source: the relationships between the people and their land, their kinship with the other living creatures that share the land, and with the spirit world.

(Daes 1993: 21)

Based on such recognition, the study highlights how the traditional division of heritage between 'cultural', 'artistic', or 'intellectual' is inappropriate in the case of Indigenous peoples as it implies a categorization of elements such as songs, stories, sciences or sacred sites, and this would imply giving different levels of protection to different elements of heritage. Recognizing the holistic cultural approach to land rights, the study raises issues regarding the inadequacy of the watertight legal regime of protection for cultural heritage. It states:

it is clear that existing forms of legal protection of cultural and intellectual property, such as copyright and patent, are not only inadequate for the protection of Indigenous peoples' heritage but inherently unsuitable. [...] Subjecting Indigenous peoples to such a legal scheme would have the same effect on their identities, as the individualization of land ownership, in many countries, has had on their territories – that is, fragmentation into pieces, and the sale of the pieces, until nothing remains.

(Daes 1993: 32)

As the UN study insists: 'All elements of heritage should be managed and protected as a single, interrelated and integrated whole' (Daes 1993: 31).

Crucially, the UN cultural heritage study proposes the adoption of international principles and guidelines for the protection of the heritage of Indigenous peoples. One of the principles proposed states:

The discovery, use and teaching of Indigenous peoples' knowledge, arts and cultures is inextricably connected with the traditional lands and territories of each people. Control over traditional territories and resources is essential to the continued transmission of Indigenous peoples' heritage to future generations, and its full protection.

(Daes 2000)

In the definition of what constitutes the cultural heritage of Indigenous peoples, the guidelines and principles point out that: 'The heritage of Indigenous peoples is comprised of all objects, sites and knowledge the nature or use of which has been transmitted from generation to generation, and which is regarded as pertaining to a particular people or its territory' (Daes 2000). While the principles and guidelines are not integrated into any internationally binding instruments, they serve as an indication of the potential evolution of international law in this area. Moreover, as highlighted in 2006 by the former UN Working Group on Indigenous Populations, it is possible 'that the guidelines might at a later stage be transformed into an international legally binding instrument, for example, a convention on the protection of Indigenous peoples' heritage' (Yokota 2005: 5). While the notion of cultural heritage does not appear as such in the International Bill of Human Rights, the principles and guidelines developed by the UN clearly establish a link between human rights law and cultural heritage for Indigenous peoples.

More generally, regarding the connection between human rights law and cultural heritage, it is worth noting that while at the international level international institutions such as the UNESCO World Heritage Centre or the International Centre for the Study of the Preservation and Restoration of Cultural Property (ICCROM) are specifically working on issues relating to cultural heritage, international human rights institutions are coming to the debate only in a derivative way based on the notion of cultural rights. However, the contribution of human rights to the notion of cultural heritage is significant as it insists on the need to take into consideration the view of minorities. As illustrated by the recognition of the specificity of Indigenous peoples' cultural heritage, human rights law advocates an understanding of cultural heritage based on a way of life. This is an important step towards the recognition of Indigenous peoples' cultural heritage, as in the words of Xanthaki: 'problems arise from the discrepancy between the Indigenous understanding of culture as a way of life and the non-Indigenous perception of culture as capital' (Xanthaki 2007: 8). From this perspective, the contribution of human rights law to the broadening of the notion of cultural heritage is crucial to preserving mankind's cultural diversity. One of the central points in such a development is the recognition of Indigenous peoples as principal actors in the development of policies relating to cultural heritage. In the past Indigenous peoples have usually been the victims of cultural heritage protection acts which did not take their own perspective into consideration. As affirmed by the draft UN principles: 'Indigenous peoples should be the source, the guardians and the interpreters of their heritage, whether created in the past, or developed by them in the future' (Daes 2000: 3). This principle highlights not only the importance of recognizing the connection between cultural heritage and land rights, but also the need to recognize that Indigenous peoples themselves are the custodians of their lands.

Conclusion

While Indigenous land tenure systems vary significantly across the world, human rights law has begun to recognize that landholding systems constitute a central aspect of Indigenous peoples' cultures, and thus represent crucial criteria of Indigenous identity. Building on such recognition, human rights law has developed a specific body of law which recognizes the need to provide protection for Indigenous peoples' rights to land. As highlighted, the notions of cultural diversity and cultural heritage have been pivotal to this development. Based on the notion of cultural diversity (protection of minorities) and cultural heritage, human rights law has recognized that Indigenous peoples' relationship with their lands underpins their cultural identity and ensures their survival. From this perspective, human rights law contributes to highlighting the inter-connection between the notions of cultural diversity and cultural heritage. Human rights law has drawn attention not only to the need to have a more diverse approach to cultural heritage, but also how a more diverse cultural heritage policy contributes to a more culturally diverse society. Human rights law's contribution shows that in order to protect cultural diversity it is necessary to reform the way cultural heritage has been approached in the past by integrating a more universal and culturally diverse approach to the meaning of heritage. This broadening of the notion of cultural heritage is not only essential for Indigenous peoples, but also for mankind. As summarized by Daes: 'The effective protection of the heritage of the Indigenous peoples of the world benefits all humanity. Cultural diversity is essential to the adaptability and creativity of the human species as a whole' (Daes 2000). Overall, the development of a human rights-based approach to cultural heritage for Indigenous peoples is contributing to the emergence and the development of a 'right to cultural integrity' which includes rights to subsistence, livelihood, cultural diversity and heritage.

Notes

1 Lars Anders Baer is a member of the United Nations Permanent Forum on Indigenous Issues, and he is the President of the Sami Parliament in Sweden, and a member of the Sami Council.
2 Estimates for the worldwide Indigenous population range from 300 million to 400 million; this would equate to just under 6 per cent of the total world population. This includes at least 5,000 distinct peoples in over 72 countries. See Office of the High Commissioner for Human Rights, 'Indigenous Peoples and the United Nations System': Office of the High Commissioner for Human Rights, United Nations Office at Geneva, 2001; *Indigenous Peoples; A Global Quest for Justice*, Zed Books, 1987; *The Indigenous World 2008* (IWGIA 2008).
3 The UN declared the decade 1994–2004 as the first World Decade on the Rights of Indigenous Peoples and 2005–2015 as the second decade; see General Assembly Reso. A/RES/48/163 (1994) and Reso. A/RES/59/174 (2005). J. Anaya, *Indigenous Peoples in International Law*, OUP (2004).
4 Supreme Court of British Columbia, *Tsilhqot'in Nation v. British Columbia*, 2007 BCSC 1700, para. 1376.
5 On 16 March 2005 the Australian Parliament passed the ATSIC Amendment Bill repealing provisions of the ATSIC Act, and in particular abolishing ATSIC.
6 The Sub-Commission called it 'a reference work of definitive usefulness' and invited the Working Group to rely on it; see Sub-Commission Res. 1985/22, § 4 (a).

References

Aboriginal and Torres Strait Islander Social Justice Commissioner (2000) *Native Title Report 2000* (Report of the Aboriginal and Torres Strait Islanders Social Justice Commissioner to the Attorney General).

African Commission on Human and Peoples' Rights (2007) Advisory Opinion on the *UN Declaration on the Rights of Indigenous Peoples*, 41st Ordinary Session, Accra, Ghana, May.

ATSIC (1997) Native Title Amendment Bill 1997, *Issues for Indigenous Peoples*, ATSIC: Australia.

Baer, L.-A. (2002) 'Protection of Rights of Holders of Traditional Knowledge, Indigenous and Local Communities,' *World Libraries* 12: 1.

Cobo, M. (1983) *Study of the Problem of Discrimination Against Indigenous Populations*, UN Doc. E/CN.4/Sub.2/1983/21/add.8 (United Nations Document).

Convention Concerning Indigenous and Tribal Peoples in Independent Countries (1989) (ILO No. 169), 72 ILO OFFICIAL BULL. 59, 1989, reprinted in I.L.M. 1382.

Convention Concerning the Protection of the World Cultural and Natural Heritage (1972), Paris, 16 November.

Daes, E. (1993) *Study on the Protection of the Cultural and Intellectual Property of Indigenous Peoples*, Sub-Commission on Prevention of Discrimination and Protection of Minorities, UN Doc. E/CN.4/Sub.2/1993/28.

Daes, E. (2000) *Protection of the Heritage of Indigenous Peoples*, UN Doc. E/CN.4/Sub.2/1994/31; see also: *Annex I, Report of the Seminar on the Draft Principles and Guidelines for the Protection of the Heritage of Indigenous Peoples*, UN Doc. E/CN.4/Sub.2/2000/26.

Gilbert, J. (2006) *Indigenous Peoples' Land Rights under International Law: From Victims to Actors*, New York: Transnational Publishers.

Human Rights Committee (1988) *Ivan Kitok v. Sweden*, Communication No. 197/1985, CCPR/C/33/D/197/1985.

Human Rights Committee (1990) *Lubicon Lake Band v. Canada*, Communication No. 167/1984 (26 March), UN Doc. Supp. No. 40 (A/45/40).

Human Rights Committee (1992) *Länsman* et al. *v. Finland*, Communication No. 511/1992, UN Doc. CCPR/C/52/D/511/1992.

Human Rights Committee (1994) General Comment No. 23: *The Rights of Minorities* (Art. 27), UN Doc. CCPR/C/21/Rev.1/Add.5.

Human Rights Committee (2000a) *J. G. A. Diergaardt (late Captain of the Rehoboth Baster Community)* et al. *v. Namibia*, Communication No. 760/1997, UN Doc. CCPR/C/69/D/760/1997.

Human Rights Committee (2000b) *Apirana Mahuika* et al. *v. New Zealand*, Communication No. 547/1993, UN Doc. CCPR/C/70/D/547/1993.

Human Rights Committee (2005) *Jouni Länsman* et al. *v. Finland*, Communication No. 1023/2001, UN Doc. CCPR/C/83/D/1023/2001.

Inter-American Court of Human Rights (2001) *The Mayagna (Sumo) Awas Tingni Community v. Nicaragua* (31 August), Inter-Am. Ct. H.R., (Ser. C) No. 79.

International Covenant on Civil and Political Rights (1966) GA Res. 2200A (XXI), UN Doc./6316 (1966), 999 UNTS171, reprinted in 6 ILM 368(1967).

International Covenant on Economic, Social and Cultural Rights (1966) GA res. 2200A (XXI), UN Doc. A/6316 (1966), 999 UNTS171, reprinted in 6 ILM 368(1967).

International Work Group for Indigenous Affairs (2004) *Land Rights: A Key Issue*, Indigenous Affairs No. 4/04.

Magdagasang, L. and Riches, L. (1999) 'Resource Development Versus Indigenous Rights in the Philippines,' *Indigenous Law Bulletin* 71.

Malezer, L. (2005) 'Permanent Forum on Indigenous Issues: Welcome to the Family of the UN,' in Joshua Castellino and Niamh Walsh (eds) *Indigenous Peoples and Human Rights*, Martinus Nijhoff.

Stewart-Harawira, M. (2005) *The New Imperial Order: Indigenous Responses to Globalization*, London: Zed Books.

Suagee, D. (1999) 'Human Rights and the Cultural Heritage of Indian Tribes in the United States,' *International Journal of Cultural Property*, pp. 48–76.

United Nations Declaration on the Rights of Indigenous Peoples (2007) adopted by General Assembly Resolution 61/295 on 13 September 2007.

UN Permanent Forum on Indigenous Issues (2007) Report on the sixth session (14–25 May) Economic and Social Council Official Records Supplement No. 23 UN Doc. E/2007/43, E/C.19/2007/12.

Universal Declaration of Human Rights (1948), GA res. 217A (III), UN Doc. A/810, at 71.

World Bank Operational Policies (2005), *OP 4.10 on Indigenous Peoples*.

Xanthaki, A. (2007) *Indigenous Peoples and United Nations Standards: Self-determination, Culture, Land*, Cambridge University Press: Cambridge.

Yokota, Yozo and the Sami Council (2005) Document Submitted to UN Working Group on Indigenous Populations, 23rd Session, July 2005 (United Nations Document Number E/CN.4/Sub.2/AC.4/2005/3).

Chapter 4

Linguistic heritage and language rights in Europe

Theoretical considerations and practical implications

Máiréad Nic Craith

Languages play an important role in the heritage mosaic of Europe – not just as a means of transmitting cultural traditions from one generation to the next, but as valuable expressions of identity and culture that are linked with particular peoples and regions. Yet this asset is extremely difficult to deal with and while Europe's linguistic pluralism is celebrated in theory, it also poses serious challenges for policy makers (Nic Craith 2006). Collectively Europe's languages form a crucial part of its cultural heritage but transnational institutions such as the European Union (EU) are barely able to cope with the challenge. With the accession of Bulgaria and Romania to the European Union in January 2007, the number of official languages in the Union rose from 21 to 23. The official languages of EU countries represent three different language families – Indo-European, Finno-Ugric and Semitic – and the Union has three alphabets – Latin, Greek and Cyrillic. Moreover, it is estimated that as many as 40 million citizens of the Union regularly speak an unofficial language that has been passed down from one generation to the next. More than 60 indigenous regional or minority language groups can be identified within the current boundaries of the EU. And then there is the issue of contested languages, dialects, non-European languages...

Over the years many trans-national European institutions have affirmed their allegiance to Europe's linguistic heritage and the commitment of organizations such as the Council of Europe to linguistic diversity on the continent is well established. Five years after its foundation in 1949, the Council of Europe pledged its commitment to the 'common cultural heritage of Europe'. Article 2a of the *European Cultural Convention* drafted in Paris in 1954 stipulated that, where possible, each party would 'encourage the study by its own nationals of the languages, history and civilization of the other Contracting Parties'. Part b was a reciprocal measure to ensure that parties would also 'endeavour to promote the study of its language or languages, history and civilization in the territory of the other Contracting Parties'.

Since then, there have been many endorsements of the linguistic dimension to Europe's heritage. At a symposium in Luxembourg on the potential of plurilingual education in the classroom in 2005, Mady Delvaux-Stehres, the then President of the Education Council of the European Union, 'reaffirmed that Europe must safeguard its heritage and the diversity of the linguistic landscape that sets it apart'. In her view, the social cohesion of Europe could be guaranteed only if schools worked to safeguard their linguistic heritage.

This view of linguistic heritage as a force for cohesion was re-affirmed in 2008 in a document initiated by the President of the European Commission, Mr José Manuel Durão Barroso, and the Commissioner for Multilingualism, Mr Leonard Orban. Proposals for intercultural dialogue were set out by a group of intellectuals chaired by Amin Maalouf. They suggested that:

> Every language is the product of a unique historical experience, each is the carrier of a memory, a literary heritage, a specific skill, and is the legitimate basis of cultural identity. Languages are not interchangeable, none is dispensable, none is superfluous. To preserve all the languages of our heritage, including the ancestral European languages such as Latin and ancient Greek; to encourage, even for languages which are very much minority languages, their development in the rest of the continent, is inseparable from the very idea of a Europe of peace, culture, universality and prosperity.
>
> (Maalouf 2008: 2)

The Treaty of Lisbon also contains a commitment to language, but the approach is functional and is formed primarily in terms of rights. Article 17 stipulates that citizens of the Union have 'the right to petition the European Parliament, to apply to the European Ombudsman, and to address the institutions and advisory bodies of the Union in any of the Treaty languages and to obtain a reply in the same language' (Treaty of Lisbon 2008). Parties to the Treaty also affirm 'the attachment of the Union to the cultural diversity of Europe and the special attention it will continue to pay to these and other languages'. Despite these and other commitments to Europe's linguistic heritage, the notion of language rights for citizens in Europe is still at an early stage and academic debates on these issues have really only begun to emerge in the past two decades (cf. Skutnabb-Kangas and Phillipson 1995; Kontra *et al.* 1999; Argenter and McKenna Brown 2004; Schneider 2005).

Protection for languages in Europe: a historical overview

Although the concept of language rights is relatively new, some historical treaties have included protection for speakers of particular languages. For example, the Treaty of Perpetual Union between the King of France and the Helvetic state (1516) contained a provision for the 'Swiss who speak no language other than German'. The Congress of Vienna (1815) included certain protections designed to maintain the nationality of Poles. In consequence, it was possible for the Polish minority in certain regions to use Polish for official business (de Varennes 1997). Overall, however, the evolution of linguistic rights in Europe was not really an issue before the nineteenth century (Wright 2001). Vieytez (2001) establishes the reasons for the lack of concern with this issue.

The linguistic landscape in medieval Europe differed considerably from its current configuration. At one end of the spectrum the linguistic landscape was very localized. Most Europeans were farmers, peasants or serfs who grew up in a specific region and spoke the local language/dialect, which had been transmitted from one generation to the next. Language difference was hardly a matter for concern as most adjacent dialects were mutually comprehensible and difficulties in communication were not an everyday occurrence. Multilingualism was more common at the upper end of the social scale. Upper classes spoke the languages of the royal families and their alliances. 'The resulting mix promoted family multilingualism' (Wright 2001: 45).

Latin was the language of the church. It was a sacred language, used across political and linguistic borders. Clerics were literate in Latin and were required to have some knowledge of it, regardless of their mother tongue. This contrasted with the Eastern, Orthodox side of the continent where Greek and Church Slavonic dominated spiritual matters. In this linguistic landscape, the notion of a linguistic minority was virtually meaningless and the issue of language rights was hardly critical.

The emergence of nations and national identity was to have a crucial impact. As the feudal system began to dissolve in sixteenth- and seventeenth-century Europe, and the notion of national identity and integrity began to emerge, languages gained a new significance. Several European dynasties gradually became more aware of the symbolism of language and began to specifically promote their own dialect as a language of power and prestige. Western nation-states worked at strengthening and standardizing specific dialects as national languages. Language academies were established in France and Spain. Britain focused on the development of English and several new languages of power began to emerge on the continent. Religious factors also contributed to the emerging complexity of the linguistic landscape. Protestants, in particular, demanded the translation of the Bible into their own language and 'print-capitalism' emerged (Anderson 1993). This process effectively consolidated prestige for particular languages across political boundaries.

Nationalist ideology encouraged linguistic homogeneity and domestic policies endorsed the notion of one people speaking one language. Many state-building protagonists ignored the multiplicity of dialects spoken within state boundaries. Moreover, as political disputes were settled and political boundaries redrawn, some language groups found themselves on alternative sides of political boundaries and living in separate nation-states. The linguistic landscape was further complicated in the twentieth century with the widespread movement of huge numbers of political refugees after the two World Wars. Economic and leisure migration have also added to the complexity.

From a strongly nationalist perspective, the notion of a linguistic minority was a problem rather than an asset. Nationalist ideology promoted a single language at the expense of other languages spoken within state boundaries (Barbour and Carmichael 2000; McColl Millar 2005). Civic nationalism in France promoted equality of its citizens through the French language. The indivisibility of the state was symbolized by the unity of the language. French was the language of the people. All were welcome to participate fully in the life of the nation, but only through the medium of French. Minorities were to be assimilated. Alternative policies were pursued in ethnic nation-states such as Germany. There, the German language was the characteristic that bound the people together. Those who did not speak German did not belong. Exclusion rather than assimilation was the policy (Nic Craith 2004).

At an international level, conditions were slightly more favourable for speakers of minority languages. Several international treaties enacted after the First World War contained language provisions for specific regions. Treaties recognizing various nation-states in the Balkans, for example, sought equality for linguistic, racial and religious minorities. However, such treaties were not always adhered to. Poulton (1998: 41) points to the campaign of assimilation that occurred in Greece at this time when all Slav minorities were deemed to be ethnically Greek. In Latvia (where independence was new), there was very limited recognition of minority languages (Druviete 1998). In its quest to re-establish the status of a long-repressed Latvian language, the state penalized other minority languages.

After the Second World War, some national minorities in Central Europe enjoyed the protection of international law. Linguistic minorities in regions such as the Åland Islands, South Tyrol and Trieste enjoyed the benefits of special protection (Alcock 2000). German minorities in Denmark and Danish minorities in Germany enjoyed reciprocal linguistic arrangements (Kockel 1999). Although there were no specific legal developments in Eastern Europe, constitutions in Yugoslavia, the German Democratic Republic, and for a time Romania, gave some protection to their linguistic minorities (Vieytez 2001: 12).

Key European initiatives

The establishment of the European Coal and Steel Community in 1951 and the subsequent Treaty of Rome in 1957 set a new trans-national context for the linguistic landscape of Europe. Article 128: 1 of the original treaty signals a commitment 'to bringing the common cultural heritage to the fore' and aims to develop 'the European dimension in education, particularly through the teaching and dissemination of the languages of the Member States' (www.hri.org/docs/Rome57/Rome57.txt). The Treaty was drawn up in the four languages of the six member states, i.e. Dutch, French, German and Italian. All four versions are regarded as equally authentic, and constituting a 'single original'. That notion of a 'single original', albeit in four different languages, is important as it highlights linguistic heritage as a potential mechanism for European cohesion, but whether all four languages can, in fact, transmit exactly the same information is debatable.

From the beginning, speakers of official languages within the European Economic Community, and subsequently the European Union, were privileged, but the question of linguistic rights for all citizens has been slow to emerge. The *Convention for the Protection of Human Rights and Fundamental Freedoms* which entered into force on 21 September 1970 was a step in this direction (www.echr.coe.int/nr/rdonlyres/d5cc24a7-dc13–4318-b457–5c9014916d7a/0/englishanglais.pdf). Article 14 of the Convention prohibits discrimination against any individual 'on any ground such as sex, race, colour, language, religion, political or other opinion, national or social origin, association with a national minority, property, birth or other status'. Article 6 guarantees the right to a fair trial. In order to ensure that correct procedures are followed, individuals charged with a criminal offence have, at a minimum, 'the right to be informed promptly, in a language which he understands and in detail, of the nature and cause of the accusation against him'. They are also entitled 'to have the free assistance of an interpreter if he cannot understand or speak the language used in court'.

Despite the protections contained within this Convention, members of the Council of Europe were uneasy about rights for speakers of regional or minority languages. Although the Convention establishes the right for individuals not to be discriminated against, it hardly offers a system of positive protection for speakers of unofficial languages. In 1961, the Parliamentary Assembly called for a protection measure which would supplement the European Convention and safeguard the rights of minorities to use their own language and enjoy their own culture. This served as the catalyst for the *European Charter for Regional or Minority Languages* which opened for signature in Strasbourg in 1992 (Nic Craith 2003).

The Charter's preamble outlines its principal aim in cultural terms. It is 'designed to protect and promote regional or minority languages as a threatened aspect of Europe's cultural heritage'. It explicitly does not confine itself to principles of non-discrimination but also seeks mechanisms to promote the use of these languages and it is aimed at the languages themselves, rather than the individuals that speak them. The explanatory report states quite clearly that the Charter does not actually 'establish any individual or collective rights for the speakers of regional or minority languages'. However, in those states that ratify the Charter, speakers of regional and minority languages would enjoy vastly improved conditions.

The preamble re-affirms the Council of Europe's commitment to the continent's 'common heritage and ideals' and states that 'linguistic diversity is one of the most precious elements of the European cultural heritage'. Since 1992, 23 nation-states have ratified the Charter and a further ten have signed but not ratified it (see Table 4.1). Some of the more notable absences from this list of member states include Belgium, Greece, Ireland and the Baltic States.

The issue of linguistic rights was also to the fore in the *Framework Convention for the Protection of National Minorities* which opened for signature in

Table 4.1 Member states of the Council of Europe that have signed or ratified the *European Charter for Regional or Minority Languages*

Member states	Signature	Ratification	Entry into force
Armenia	11/05/2001	25/01/2002	01/05/2002
Austria	05/11/1992	28/06/2001	01/10/2001
Azerbaijan	21/12/2001		
Bosnia and Herzegovina	07/09/2005		
Croatia	05/11/1997	05/11/1997	01/03/1998
Cyprus	12/11/1992	26/08/2002	01/12/2002
Czech Republic	09/11/2000	15/11/2006	01/03/2007
Denmark	05/11/1992	08/09/2000	01/01/2001
Finland	05/11/1992	09/11/1994	01/03/1998
France	07/05/1999		
Germany	05/11/1992	16/09/1998	01/01/1999
Hungary	05/11/1992	26/04/1995	01/03/1998
Iceland	07/05/1999		
Italy	27/06/2000		
Liechtenstein	05/11/1992	18/11/1997	01/03/1998
Luxembourg	05/11/1992	22/06/2005	01/10/2005
Malta	05/11/1992		
Moldova	11/07/2002		
Montenegro	22/03/2005	15/02/2006	06/06/2006
Netherlands	05/11/1992	02/05/1996	01/03/1998
Norway	05/11/1992	10/11/1993	01/03/1998
Poland	12/05/2003		
Romania	17/07/1995	29/01/2008	01/05/2008
Russia	10/05/2001		
Serbia	22/03/2005	15/02/2006	01/06/2006
Slovakia	20/02/2001	05/09/2001	01/01/2002
Slovenia	03/07/1997	04/10/2000	01/01/2001
Spain	05/11/1992	09/04/2001	01/08/2001
Sweden	09/02/2000	09/02/2000	01/06/2000
Switzerland	08/10/1993	23/12/1997	01/04/1998
The former Yugoslav Republic of Macedonia	25/07/1996		
Ukraine	02/05/1996	19/09/2005	01/01/2006
United Kingdom	02/03/2000	27/03/2001	01/07/2001

Source: adapted from: http://conventions.coe.int/Treaty/Commun/ChercheSig.asp?NT=148&CM=8&DF=5/27/2008&CL=ENG.

Strasbourg in February 1995. This was the first legally binding instrument which was specifically devoted to the protection of national minorities. Significantly, the Convention contained no definition of the concept of 'national minority', preferring instead a more pragmatic solution of allowing each member state to define it in its own terms.

Unlike the *European Charter for Regional or Minority Languages*, the Framework Convention was aimed at individuals rather than languages, and rights were clearly expressed at individual rather than collective levels. In Article 5, for example, parties to the Convention 'undertake to promote the conditions necessary for persons belonging to national minorities to maintain and develop their culture, and to preserve the essential elements of their identity, namely their religion, language, traditions and cultural heritage'. Article 9 upholds 'the right to freedom of expression of every person belonging to a national minority'. This includes the 'freedom to hold opinions and to receive and impart information and ideas in the minority language, without interference by public authorities and regardless of frontiers'. Throughout, the emphasis is on the protection of individuals belonging to national minorities and there is no recognition of any collective rights. In this regard, the Framework Convention is in keeping with texts such as the *Universal Declaration of Human Rights*.

The Convention focuses on the freedom of individuals to use their minority languages, but also implies the freedom to receive information in those same languages. It specifically deals with language issues in the fields of education, culture and the media as these are deemed to be crucial sectors for the transmission and enhancement of languages. The document is keen to emphasize a positive relationship between speakers of minority languages and the nation-state, and in particular to ensure that the status of official languages is not threatened. This gesture of tolerance and dialogue is probably a necessary pre-condition for the support of nation-states who might feel some concern regarding the status of their national languages.

The Convention avails of flexible wording throughout, giving parties involved a good deal of discretion in their application of the document. Phrases such as 'sufficient demand' and 'as far as possible' are designed to encourage partners to participate without fear of threat to national resources, but not everyone agrees with such a strategy. Phillipson *et al.* (1995: 5) suggest that such '"legitimate" flexibility' and 'many escape clauses' substantially undermine the linguistic rights of the speakers within state boundaries. They also allow states that want to be seen as doing something, to refrain from committing themselves fully. It is true that such phrases may be regarded as weaknesses, as they permit great flexibility in the application of the document at national levels, but without such flexibility, it might prove exceptionally difficult to persuade states to commit themselves. Since it opened for signature in 1995, 39 nation-states have ratified the document (see Table 4.2). A further four signatures were not followed by ratification.

Table 4.2 Member states of the Council of Europe that have signed or ratified the *Framework Convention for the Protection of National Minorities*

Member states	Signature	Ratification	Entry into force
Albania	29/06/1995	28/09/1999	01/01/2000
Armenia	25/07/1997	20/07/1998	01/11/1998
Austria	01/02/1995	31/03/1998	01/07/1998
Azerbaijan		26/06/2000	01/10/2000
Belgium	31/07/2001		
Bosnia and Herzegovina		24/02/2000	01/06/2000
Bulgaria	09/10/1997	07/05/1999	01/09/1999
Croatia	06/11/1996	11/10/1997	01/02/1998
Cyprus	01/02/1995	04/06/1996	01/02/1998
Czech Republic	28/04/1995	18/12/1997	01/04/1998
Denmark	01/02/1995	22/09/1997	01/02/1998
Estonia	02/02/1995	06/01/1997	01/02/1998
Finland	01/02/1995	03/10/1997	01/02/1998
Georgia	21/01/2000	22/12/2005	01/04/2006
Germany	11/05/1995	10/09/1997	01/02/1998
Greece	22/09/1997		
Hungary	01/02/1995	25/09/1995	01/02/1998
Iceland	01/02/1995		
Ireland	01/02/1995	07/05/1999	01/09/1999
Italy	01/02/1995	03/11/1999	01/03/1998
Latvia	11/05/1995	06/06/2005	01/10/2005
Liechtenstein	01/02/1995	18/11/1997	01/03/1998
Lithuania	01/02/1995	23/03/2000	01/07/2000
Luxembourg	20/07/1995		
Malta	11/05/1995	10/02/1998	01/06/1998
Moldova	13/07/1995	20/11/1996	01/02/1998
Montenegro		11/05/2001	06/06/2006
Netherlands	01/02/1995	16/02/2005	01/06/2005
Norway	01/02/1995	17/03/1999	01/07/1999
Poland	01/02/1995	20/12/2000	01/04/2001
Portugal	01/02/1995	07/05/2002	01/09/2002
Romania	01/02/1995	11/05/1995	01/02/1998
Russia	28/02/1996	21/08/1998	01/12/1998
San Marino	11/05/1995	05/12/1996	01/02/1998
Serbia		11/05/2001	01/09/2001
Slovakia	01/02/1995	14/09/1995	01/02/1998
Slovenia	01/02/1995	25/03/1998	01/07/1998
Spain	01/02/1995	01/09/1999	01/02/1998
Sweden	01/02/1995	09/02/2000	01/06/2000
Switzerland	01/02/1995	21/10/1998	01/02/1999
The former Yugoslav Republic of Macedonia	25/07/1996	10/04/1997	01/02/1998
Ukraine	15/09/1995	26/01/1998	01/05/1998
United Kingdom	01/02/1995	15/01/1998	01/05/1998

Source: adapted from http://conventions.coe.int/Treaty/Commun/ChercheSig.asp?NT=15 7&CM=8&DF=5/27/2008&CL=ENG.

A notable absence from this list of signatories is France which also has problems with the *European Charter for Regional or Minority Languages*.

Despite these initiatives on behalf of speakers of minority languages, the notion of language rights is a contested issue. One of the key issues is the significance of language for identity. If language is a critical factor, then the notion of linguistic rights is crucial for the well-being of individuals in a society. If, on the other hand, language is contingent for a sense of identity, then the implementation of linguistic rights is less essential.

Linguistic diversity and identity

Some eminent sociolinguists have argued that language is not necessarily an essential element of identity (Eastman 1984; Edwards 1985, 1994). If this is true, then linguistic rights are not necessarily crucial. If individuals do not have the right to use their preferred language – particularly if this is a language that offers no economic potential – they can simply begin speaking another. From this perspective, giving people the right to speak a language that is 'backward' is not necessarily beneficial and may even be harmful. This is an argument that could equally be used against the preservation of any traditional skills. Maintaining people in a traditional setting with traditional skills may deprive them of the benefits of modernity and progress.

The suggestion that language is not an essential component of identity should be set in the context of current social theory which emphasizes the fluidity of culture and identity at all levels (Hall 1992; Bhabha 1994). Personalities are regarded as fluid. Billig (1995: 69) uses the term 'pastiche personality' for the multi-faceted nature of our personalities. He places great emphasis on the contextual nature of identity. Some postmodernist academics argue for the absence of any 'inner core'.

The notion of a stable identity has become branded with the 'negative characteristics of essentialism, closure and conflict' (May 2001: 39). Yet to regard identity as completely un-rooted seems illogical and it is surely the case that there is some element of stability in the concept of identity. Although models of culture and identity are fluid, they do have substance and are hardly ephemeral. This would explain the attachment to traditional mother tongues:

> hybridity of identity doesn't change the fact that ethnicity and mother tongue have always been potent forces in community relations ... Change doesn't mean irrelevance or irreverence. Attachments to ethnicity and mother tongue are resilient, despite their limited value in pragmatic and material terms.
>
> (May 2001: 439)

Stephen May (2005: 330) goes to the kernel of this argument when he suggests that 'to say that language is not an inevitable feature of identity is thus *not* the same as saying it is unimportant' (italics original). Although language and linguistic heritage are contingent elements of one's identity, this does not imply that they are unimportant. Contingency does not imply peripherality. This explains the significance of language in many contemporary conflicts in Europe where the will to maintain a traditional language, despite considerable adversity, is a rational choice (Maguire 1991; Conversi 1997; O'Reilly 1999). But does that explain the importance of linguistic diversity?

Despite the empathy felt with a traditional language, how does one counter the argument that life would be considerably easier if all Europeans spoke the same language – perhaps English. Then the issue of linguistic rights would become totally irrelevant on the continent as everyone would speak the same language. This argument ignores the fact that not all individuals speak English as a mother tongue and to operate solely in English would seriously disadvantage those having to learn it as a second language.

Here one might also appeal to the significance of heritage and biodiversity arguments. Linguistic diversity is increasingly challenged in contemporary, globalized society. At the turn of the millennium, surveys by the United States Summer Institute of Linguistics calculated that there were approximately 6,809 languages in existence (Grimes 2000). Experts concur that language loss is occurring at an unprecedented rate at the beginning of the twenty-first century. Krauss (1992, 1995) has calculated that half of the languages currently spoken may die within the next century. Moreover, a further 40 per cent are 'endangered' (Nic Craith 2007). Biodiversity is also threatened and it is generally accepted that a proportion of the world's biological species are becoming extinct.

Skutnabb-Kangas (2002) makes an interesting connection between these two, suggesting that when linguistic and cultural diversity is high, it has a positive impact on biodiversity. She supports her argument with reference to David Harmon (1995, 2002) who finds a high degree of overlap between linguistic diversity and biodiversity in 16 of the top 25 countries that he examined. When comparing languages and plants, language and butterflies, etc., he found a high correlation between biological and linguistic diversity. There may be a logical reason for the link. Traditional languages are reservoirs of local knowledge. When languages die, traditional knowledge concerning the local environment and its species is also lost. This particularly applies to indigenous knowledge which has not necessarily been acquired or endorsed by science. 'If the long-lasting coevolution which people have had with their environments since time immemorial is abruptly disrupted (as we are doing today), without nature (and people) having enough time to adjust and adapt, we are also seriously undermining our chances of life on earth' (Skutnabb-Kangas 2002: 14). The ecological argument applies to all aspects of heritage and not just language.

To link languages with the environment is a powerful argument but it also can imply that languages are self-sustaining and have natural life-cycles.

They emerge, flourish and die, like other species in the environment. As long as there is respect for and attachment to a particular language, it will be transmitted from one generation to the next. Natural selection can decide on the fate of all languages, and there is no need to offer support structures such as linguistic rights for speakers of languages which cannot cope with modernity. Such arguments assume that the universality of languages such as English and French is an inevitable consequence of their 'natural' ability to cope with modernity. These languages are 'naturally' superior to minority and regional languages which seem constantly under threat. But the most powerful languages in contemporary Europe have not emerged naturally. Instead, intense planning and government support has preceded their proliferation across the continent and further afield. The adaptability of these major languages to modernity has been greatly aided by centuries of official support – a support that has not been available to regional or minority languages and their speakers (Nic Craith 2007).

Linguistic rights in the context of human rights

A crucial issue that has emerged in this debate is the extent to which linguistic rights are really human rights at all. The *Universal Declaration of Human Rights* (1948) does make some allusion to culture but not specifically to language. Article 2 of this Declaration suggests that every individual is entitled to the rights and freedoms specified in the document 'without distinction of any kind, such as race, colour, sex, language, religion, political or other opinion, national or social origin, property, birth or other status' (www.un.org/Overview/rights.html). Article 27 is more explicit in relation to the cultural sphere, suggesting that '[e]veryone has the right freely to participate in the cultural life of the community, to enjoy the arts and to share in scientific advancement and its benefits'. (Silverman and Ruggles (2007: 4) note of this Article, in particular, that it effectively 'introduced the idea that culture was an aspect of human rights', although it failed to comment on relationships between individuals, communities and nations, and how tensions between these relationships might be resolved. Moreover, one might add that the Article seems to imply a mono-cultural context generally. Everyone has the right to enjoy the single cultural life of the community, which is inevitably that of the majority. There is no mention here of minority cultures or multiple cultural contexts.

The notion of cultural rights was further promoted with the *Declaration on the Rights of Persons Belonging to National or Ethnic, Religious and Linguistic Minorities*, a resolution promoted by the General Assembly of the United Nations in 1992 (www.unhchr.ch/html/racism/minorpart1–1.doc). The first Article requires of states that they 'protect the existence and the national or ethnic, cultural, religious and linguistic identity of minorities' within their territorial boundaries, but also that they encourage the conditions necessary for the promotion of that identity. Article 2 specifies that individuals belonging to linguistic (and other) minorities 'have the right to enjoy their own culture' and 'to use their own language, in private and in public, freely and without interference or any form of discrimination'. Article 4 urges states to 'take measures to create favourable conditions to enable persons belonging to minorities ... to develop their culture, language, religion, traditions and customs', except in those circumstances where specific cultural customs violate national law and are contrary to international standards.

Four years later, the *Declaration of the Principles of International Cultural Co-operation* highlighted the value and dignity of each culture which ought to be preserved and respected (www.wwda.org.au/deccultcoop1.pdf). The first Article notes both the right and the duty of each community to develop its cultures. It also re-affirms the importance of all cultures 'in their rich variety and diversity and in the reciprocal influences they exert on one another', which 'form part of the common heritage belonging to all mankind'.

The *International Covenant on Civil and Political Rights* opened for signature in 1966 also features language rights, although in this instance these rights are primarily instrumental rather than cultural (http://www1.umn.edu/humanrts/instree/b3ccpr.htm). Article 9 requires certain minimum guarantees when criminal charges are brought against an individual. Any person in these circumstances is entitled 'to be informed promptly and in detail in a language which he understands of the nature and cause of the charge against him' and 'to have the free assistance of an interpreter if he cannot understand or speak the language used in court'. This language is similar to the *Convention for the Protection of Human Rights and Fundamental Freedoms* mentioned earlier. Article 27 is more significant. Focusing on states where linguistic, religious or ethnic minorities exist, that Covenant stipulates that 'persons belonging to such minorities shall not be denied the right, in community with the other members of their group, to enjoy their own culture, to profess and practise their own religion, or to use their own language'.

All of the Articles cited above imply both an individual and a communal element in the promotion of language rights. This is problematic for a number of reasons, not least of which is the question of whether linguistic human rights can deal with both collective and individual dimensions. If human rights operate at the level of the individual only, this might suggest that the collective nature of language rights disallows them from being classified as human rights. Fernand de Varennes (2001), one of the leading proponents of language rights, suggests that the distinction is irrelevant. 'It is therefore an oft repeated error to assume that the protection of the rights of minorities is somehow inconsistent with "individual" human rights which have emerged as an integral feature of international law this century.' From his perspective, language rights are recognition of individual human diversity. 'To deny minority individuals access to certain benefits, or to disadvantage them because of their religion or language is – under certain conditions – no longer permissible. Their human differences must be respected and acknowledged to some degree beyond mere tolerance.'

Phillipson *et al.* (1995: 2) argue that both the individual and the collective aspects are highly significant for linguistic human rights. These academics define the notion of a linguistic human right at an individual level as allowing everybody 'to identify positively with their mother tongue, and have that identification respected by others, irrespective of whether their mother tongue is a minority language or a majority language'. This implies the right to basic education in one's mother tongue but also includes the right to acquire at least one of the official languages in one's country of residence. However, it does not take account of the contemporary hybrid world where children can have several, rather than one, native languages.

At group level, Phillipson *et al.* (1995: 2) define the observation of linguistic human rights as implying the right of minority groups to exist. 'It implies the right to enjoy and develop their language and the right for minorities to establish and maintain schools and other training and educational institutions, with control of curricula and teaching in their own language' (Phillipson *et al.* 1995: 2). But the potential recognition of a minority can cause immense anxieties for states. If, for example, France were to sanction linguistic rights for individual speakers of Arabic, does that not automatically legitimate the Arabic minority? If Germany were to give formal linguistic rights to speakers of Turkish, would that not imply that Turks are a legal minority within state boundaries? Many states are not necessarily happy with such consequences.

France, in particular, has been very uncomfortable with the *European Charter for Regional or Minority Languages* for precisely this reason. Although the Charter does not actually give rights to speakers of minority languages, the indivisibility of the state (from the French perspective) was under threat. When initially France appeared in favour of the Charter, the French President felt it necessary to declare that 'the Charter does not aim at recognizing and protecting minorities, but only at promoting European linguistic heritage'. For this reason, the notion of language groups does not imply collective rights for such groups. In that context only, the French Government understood the Charter 'to be compatible with the preamble to the French constitution, which guarantees the equality of all its citizens before the law and recognizes only the French people, comprising all citizens without any distinction as to origin, race or religion' (cited in Oellers-Frahm 1999: 940). France subsequently failed to ratify the Charter (Judge and Judge 2000).

Sue Wright (2007: 204) argues that although positive language rights may be presented as individual rights, they are in reality group rights. 'Where governments accord access to government, participation in the legal process and educational provision in the minority language, they tend to cater for the group as a whole.' When this happens, one language will inevitably tend to come to the fore. 'The local school will have a dominant language in the institution, even if others are taught. There will be a dominant language in the court, even if there is provision for translation.' In order to fully implement language rights, they must become group rights.

Such complications have not deterred those campaigning for a more formal recognition of the concept of universal linguistic human rights. As 2008 was declared the International Year of Languages by the UN, organizations such as the European Bureau for Lesser Used Languages and CIEMEN (an international network to promote linguistic diversity) took the opportunity to press the case for a *Universal Declaration of Linguistic Rights*. In June 2008, CIEMEN co-organized a symposium in Geneva to coincide with the eighth session of the UN Human Rights Council. Attendees at the event entitled 'Linguistic Rights to Enhance Human Rights' penned a draft resolution on linguistic human rights which was then presented at a September session of the Human Rights Council. Aureli Argemí (President of CIEMEN) in a speech at the 14th plenary meeting of the UN Human Rights Council, proposed the adoption of a *Universal Declaration of Linguistic Rights* to complement the *Universal Declaration of Human Rights*, arguing that this responsibility is incumbent on the Human Rights Council because, 'although languages must be considered in the context of culture, and may therefore fall within the ambit of UNESCO, languages do not have rights; but individuals, they have linguistic rights'. For this reason, he explained, it is common to distinguish between languages and cultures (www.nationalia.info/en/news/271).

The text of the draft resolution notes that 'no single UN declaration specifically defines linguistic rights in positive terms and sets forth which rights constitute linguistic rights'. Four Articles are presented for consideration. The first of these recognizes that 'all languages are of equal value and deserve equal respect'. This is linked to the premise that 'each language is an expression of the identity of the speaker and of the speaker's community'. Article 2 asserts that greater recognition of linguistic diversity will promote a 'constructive peace between peoples'. The subsequent Article urges states to continue policies to ensure that 'all languages are respected, promoted and used in society, in all domains that affect the life of the individual and the community'. The fourth and final Article urges the pursuance of linguistic rights across the world (www.eblul.org/images/stories/hrc_resolution_proposal_linguistic_rights.doc).

Conclusion

There is still no broad agreement on the meaning of the concept of linguistic human rights, and the full implications of language rights for speakers of all languages in Europe is still at an early stage of the debate. Apart from the issues that I have dealt with in this chapter, there are many concerns that I have not had the scope to deal with here. This applies in particular to the notion of a hierarchy of linguistic human rights. Do linguistic human rights have a universal application or are some (i.e. indigenous groups) more entitled to these rights than others. In a European context, there is the question of whether non-Europeans should be excluded from the terms of reference of any language rights that might apply in a European context – or do such questions negate the concept of a human right that is conceptually intended to apply to all? These debates notwithstanding, it is clear that proponents of linguistic human rights are more determined than ever to push forward the campaign. With the proper legislation, the linguistic heritage of Europe could be stabilized and enhanced. Without the proper structures, many of the languages currently spoken could become linguistic relics, and this would result in the impoverishment of Europe's intangible heritage. The debate has only begun.

Bibliography

Alcock, A. (2000) *A History of the Protection of Regional Cultural Minorities in Europe from the Edict of Nantes to the Present Day*, Basingstoke: Palgrave Macmillan.

Anderson, B. (1993) *Imagined Communities*, London: Verso.

Argenter, J. and McKenna Brown, R. (eds) (2004) *On the Margins of Nations: Endangered Languages and Linguistic Rights*, Barcelona: Foundation for Endangered Languages.

Barbour, S. and Carmichael, C. (eds) (2000) *Language and Nationalism in Europe*, Oxford: University Press.

Bhabha, H. (1994) *The Location of Culture*, London: Routledge.

Billig, M. (1995) *Banal Nationalism*, London: Sage.

Canagarajah, A. S. (2005) 'Dilemmas in Planning English/Vernacular Relations in Post-colonial Communities,' *Journal of Sociolinguistics* 9 (3): 418–47.

Convention for the Protection of Human Rights and Fundamental Freedoms. Available at www.echr.coe.int/nr/rdonlyres/d5cc24a7-dc13–4318-b457–5c9014916d7a/0/englishanglais.pdf (accessed 27 November 2008).

Conversi, D. (1997) *The Basques, the Catalans and Spain: Alternative Routes to Nationalist Mobilization*, London: Hurst and Co.

Declaration of the Principles of International Cultural Co-operation. Available at www.un-documents.net/a47r135.htm da.org.au/deccultcoop1.pdf (accessed 27 November 2008).

Declaration on the Rights of Persons Belonging to National or Ethnic, Religious and Linguistic Minorities. Available at www.un-documents.net/a47r135.htm (accessed 27 November 2008).

de Varennes, F. (1997) 'To Speak or not to Speak.: The Rights of Persons Belonging to Linguistic Minorities,' Working Paper prepared for the UN Sub-Committee on the rights of minorities. Available at www.unesco.org/most/ln2pol3.htm (accessed 27 November 2008).

—— (2001) 'Language Rights as an Integral Part of Human Rights,' *International Journal of Multicultural Studies* 3 (1): 15–25.

Draft Resolution of Linguistic Human Rights. Available at www.eblul.org/images/ stories/hrc_resolution_proposal_linguistic_rights.doc (accessed 27 November 2008).

Druviete, I. (1998) 'Republic of Latvia,' in C. B. Paulston and D. Peckham (eds) *Linguistic Minorities in Central and Eastern Europe*, Clevedon: Multilingual Matters, pp. 160–83.

Eastman, C. (1984) 'Language, Ethnic Identity and Change,' in J. Edwards (ed.) *Linguistic Minorities, Policies and Pluralism*, London: Academic Press, pp. 259–76.

Edwards, J. (1985) *Language, Society and Identity*, Oxford: Blackwell.

—— (1994) *Multilingualism*, London: Routledge.

European Charter for Regional or Minority Languages. Available at http://conventions. coe.int/Treaty/en/Reports/Html/148.htm (accessed 27 November 2008).

European Cultural Convention. Available at http://conventions.coe.int/Treaty/EN/ Treaties/Html/018.htm (accessed 27 November 2008).

Framework Convention for the Protection of National Minorities: Explanatory Report. Available at http://conventions.coe.int/Treaty/EN/Reports/Html/157.htm (accessed 27 November 2008).

Grimes, B. (2000) *Ethnologue: Languages of the World*, Vol. 1, 14th edn, Texas: US Summer School of Linguistics.

Hall, S. (1992) 'The Questions of Cultural Identity,' in S. Hall, D. Held and T. McGrew (eds) *Modernity and its Futures*, Cambridge: Polity Press, pp. 274–325.

Harmon, D. (1995) 'The Status of the World's Languages as Reported in the "Ethnologue",' *Southwest Journal of Linguistics* 14 (1&2), pp. 1–28.

—— (2002) *In Light of Our Differences: How Diversity in Nature and Culture Makes Us Human*, Washington: Smithsonian.

Judge, A. and Judge, S. (2000) 'Linguistic Policies in France and Contemporary Issues: the Signing of the Charter for Regional or Minority Languages,' *International Journal of Francophone Studies* 3 (2): 106–27.

Kontra, M., Phillipson, R., Skutnabb-Kangas, T. and Varady, T. (eds) (1999) *Language: A Right and a Resource – Approaches to Linguistic Human Rights*, Budapest: Central European University Press.

Kockel, U. (1999) *Borderline Cases: Ethnic Frontiers and European Integration*, Liverpool: University Press.

Krauss, M. (1992) 'The World's Languages in Crisis,' *Language* 68: 4–10.

—— (1995) 'Language Loss in Alaska, the United States and the World. Frame of Reference,' *Alaska Humanities Forum* 6 (1): 2–5.

Maalouf, A. (2008) *A Rewarding Challenge: How the Multiplicity of Languages Could Strengthen Europe*, Brussels. Available at http://ec.europa.eu/education/policies/ lang/doc/maalouf/report_en.pdf (accessed 27 November 2008).

McColl Millar, R. (2005) *Language, Nation and Power: an Introduction*, Basingstoke: Palgrave Macmillan.

Maguire, G. (1991) *Our Own Language: an Irish Initiative*, Clevedon: Multilingual Matters.

May, S. (2001) *Language and Minority Rights: Ethnicity, Nationalism and the Politics of Language*, Essex: Longman.

—— (2005) 'Language Rights: Moving the Debate Forward,' *Journal of Sociolinguistics* 9 (3): 319–47.

Nic Craith, M. (2003) 'Facilitating or Generating Linguistic Diversity: the European Charter for Regional or Minority Languages,' in S. Wolff and G. Hogan-Brun (eds) *Minority Languages in Europe: Frameworks – Status – Prospects*, Basingstoke: Palgrave, pp. 59–72.

—— (2004) 'Culture and Citizenship in Europe: Questions for Anthropologists,' *Social Anthropology* 12 (3): 289–300.

—— (2006) *Europe and the Politics of Language: Citizens, Migrants, Outsiders*, Basingstoke: Palgrave Macmillan.

—— (2007) 'Rethinking Language Policies: Challenges and Opportunities,' in C. Williams (ed.) *Language and Governance*, Cardiff: University of Wales Press, pp. 159–84.

Oellers-Frahm, K. (1999) 'European Charter for Regional and Minority Languages – Minority Group Rights and Compatibility with Concepts of Equality, Nondiscrimination and National Unity in French Constitution – Reconciling Official Language with Freedom of Speech,' *The American Journal of International Law*, 93: 938–42.

O'Reilly, C. (1999) *The Irish Language in Northern Ireland: the Politics of Culture and Identity*, Basingstoke: Palgrave Macmillan.

(The) Path towards a Universal Declaration. Available at www.nationalia.info/en/news/271 (accessed 27 November 2008).

Paulston, C. B. (1997) 'Language Policies and Language Rights,' *Annual Review of Anthropology* 26: 73–85.

Phillipson, R., Rannut, M. and Skutnabb-Kangas, T. (1995) 'Introduction' in T. Skutnabb-Kangas and R. Phillipson (eds) *Linguistic Human Rights: Overcoming Linguistic Discrimination*, Berlin, New York: Mouton de Gruyter, pp. 1–22.

Poulton, H. (1998) 'Linguistic Minorities in the Balkans (Albania, Greece and the Successor States of former Yugoslavia),' in C. B. Paulston and D. Peckham (eds) *Linguistic Minorities in Central and Eastern Europe*, Clevedon: Multilingual Matters, pp. 37–79.

Schneider, B. (2005) *Linguistic Human Rights and Migrant Languages: a Comparative Analysis of Migrant Language Education in Great Britain and Germany*, Bern, Berlin: Peter Lang.

Silverman, H. and Fairchild Ruggles, D. (2007) 'Cultural Heritage and Human Rights,' in H. Silverman and D. Fairchild Ruggles (eds) *Cultural Heritage and Human Rights*, New York, Berlin: Springer, pp. 3–22.

Skutnabb-Kangas, T. (2002) *Why Should Linguistic Diversity Be Maintained and Supported In Europe? Some Arguments*, Strasbourg: Council of Europe. Available at www.coe.int/t/dg4/linguistic/Source/Skutnabb-KangasEN.pdf (accessed 27 November 2008).

Skutnabb-Kangas, T. and Phillipson, R. (eds) (1995) *Linguistic Human Rights: Overcoming Linguistic Discrimination*, Berlin, New York: Mouton de Gruyter.

Spolsky, B. (2004) *Language Policy*, Cambridge: University Press.

Treaty of Lisbon. Available at http://eurlex.europa.eu/JOHtml.do?uri=OJ:C:2007:306:SOM:EN:HTML (accessed 27 November 2008).

Treaty of Rome. Available at www.hri.org/docs/Rome57/Rome57.txt (accessed 27 November 2008).

Universal Declaration of Human Rights. Available at www.un.org/Overview/rights.html (accessed 27 November 2008).

Vieytez, E. J. R. (2001) 'The Protection of Linguistic Minorities: a Historical Approach,' *International Journal on Multicultural Societies* 3 (1): 5–14.

Wright, S. (2001) 'Language and Power: Background to the Debate on Linguistic Rights,' *International Journal on Multicultural Societies* 3 (1): 44–54.

—— (2007) 'The Right to Speak One's Own Language: Reflections on Theory and Practice,' *Language Policy* 6: 203–24.

Part II

National versus local rights

Chapter 5

Unravelling the cradle of civilization 'layer by layer'

Iraq, its peoples and cultural heritage

Ana Filipa Vrdoljak

> Our history was in the building. It was the soul of Iraq. If the museum doesn't recover the looted treasures, I will feel like a part of my own soul has been stolen.
>
> (Lemonick 2003: 46)

The modern state of Iraq came into being with its demarcation by outside Powers following the First World War. This moment threw into stark relief two characteristics which have prevailed to the present day. On the one hand, there is the diversity of its constituent peoples, that is, the multifarious ethnic, religious and linguistic minorities which live within its territorial boundaries. On the other, its rich cultural heritage has been deployed consistently to imbue its populace with a unified, *national* sentiment. Iraq has been an often tragic testing ground for the themes of this book: cultural heritage, diversity and human rights.

In this chapter, I concentrate on the two (often contradictory) forces which have defined the state of Iraq and the antagonisms and efforts at reconciling them which have marked it since its inception. The centrifugal force of diversity was an inevitable consequence of the emergence of a nation hewed from the remnants of a collapsing empire. The mixing of people and their cultures and religions over vast territories and existing side by side is emblematic of most empires, and the Ottoman Empire in particular. While the empire dissolved, this diversity on the ground often remained unchanged. The territorial boundaries of the new nation state made few concessions to this reality. Instead, individuals and communities which found themselves within its borders were provided with some guarantees designed to ensure their enjoyment of their languages, cultures and religious practices. These minority guarantees were a precursor to contemporary human rights. However, the reality for these groups and their individual members often fell far short of these laws.

This motion was counterbalanced by the centripetal force of the new state which strove to engender a cohesive whole within its borders. The harnessing of a rich cultural heritage was essential to fostering a *national* identity to unify the populace. Detailed legislation and sanctions for the protection of historic monuments and archaeological sites was a central plank of this effort. The promotion and protection of both the diversity of minority cultures and religions (and related human rights of its practitioners) and the protection of cultural heritage lay largely in the lap of the same entity, the government and officials of the state. The history of Iraq bears witness to the problematic nature of these multiple forces and responsibilities.

This chapter considers the twin forces of diversity and the pursuit of national unity as they have been played out in Iraq through the twentieth and twenty-first centuries. It is divided into three parts which follow a chronological line: first, the period from the British mandate to the establishment of the Kingdom of Iraq and the internalization of external norms; second, the period from the Republic to the dictatorship of Saddam Hussein, and the rise of nationalism and socialism during decolonization; and finally, the invasion of Kuwait, the 1990–1991 Gulf War, 2003 coalition invasion and occupation, and post-war reconstruction and transition from occupier to occupied.

Mandate to kingdom

The first half of the twentieth century saw the emergence of the Iraqi state following the dismantling of the Ottoman Empire, its administration during the British mandate, and then its gradual transition to statehood as the Kingdom of Iraq. The period is marked by the imposition of standards and norms from above (by the international community through its interlocutor, Britain), including a constitution which guaranteed certain rights to all Iraqi citizens, and recognized the right of minorities to preserve and practise their languages, cultures and religions, and antiquities legislation protecting a cultural heritage deemed the inheritance not only of a particular nation, but all humanity.

British mandate: defining a nation from the top down

From the mid-nineteenth century, Mesopotamia experienced the brunt of escalating Western interest in antiquities which fuelled a myriad of excavations of archaeological sites in this 'neglected province of a decaying empire' (Lloyd 1980: 173). This situation was tempered somewhat from 1881, when the Ottoman statesman, Hamdi Bey founded the Archaeological Museum of Istanbul. Henceforth, in an effort to build a collection befitting an imperial capital, this museum retained unique finds and divided duplicates between itself and the excavator (Lloyd 1980: 170). In addition, the Ottoman Empire had in place minority protection for particular religious communities, which protected their right to practise their faith and protected communal property.

Following the First World War, the Ottoman Empire was partitioned and a mandate, administered by Britain, was established over the newly defined and designated state of Iraq. As the mandating power, Britain undertook the responsibility encapsulated in 'the principle that the well-being and development of such peoples form[ed] a sacred trust of civilization'.[1] The redefinition and internationalization of the colonial relationship in the aftermath of the First World War meant that Britain held the territory on a double trust: to guide the territory to self-rule and ensure equal access to all member states of the League of Nations to Iraq's resources, including cultural 'resources'.

At the commencement of the British mandate, British official, Gertrude Bell was appointed the first Director of Antiquities in Iraq. She was keenly aware of the 'Arab awakening' of national consciousness which inextricably wove political nationalism with a cultural resurgence (Lloyd 1980: 179). She was instrumental in mapping not only the first physical borders of the new, multi-ethnic Iraqi state but also its 'national', cultural parameters through the establishment of the Baghdad Museum and the drafting of the first Iraqi antiquities legislation (Russell 2001: 44).

1924 Antiquities Law

Unable to maintain the costs of occupation but determined to protect its oil fields in southern Iraq, the British finally signed the Treaty of Alliance with Iraq on 10 October 1922 ('1922 Treaty'), creating the kingdom of Iraq with the newly installed monarch, King Faisal I as its titular head.[2] Under Article XIV of the 1922 Treaty, the relevant Iraqi authorities undertook 'to ensure the execution of a Law of Antiquities based on the rules annexed to Article 421' of the Treaty of Peace with Turkey ('Treaty of Sèvres') which had been signed but not ratified (Visscher 1937: 700).[3] Bell drafted and lobbied for the passage of legislation to regulate the excavation and export of antiquities (Bell 1927: II, 654). The Antiquities Law No. 40 of 1924 ('1924 Antiquities Law') was finally passed in the same year the Iraqi National Assembly ratified the 1922 treaty with Britain.

While Gertrude Bell discharged her duty under the 1924 Antiquities Act with her primary concern being Iraqi interests, her understanding of how these obligations were to be fulfilled was defined in Anglo-American terms. Like other mandated territories, the antiquities department established by the mandating power encouraged excavation by large foreign archaeological expeditions. At the end of the British mandate in 1932, there were 11 expeditions of five different nationalities working in Iraq (O'Keefe and Prott 1984: 46–7). The division of antiquities was determined by Bell, as Director of Antiquities. For Bell, 'the interests of science' dictated that because of the scarcity of resources and expertise in Iraq to restore and preserve objects meant they were relinquished to museums in other states (Bell 1927: 725).

1925 Constitution of the Kingdom of Iraq

Bell's letters during the 1920s detail the deep ethnic and religious fracture lines which plague Iraq to this day and which she even then saw as threatening the very existence of the state. The League of Nations' mandate system under which Britain administered Iraq provided for a rudimentary guarantee of minority rights. The victorious Allied Powers had been aware of the need for such guarantees when drawing up territorial boundaries in Europe during the Versailles Peace Conference in 1919. The potential instability arising from newly formed multi-ethnic states applied with equal force to Iraq. Accordingly, when the Iraqi constitution was adopted on 21 March 1925 it provided various rights to its constituent peoples.[4] Whilst Islam was recognized as the official religion of the new kingdom, Article 13 also guaranteed religious freedom for all. In addition to the guarantee of non-discrimination (Article 6), Article 18 ensured equal enjoyment of civil rights by all Iraqis. The constitution also provided some measure of cultural preservation and reproduction for minorities (Article 16). However, these guarantees did little to prevent inter-ethnic violence and protect certain minorities in the new state.

Kingdom of Iraq: self-definition and internalization of external norms

The transition of Iraq from British administration to independence was defined unsurprisingly by its leaders' efforts to assert their distinction from those that had preceded them. Yet, the mechanisms which they employed manifested their internalization of external norms and standards in respect of minorities and cultural heritage, some imposed from outside, others voluntarily adopted.

Minority protection declaration and League of Nations membership

On 30 May 1932, upon its admission to the League of Nations (and as part of its condition of entry), Iraq unilaterally declared its acceptance of the obligations arising from the organization's minority protection regime. However, as noted above, this framework had been significantly internalized into the legal order of the Iraqi state through its 1925 constitution. The League minority guarantee had several levels. First, the nationality of members of the minority was guaranteed – this served as a starting gate issue for the remaining rights. Second, the state would have to provide equal treatment in respect of civil and political rights of nationals. Finally, special measures would be established for minority groups covering cultural reproduction. This minority guarantee became part of the fundamental law, which could not be altered by its domestic legislation, and with compliance subject to external oversight. This international guarantee proved largely ineffective in preventing growing ethnic strife in the country and the repression of minorities (Iraq 1932).

Iraqi nationalism and the Samarra controversy

During the 1920s and '30s, the increasing interest exhibited by populations in the Middle East in antiquities located within their territory was reflected in the introduction of stricter regulations governing their excavation and export. Iraqi officials made a firm connection between people, territory and cultural identity (Bernardsson 2001a). While archaeology was a Western discipline it became 'an integral aspect of the indigenous cultural perception' (Masry 1982: 222).

Iraq's admission as the first independent Arab state into the League of Nations in 1932, led to significant changes within the Department of Antiquities. Briton, Sidney Smith, was recalled to the British Museum and an Arab nationalist, Sati al-Husri, replaced him as Director of Antiquities. Al-Husri's impact was immediate. He directed his attention to protecting and preserving the Iraqi national heritage through restitution requests to reverse prior cultural loss; passage of a new antiquities law and seeking international enforcement of export controls to prevent ongoing cultural loss; and training Iraqi nationals and educating the population generally to ensure the future preservation of this cultural heritage.

During the mid-1930s, Iraqi authorities commenced investigating the holdings of Mesopotamian artefacts in Western museums. These searches uncovered that the Samarra collection of ninth-century Islamic antiquities which had been excavated in 1914 was located at the British Museum (Bernardsson 2001b: 17). In 1919, then Colonial Secretary Winston Churchill ordered the collection which had been captured during the First World War be 'removed to England, in order to prevent [its] deterioration' and before the 1922 Treaty was signed (British Museum 1933: 5004). In response to a restitution claim for the Samarra collection, the British Museum trustees concluded the Iraqi government 'could have no legal claim to these antiquities...' (British Museum 1933: 5004). After much pressure from the British government, the museum finally relinquished a fraction of the original collection which was greeted with jubilation on its arrival in Baghdad in 1936.

1936 Antiquities Law

During the 1920s, there had been some legal antiquities dealing in Baghdad. However, this trade had steadily dwindled during the 1930s (Gibson 1997). Al-Husri sought to further inhibit it through the passage of new antiquities legislation. British Museum officials were perturbed by the new law prior to its passage (British Museum 1933: 5004). The leader of the Museum's Ur expedition, Charles Leonard Woolley, maintained the Iraqi antiquities bill was proceeded by a campaign which alleged that the earlier 1924 Act had 'robbed [Iraq], by concessions made to foreign missions, of the treasures which were legally and morally hers' (Woolley 1935: 84).

The Iraqi Antiquities Law No. 59 of 1936 (as amended in 1974 and 1975) covering the excavation, export and importation of antiquities in Iraq remained in force until 2002. The law vested ownership of all antiquities in the Iraqi state (Article 3). Export was prohibited. Unauthorized exportation or attempted exportation was punishable by imprisonment of up to five years and the confiscation of the antiquities (Article 60 (1)). The law also regulated the excavation of antiquities (Part V). All antiquities discovered by the excavators were the property of the Iraqi state and the excavator would be given a reward (Article 49).

An *Antiquity* editorial in early 1935 concluded that whilst foreign scientists were discouraged and penalized under the reforms, Iraq had no means of undertaking such research itself nor did the law provide 'efficient means to prevent wholesale spoliation and destruction of ancient sites' (Anon. 1935: 1–2). Al-Husri had worked to enable the Department's own people to conduct excavations in the country; however, it quickly became clear to him that his staff were inadequately trained in the archaeological method. To remedy this situation, Iraqi authorities attached local inspectors to ensure that they acquired the necessary scientific training (British Museum 1933: 5004).

Iraqi authorities, like other archaeologically rich nations, were aware that their national antiquities law had limited effect beyond their territorial borders. Hence, Iraq's official response to the draft *International Convention for the Protection of National Historic or Artistic Treasures* prepared in 1936 by the International Museums Office, of the League of Nations' International Committee for Intellectual Cooperation (Iraq 1936: 162). Iraq lobbied for the adoption of a restitution regime triggered by the non-possession of an 'exportation certificate' issued by government authorities upon leaving the country. It noted that the identification prior to the theft may be possible in other states but this did not work in countries like Iraq with innumerable archaeological sites. Its recommendation was ignored (League of Nations 1937).

Republic to dictatorship

For Iraq, the decades following the Second World War bore witness to the fall of the Kingdom and its replacement by a self-styled republic based on socialist principles which necessarily reinterpreted existing constitutional principles and norms for the protection of cultural heritage in pursuit of this agenda. The role of cultural heritage and tolerance of diversity among the populace was necessarily affected by the consolidation of power in the hands of one individual by the late twentieth century. The physical reminders of past civilizations were redefined to provide legitimacy to the regime. Repression, disappearances and executions against entire religious or ethnic communities was the response to political dissent.

Decolonization and the creation of the republic

The proposed inclusion of the concept of trusteeship over colonial peoples into the Charter of the United Nations led to heated disputation between anti-colonial and colonial states about the role of the 'civilizing mission' in the new international order being articulated at the close of the Second World War. Iraq strenuously argued: '[C]olonialism must give place to self-government ... *People of one language, culture and thought could not submit forever to domination and division by a different culture.*'[5]

In 1958, the monarchy and parliamentary system established under the British mandate was swept away following a military coup d'état. Power was eventually consolidated in the hands of the Ba'ath Socialist Party. The Iraqi Constitution was overhauled in 1970 to centralize authority in the hands of the President, with the National Council having enumerated powers.[6] The constitution embodied the socialist ethos contained in various constitutions overhauled during the same period in the Soviet sphere of influence. Also, it continued to recognize and notionally protect the rights of minorities. Article 5 provided that: 'This Constitution acknowledges the national rights of the Kurdish People and the legitimate rights of all minorities within the Iraqi unity.' Chapter III outlined the fundamental rights and duties bestowed on all Iraqis. Again, the principle of non-discrimination was affirmed (Article 19). Article 25 guaranteed freedom of religious observance as long as they did not contravene the 'moral and public order'. These provisions were replicated in the 1990 Interim Constitution.[7]

The international obligations in respect of minority protection made upon Iraq's independence in 1932 remained binding (United Nations 1950: 51). In the years following the Second World War, Iraq become party to various international instruments, including the 1948 *Convention on the Prevention and Punishment of the Crime of Genocide* and 1966 *International Covenant on Civil and Political Rights*. However, in reality for many (if not most) minorities there was ongoing systematic and persistent flagrant violation of these obligations by the regime (United Nations 1992a: 96ff.)

Cultural heritage as a national resource

Given the history of colonization, it was no coincidence that the articulation of the legal right to self-determination during the 1960s and '70s was firmly tied to development and control of resources. No longer would the rights and interests of 'colonized' peoples be subordinated to the interests of other states in their resources, including cultural 'resources'. This emphasis on national cultural patrimony asserted itself through the concerted push via international fora for the return of cultural materials removed during foreign occupation, and the realization of a multilateral instrument to stem the flow of cultural objects from these states onto the international art market following independence.

The inter-war efforts to prepare a multilateral instrument regulating the transfer and restitution of cultural objects was revived by UNESCO in the late 1960s, and realized with the adoption of the *Convention on the Means of Prohibiting and Preventing the Illicit Import, Export and Transfer of Cultural Property* in November 1970 ('1970 UNESCO Convention').[8] Iraq's formal reply to the draft convention referred to its 'natural interest' in the treaty given its rich cultural patrimony and 'more so as we have greatly suffered in the past from ... illicit practices' concerning cultural objects (UNESCO 1970: Annex I, 10). Its efforts to seek amendments to the draft convention which would have entailed redress of past depredations proved largely unsuccessful.

Following a series of coups, Saddam Hussein grabbed the key leadership roles of the party and the state in 1979. Previously, as second-in-command, he had displayed a keen interest in the importance of antiquities for his own and the state's self-image. It was not until the consolidation of his power that Iraq co-sponsored the UN General Assembly *Resolutions on Restitution of Works of Art to Countries Victims of Expropriation*. These resolutions were a concerted call for the return of cultural objects during colonial occupation.

Iraq based its successive sponsorship of these resolutions on the following grounds. First, the return of cultural objects was articulated as an extension of Iraq's exercise of sovereignty over its territory and resources.[9] Second, an intrinsic component of the Iraqi people's right to self-determination was the right to determine the course of their cultural development which included the manner in which their cultural heritage was protected and preserved.[10] Third, Iraq rejected the argument that developing states were unable to safeguard, preserve and protect such objects. Iraq's Department of Antiquities and Heritage systematically educated the general public about the 'national' cultural history through a network of regional museums. This programme, together with draconian penalties meted out to offenders, meant that clandestine excavation of archaeological sites became rare (Russell 2001). Fourth, Iraqi representatives argued that restitution was vital to ensuring 'friendly relations between countries and strengthening international solidarity'.[11]

Occupier to occupied

Since the consolidation of his power in the late 1970s, Saddam Hussein oversaw a period of near continuous armed conflict with Iraq's neighbours, including the decade-long war with Iran during the 1980s, the invasion of

Kuwait in 1990–1991, and the ensuing first Gulf War; and barbaric attacks on minority ethnic and religious groups within Iraq. All of these events adversely affected the two intrinsic features of the modern Iraqi state – its cultural and religious diversity and rich cultural heritage.

Invasion of Kuwait

The invasion of Kuwait by Iraq on 3 August 1990 had long-term ramifications not only for Kuwait's cultural heritage but a devastating and recurring impact on Iraq's archaeological sites, monuments and museum collections, also. The international instruments to which both Iraq and Kuwait are parties, prohibits the destruction, damaging and removal or transfer of cultural heritage under compulsion during armed conflict and occupation.[12] During the seven-month occupation, Iraqi museum officials had headed a well-organized confiscation of cultural objects from Kuwaiti museums and libraries (Oyer 1999: 58–9). These actions clearly violated Iraq's existing international obligations. International law permits and encourages the removal of cultural objects for safekeeping, from the places which may be exposed to hostilities. Yet, it is an obligation on the national authorities of the state whose cultural objects are being sheltered, not the occupying force. Indeed, the occupying power is required to cooperate with the relevant national authorities of the occupied territory. Iraq did not have the consent of Kuwaiti authorities for the initial removals.[13]

Tariq Aziz, the Iraqi Foreign Minister, informed the United Nations that cultural objects removed from Kuwait would be returned pursuant to Security Council Resolution 686 of 1991 (United Nations 1992b: Part II, para. 25; United Nations 1992c). Under the supervision of the United Nations Return of Property Unit, over 25,000 items from the Dar-Al-Athar Al-Islamiyya and Kuwait National Museum were handed over in Baghdad to the Kuwaiti representatives in late 1991 (UNESCO 1993: paras. 11–12). Nonetheless, Kuwait continued to implore the UN and UNESCO to pressure Iraq to comply fully with Security Council resolutions relating to restitution particularly in relation to archives (United Nations 1994).[14]

Also, the UN Compensation Commission, established by the Security Council to assess a compensation claim arising from the invasion of Kuwait, considered (but ultimately rejected) an Iranian claim for damage to historic artefacts and sites caused by contaminants released from oil well fires (UN Compensation Commission 2005: paras. 204–7).

First Gulf War and its aftermath

The impact of civil, economic and social instability on the enjoyment of cultural rights and the protection of cultural heritage was increasingly recognized by the international community from the 1990s onwards. UNESCO and leading archaeologists acknowledged the damage sustained to Iraqi archaeological sites and museum collections following the first Gulf War which was triggered in response to the invasion of Kuwait. The repression that followed the popular uprisings in the aftermath of the war had a devastating impact on the populace, especially minorities.

Loss of cultural heritage

Three distinct phases can be identified in respect of loss or damage of cultural heritage. The first phase was during hostilities. Iraqi officials maintained that the aerial bombardment by coalition forces during the conflict and in the so-called 'No-Fly zone' until the invasion by coalition forces in 2003 resulted in the partial or total destruction of Iraqi cultural sites, including religious and archaeological sites (Boylan 1993).

The second phase encompassed the civil instability following the war which coincided with the looting and destruction of museum collections, and religious, cultural and historic sites. The collections of regional museums that were used to store objects from the Iraq National Museum for safekeeping during the war were badly affected. Significantly, there was an exponential increase in the number of Iraqi antiquities on sale in Europe and the United States after this period (Gibson 1997; Gibson and McMahon 1992; Baker et al. 1993).

The third phase was the exacerbation of these conditions by Security Council sanctions. The Security Council embargo on Iraq prohibited UN member states from trading in Iraqi cultural objects. Ironically, this same Security Council resolution applied to all goods and services (except in respect of humanitarian needs). As a consequence, looting and clandestine excavations flourished because of the ensuing economic hardship and ongoing social upheaval (UNESCO 1995; Russell 1998).

In 2002, the 1936 Antiquities Law was superseded by the passage and entry into force of the Antiquities and Heritage Law. It stipulated that the purpose of the Act is: first, to protect the Iraqi Republic's antiquities and heritage, the country's most important national resources; and second, to uncover the country's antiquities and heritage and to make them known to citizens and to the international community, thereby highlighting the singular role played by the civilization of Iraq in advancing the civilization of mankind.[15]

This law largely mirrored the provisions of the earlier law, but with more draconian sanctions including the death penalty. However, there was an additional obligation on the Antiquities Department to use all legal and diplomatic means 'to bring back to Iraq antiquities that were stolen from Iraq and taken outside the country' (Article 37).

Repression of minorities and violation of cultural rights

The uprisings by ethnic and religious groups in north and south-eastern Iraq in the wake of the first Gulf War were brutally suppressed by the regime. These and other acts against minorities were in clear violation of Iraq's obligation under the Genocide Convention which it had acceded to in 1959 (United Nations 1992a: 27);[16] and the *International Covenant on Civil and Political Rights* in 1976.[17] In addition to the mass executions, deportations, displacement, use of chemical weapons and confiscation of property, minorities suffered systematic discrimination and violation of their cultural rights. These abuses included the destruction of religious and cultural sites, monuments and movable heritage (e.g. manuscripts), targeting of community leaders, and suppression of language and schools.[18] The UN General Assembly, the UN Special Rapporteur on the human rights situation in Iraq and various UN human rights committees repeatedly condemned the regime's repression of and discrimination against minorities.[19]

2003 Iraq War

In March 2003, the United States and the United Kingdom led a military invasion and subsequent occupation of Iraq. Despite warnings from international agencies and professional bodies and the lessons learnt following the 1990–1991 Gulf War, the coalition forces failed to effectively protect Iraq's museums, libraries, and religious, historical, cultural and archaeological sites from the looting and destruction fuelled by the civil and security void created following the fall of Saddam Hussein's regime (Anon. 2003: 465). As occupying powers, they were bound under international law to protect cultural heritage located in Iraq. Furthermore, unless 'absolutely prevented', they were bound to respect existing Iraqi law vesting ownership of movable heritage in the Iraqi state which provides significant criminal penalties for exportation.[20]

Legal obligations arising from occupation forced the United States and the United Kingdom to reassess the limitations of their existing domestic legislative frameworks regulating dealings with the cultural property of other states. Like all member states of the United Nations, they were bound by the existing Security Council Resolution 661 of 1990 which placed a general trade embargo on Iraq, following its invasion of Kuwait.[21] Although the embargo was lifted by Security Council Resolution 1483 of 2003, UN member states were required to prohibit the transfer and facilitate the return of cultural property illegally removed from 'the Iraq National Museum, the National Library and other locations in Iraq' after 6 August 1990.[22]

The implementation of these obligations at the national level took place against a backdrop of escalating international and domestic concern surrounding the removal and destruction of cultural objects from museum collections and archaeological sites in Iraq. Archaeological and museum organizations fostered broad public and governmental awareness of these cultural losses.[23] They argue that, to the detriment of all humanity, clandestine excavations destroy the historical and scientific record and the illicit traffic of cultural objects depleted a finite resource, best understood *in situ* (Brodie *et al.* 2000). These efforts proved instrumental in the eventual ratification of the 1970 UNESCO Convention by many states which host the leading art market centres (UNESCO 2003a).

Post-conflict reconstruction

As the opening quotation highlights, the recovery and return of these cultural objects and cultural reconstruction were important tasks facing coalition forces and the future Iraqi government as they commenced to reconstruct the country and sought to reassure Iraqis and the international community.

Security Council Resolution 1483 of 2003 laid down the obligations of the occupying powers, the United States and the United Kingdom, and detailed the role of the United Nations and other international organizations in the provision of humanitarian and post-war reconstruction. UNESCO, because of its specialized mandate in the UN system, was endowed with responsibility in respect of cultural matters.[24] Its initial activities were designed to ameliorate the impact of the conflict on cultural heritage. In particular, UNESCO strove to stem the tide of cultural loss from museum collections and archaeological sites and facilitate returns in cooperation with scientists and scholars, relevant intergovernmental and non-governmental agencies (UNESCO 2003b: 9–10). This work together with the rehabilitation of conflict-damaged sites remained a significant component of the organization's remit to date.[25]

However, as the situation in Iraq moved from one of occupation to reconstruction and nation-building, the concerns of Iraqis and the international community in respect of priorities pertaining to cultural rights and cultural heritage similarly shifted. The United Nations' mandate and various humanitarian and reconstruction roles were complicated by the escalating civil strife on the ground (United Nations 2003). Security Council Resolution 1511 of 16 October 2003 provided for the termination of the occupation by the Coalition Provision Authority (CPA) and its replacement by representative government chosen by the Iraqi people. The Security Council recognized that: '[S]overeignty of Iraq resides in the State of Iraq . . .'. The interim administration was charged with preparing a constitution through a process of national dialogue and consensus-building. It affirmed a commitment to 'work[ing] towards a federal, democratic, pluralist and unified Iraq, in which there [was] full respect for political and human rights'.[26] Whilst sanctioning this transfer of power, the Security Council 'stress[ed] the need for all parties to respect and protect Iraq's archaeological, historical, cultural, and religious heritage'.[27]

After the transfer of power to the Interim Government in mid-2004, UNESCO began liaising with national staff in Iraq and its own staff in neighbouring Amman to undertake reconstruction efforts in the fields of culture and education (UNESCO 2004a). The first Iraqi Cultural Forum hosted by UNESCO in May 2004 recognized the importance of 'Iraq's contribution to world civilization over many thousands of years' whilst acknowledging the 'plural ethnic and religious identity of Iraq' (UNESCO 2004b). While the first principle no doubt guided the work of the international community in the protection and preservation of cultural heritage on Iraqi territory after the commencement of the Iraq War, it was the civil strife and inter-ethnic and religious sectarianism which dominated the post-conflict efforts to 'reconstruct' the Iraqi state. The appeal arising from the 2004 meeting set a number of priorities for the relevant national authorities, including: (1) respecting cultural diversity which included a constitution enshrining the religious, linguistic and cultural rights of all elements of the Iraqi people, as well as freedom of expression and academic freedom; (2) promoting the participation of all in cultural life which encompasses the free flow of ideas and images, public access to information, and integrity of the artist and intellectual; and (3) the safeguarding of heritage.

The term of the Interim Government come to an end in early 2005 with the holding of national elections for a Transitional National Assembly (TNA) which led to the formation of the Transitional Government of Iraq (TGI) (UNESCO 2005a: 1–2).[28] This transition period lasted until late 2005 during which time the Iraqi people voted for a new constitution and in parliamentary elections for the Iraqi House of Representatives. The TGI was replaced by the new government when it was sworn in, in 2006.

2005 Permanent Constitution

The Permanent Constitution of the Republic of Iraq was accepted by referendum by the Iraqi people in October 2005 and is a compromise document.[29] In its preamble it refers to the revenge against people and their cultural heritage by the previous regime following uprisings in the North and South following the first Gulf War particularly Sha'abaniyya, Al-Dujail and others; and the subsequent massacres of Halabcha, Barzan, Anfal and the Fayli Kurds; and Turkmen in Basheer. It also embraces the striving toward a 'pluralist' state and the 'spread of a culture of diversity'.

The 2005 Permanent Constitution likewise enunciates certain rights and liberties. It recognizes an individual right to religious freedom (Article 2(2)). However, Article 10 reflects a more communal right in respect of the cultural property of the related religious communities and states that: 'The holy shrines and religious places in Iraq are religious and cultural entities.

The State is committed to confirming and safeguarding their sanctity, and guaranteeing the free practice of rituals in them.' It recognizes Arabic and Kurdish as the official languages of the state throughout the country, with Turkmen and Syriac also listed as official languages in those regions where it is the predominant language of the populations (Article 4). Regions may choose another language as an additional official language if sanctioned by a referendum. As in previous constitutions since the early twentieth century, there is a general equality provision (Article 14), and a right to nationality (Article 18). In the chapter covering liberties, Article 35(4), inserted after a late revision to the draft text, provides that: 'The State shall promote cultural activities and institutions in a way that is appropriate with Iraq's civilizational history and culture. It will take care to depend on authentic Iraqi cultural trends.'

This period also witnessed a sharp increase in sectarian violence during which monuments and sites of significance to particular communities were targeted. The most prominent was the bombing of the Al-Askari shrine in Samarra. The bombing destroyed its golden dome and precipitated sectarian violence throughout the country. In 2007, the Samarra Archaeological City was inscribed on the UNESCO World Heritage List and List of Heritage in Danger, because of the 'disastrous impact' of hostilities and widespread looting of archaeological sites.[30] Not surprisingly, UNESCO saw its role as including the enhancement of the 'bridging role' of culture for the fostering of 'tolerance, mutual respect and understanding' within the emerging state (UNESCO 2007a: 3). A second bombing of the Al-Askari shrine a year later led to the destruction of its twin minarets. The violence has also deliberately targeted educators, students, journalists and religious figures (UN Assistance Mission for Iraq 2007c: paras. 21ff.).

The fate of minorities and their cultural heritage has worsened with the deteriorating security situation (UNESCO 2007b: paras. 34–44). The Human Rights Office of the UN Assistance Mission for Iraq noted in March 2007 that: 'Attacks against religious and ethnic minorities continued unabated in most areas ... prompting sections of these communities to seek ways to leave the country' (UN Assistance Mission for Iraq 2007a: para. 39). It has called on the Iraqi Government and the Kurdish Regional Government to ensure the protection of vulnerable religious and ethnic communities (UN Assistance Mission for Iraq 2007b: para. 32; and 2007c: para. 13(b)).

Conclusion

At its inception, the twin requirements imposed by the international community on the newly independent state of Iraq guaranteed the rights of minority individuals, the enjoyment of their languages, cultures and religion (and by default the preservation of diversity); and the legal protection of a rich cultural heritage perceived to be the inheritance not only of Iraqis but all humanity. However, through its persistent, often large-scale, gross violations of its international obligations and human rights norms, the Iraqi state often belied the rhetoric which it repeatedly proclaimed.

In recent decades, the international community has increasingly become aware of the impact upon diversity and human rights of deliberate and systematic attacks on the cultural heritage of minority groups which was often designed to eradicate their identity and difference. There is a growing appreciation that cultural heritage (tangible and intangible, movable and immovable) is vital to maintaining diversity and enjoying human rights. This concern has translated into the criminalization of genocide and the renewed emphasis on minority protection. As noted by scholars after the first Gulf War: 'the destruction or theft of cultural markers is an important issue, for such violation of cultural markers is a conscious or unconscious negation of the people involved' (Gibson and McMahon 1992: v). It is in effect the erasure of their memory and presence from the collective national consciousness.

Notes

1 Article 22 of the Treaty of Peace with Germany and the Allied and Associated Powers, Versailles, 28 June 1919, into force 10 January 1920, *Parry's Consolidated Treaty Series*, vol. 225, p. 188 ('Versailles Treaty').

2 Treaty of Alliance between Great Britain and Iraq, with Protocol, 10 October 1922 and 30 April 1923, *League of Nations Treaty Series*, 1925, vol. 35, 13 (No. 890).

3 *League of Nations Official Journal* (December 1922) 3rd Year, No. 12, 1505ff.

4 Constitution of the Kingdom of Iraq, adopted 21 March 1925, as amended 29 July 1925, in *British and Foreign State Papers 1926*, HMSO: London, 1931, Vol. CXXIII, Part I, 383–402.

5 UN Doc.A/C.4/257, para.11, Khalidy (Iraq) (emphasis added).

6 Interim Constitution of the Republic of Iraq, 16 July 1970. Available at www.oceanalaw.com (accessed 15 January 2008).

7 Interim Constitution of Iraq of 1990. Available at http://confinder.richmond.edu/admin/docs/local_iraq1990.pdf (accessed 15 January 2008).

8 14 November 1970, entered into force 24 April 1972, *United Nations Treaty Series*, vol. 823, 231.

9 UN Doc.A/32/PV.65, p. 1121, para. 19.

10 UN Doc.A/32/PV.65, p. 1120, para. 16.

11 UN Doc.A/32/PV.65, p. 1121, para. 18.

12 Para. 1, Protocol to the *Convention for the Protection of Cultural Property in the Event of Armed Conflict*, 14 May 1954, entered in force 7 August 1956, *United Nations Treaty Series*, vol. 249, 240; Article 53 of Protocol Additional I to 1949 Geneva Conventions, 8 June 1977, entered in force 7 December 1978, *United Nations Treaty Series*, vol. 1125, 3 (Iraq is not a party to this treaty); and Article 11 of the 1970 UNESCO Convention.

13 Articles 5 and 15, 1954 *Hague Convention*.

14 UN Doc.A/52/PV.55.

15 Article 1 of the *Antiquities and Heritage Law* No. 55 of 2002.

16 *Convention on the Prevention and Punishment of the Crime of Genocide*, 9 December

1949, entered into force 12 January 1951, *United Nations Treaty Series*, vol. 78, 277.
17 Article 27, *International Covenant on Civil and Political Rights*, 16 December 1966, entered into force 23 March 1976, *United Nations Treaty Series*, vol. 999, 171.
18 UN Doc.E/CN.4/1992/31, paras. 96ff.; and E/CN.4/1994/58, paras. 91ff.
19 GA Resolution 49/203 of 13 March 1995, paras. 8 and 9; 53/157 of 25 February 1999, para. 13; 54/178 of 24 February 2000, para. 3(g); 55/115 of 20 December 2000, para. 3(h).
20 Article 43, *Convention (IV) Respecting the Laws and Customs of War on Land*, and Annex, The Hague, 18 October 1907, entered into force 26 January 1910, *Parry's Consolidated Treaty Series*, 1907, vol. 208, 77; and Articles 17 and 41, *Antiquities and Heritage Law*, No. 55 of 2002.
21 Para. 3, SC Resolution 661 of 6 August 1990; Iraq (United Nations Sanctions) Order 2003 (UK); *Dealing in Cultural Objects (Offences) Act* 2003 (UK); *Iraqi Sanctions Regulations*, 31 CFR 575.533 (2003); and Executive Order 13315.
22 Para.7, SC Resolution 1483 of 22 May 2003. See also Declaration of the Council of the European Union of 26 May 2003 on the tragic destruction of cultural goods, archaeological sites, monuments and libraries in Iraq, OJ 2003/C 136/01.
23 See ICOMOS Communiqué, 6 March 2003; ICOM Press Release, 15 April 2003; and UNESCO Experts Meeting, Press Release, 17 April 2003.
24 UNESCO Doc.166 EX/Decision 3.1.1.
25 See, for example, the work of the International Coordination Committee for the Safeguarding of the Cultural Heritage of Iraq, created pursuant to decision of the UNESCO Executive Board, UNESCO Doc.166 EX/Decision 9.2.
26 SC Resolution 1546 of 8 June 2004.
27 Ibid.
28 Para. 1, SC Resolution 1546 of 8 June 2004.
29 The Permanent Constitution of the Republic of Iraq of 2005. Available at www. oceanalaw.com (accessed 12 November 2007).
30 See Decision 31 COM 8B.23.

References

Anon. (1935) 'Editorial Note,' *Antiquity* IX (33): 1.
Anon. (2003) 'Editorial: Recovering from Cultural Devastation,' *Nature*, 29 May 2003, vol. 432, 465.
Baker, H. D., Matthews, R. J. and Postgate, J. N. (1993) *Lost Heritage: Antiquities Stolen From Iraq's Regional Museums*, Fascicle 2, London: British School of Archaeology in Iraq.
Bell, G. (1927) *The Letters of Gertrude Bell*, selected and edited by Lady Bell, DBE, London: Ernest Benn Limited, 2 vols.
Bernardsson, M. (2001a) 'Negotiating History: Nationalism and Cultural Property in Modern Iraq,' *The Middle East: Interpreting the Past*, Nordic Society of Middle East Studies, 5th Conference, Lund, Sweden, 27 October. Available at www.smi. uib.no/pal/Abstract_Lund_07MB.pdf (accessed 12 November 2007).
Bernardsson, M. T. (2001b) 'The Spoils of History: The Return of Cultural Property and the Samarra Collection Episode,' *Hofstra Horizons*, Fall, 17.
Boylan, P. J. (1993) Review of the *Convention for the Protection of Cultural Property in the Event of Armed Conflict* (The Hague Convention of 1954), UNESCO Doc. CLT-93/WS/12.

British Museum (1933) British Museum Trustees' Committee Minutes, Excavations in Iraq, 14 October.

Brodie, N., Doole, J. and Watson, P. (2000) *Stealing History: The Illicit Trade in Cultural Material*, Cambridge: MacDonald Institute.

Gibson, M. (1997) 'The Loss of Archaeological Context and the Illegal Trade in Mesopotamian Antiquities,' *Culture Without Context*, Autumn, issue 1. Available at www.mcdonald.cam.ac.uk/projects/iarc/culturewithoutcontext/issue1/gibson. htm (accessed 30 June 2003).

Gibson, M. and McMahon, A. (1992) *Lost Heritage: Antiquities Stolen from Iraq's Regional Museums*, Fascicle 1, Chicago: American Association for Research in Baghdad.

Iraq (1932) *Iraq – Petitions de la Communauté Assyrienne – Projet de Résolution Présenté par le Comité Constitué par la Décision du Conseil du 5 décembre 1932*, LN Doc. C.837.1932.VI.

Iraq (1936) Letter from the Iraqi delegation to Secretary-General of the League of Nations, 21 May 1936, International Museum Office Archives, OIM.IV.27, II, 162–3, UNESCO Archives, Paris.

League of Nations (1937) Report of the Committee on the Work of its Nineteenth Plenary Session, International Charter of Antiquities and of Excavations. The Cairo Conference – *The International Conference on Excavations*, Cairo, 9–15 March, League of Nations Doc.C.327M.2201.1937.XII.

Lemonick, M. D. (2003) 'Lost to the ages: could the U.S. have stopped the looting of Iraq's priceless antiquities? The answer is not that simple,' *Time*, 28 April 161: 46.

Lloyd, S. (1980) *Foundations in the Dust: The Story of Mesopotamian Exploration*, London: Thames and Hudson.

Masry, A. H. (1982) 'Traditions of Archaeological Research in the Near East,' *World Archaeology*, 1981–1982, 13: 222.

O'Keefe, P. J. and Prott, L. V. (1984) *Law and the Cultural Heritage, Vol. 1: Discovery and Excavation*, London: Professional Books.

Oyer, H. E. (1999) 'The 1954 Hague Convention for the Protection of Cultural Property in the Event of Armed Conflict – Is it working? A Case Study: the Persian Gulf War Experience,' *Columbia – VLA Journal of Law and Arts*, 23: 49.

Russell, J. M. (1998) *The Final Sack of Nineveh*, New Haven: Yale University Press.

Russell, J. M. (2001) 'Robbing the Archaeological Cradle,' *Natural History*, 110 (1): 44.

UNESCO (1970) *Means of Prohibiting and Preventing the Illicit Import, Export and Transfer of Ownership of Cultural Property: Final Report*, UNESCO Doc.SHC/MD/5.

UNESCO (1993) *Report of Intergovernmental Committee for Promoting the Return of Cultural Property to its Countries of Origin or its Restitution in Case of Illicit Appropriation on its Activities (1991–1993)*, UNESCO Doc.27C/102.

UNESCO (1995) 'Scholars Confirm Continuing Losses of Iraqi Antiquities,' UNESCO Press Release, 31 March.

UNESCO (2003a) Address of K. Matsuura, UNESCO Director-General, On the occasion of the opening of the Meeting of Experts on the Iraqi Cultural Heritage, DG/2003/064.

UNESCO (2003b) *Report of the Director-General on the Cultural and Educational Institutions in Iraq*, UNESCO Doc.167 EX/45.

UNESCO (2004a) *Report by the Director-General on the Cultural and Educational Institutions in Iraq*, UNESCO Doc.170 EX/34.

UNESCO (2004b) *Appeal of the First Iraqi Cultural Forum, UNESCO, 26–27 May 2004*. Available at http://portal.unesco.org/culture/en/files/20791/10861931843Appeal_Iraq_En_27May04.pdf/Appeal_Iraq_En_27May04.pdf (accessed 20 November 2007).

UNESCO (2005a) *Report by the Director-General on the Cultural and Educational Institutions in Iraq*, UNESCO Doc.172 EX/48.

UNESCO (2007a) Address of UNESCO Director-General to the Third Session of the International Coordination Committee for the Safeguarding of Iraqi Cultural Heritage, DG/2007/171.

UNESCO (2007b) *Report by the Director-General on the Cultural and Educational Institutions in Iraq*, UNESCO Doc.177 EX/64 Rev.

United Nations (1950) *Study on the Legal Validity of the Undertakings Concerning Minorities*, UN Doc.E/CN.4/367.

United Nations (1992a) *Report on the Situation of Human Rights in Iraq*, UN Doc.E/CN.4/1992/31.

United Nations (1992b) *Further Report of the Security Council on the Status of Compliance by Iraq with Obligations Placed upon it under certain Security Council Resolutions on the Situation between Iraq and Kuwait*, UN Doc.S/23687.

United Nations (1992c) *Statement of the President of the Security Council concerning General and Specific Obligations of Iraq under various Security Council Resolutions relating to the Situation between Iraq and Kuwait*, UN Doc.S/23699.

United Nations (1994a) *Report of the Secretary-General on the Returning of Kuwaiti Property Seized by Iraq, 2 March*, UN Doc.S/1994/243.

United Nations (2003) *Report of the Secretary-General pursuant to paragraph 24 of Resolution 1483 and paragraph 12 of Resolution 1511* (2003), UN Doc.S/2003/1149.

UN Assistance Mission for Iraq (2007a) Human Rights Office, *Human Rights Report 1 January–31 March 2007*, www.uniraq.org/aboutus/HR.asp (accessed 15 May 2008).

UN Assistance Mission for Iraq (2007b) Human Rights Office, *Human Rights Report 1 April–30 June 2007*, www.uniraq.org/aboutus/HR.asp (accessed 15 May 2008).

UN Assistance Mission for Iraq (2007c), Human Rights Office, *Human Rights Report 1 July–31 December 2007*, www.uniraq.org/aboutus/HR.asp (accessed 15 May 2008).

UN Compensation Commission (2005) *Report and Recommendations Made by the Panel of Commissioners Concerning the Fifth Instalment of 'F4' Claims*, UN Doc.S/AC.26/2005/10.

Visscher, C. de (1937) 'La Conférence Internationale des Fouilles et l'Œuvre de l'Office International Musées,' *Revue de Droit International et de Législation Comparée*, 18: 700.

Woolley, C. L. (1935) 'Antiquities Law, Iraq, Antiquity,' *A Quarterly Review of Archaeology*, IX (33): 84.

Chapter 6

The political appropriation of Burma's cultural heritage and its implications for human rights

Janette Philp

Burma's cultural heritage has become highly politicized under the authoritarian military rule of the State Peace and Development Council (SPDC) and appropriated as a powerful political tool in the construction of a national identity that is both ethnically Burman and Buddhist. Since coming to power in 1988, the SPDC has pursued its nation-building goals, in particular the achievement of national unity. More specifically, the reconstruction of Buddhist cultural heritage sites and the revival or reinvention of Burmese cultural traditions and rituals have played a significant role in the SPDC's attempts to establish a sense of continuity with the past. Burma, geographically located in South-East Asia, has drawn on its historical traditions, in particular with the political system of monarchical rule in the pre-colonial period, when political authority was legitimated through the moral authority of Theravada Buddhism.

Hobsbawm and Ranger (1983: 1–2) first coined the term 'invented tradition' to refer to a set of practices 'of a ritual or symbolic nature, which seek to inculcate certain values and norms of behaviour by repetition, which automatically implies continuity with the past'. They identify three types of invented traditions: traditions that establish or legitimize institutions, status or relations of authority; traditions that establish or symbolize social cohesion of communities; and traditions that inculcate beliefs, values and conventions of behaviour in a society. The SPDC has sought to revive or reinvent Burmese cultural traditions for all three purposes: to promote the legitimation of authoritarian military rule; to promote the national unity of Burma's diverse ethnic and religious groups; and to promote those Theravada Buddhist beliefs and values that serve its political ambitions.

Theravada Buddhist practices in contemporary Burma

Buddhism in Burma has its roots in Indian–Sinhalese culture, principally Theravada Buddhist and Mahayana Buddhist beliefs,[1] which, in turn, have their roots in Hinduism. Buddhist beliefs, in common with other Buddhist countries in South-East Asia, have been localized in the Burmese context and represent a blending of religious ideological influences. Importantly, Buddhism in Burma also coexists in a syncretic relationship with indigenous beliefs, which throughout Burmese history have been an integral part of Burmese culture. But it is principally Theravada Buddhism that most aptly describes the doctrine adopted by the monarchy and post-independence political leaders in Burma.[2]

State-sponsored Theravada Buddhist merit-making rituals of patronage include the restoration and reconstruction of Burma's cultural heritage sites (for example, pagodas, temples and monasteries) and the revival or reinvention of Burmese cultural traditions (for example, the giving of *dana* [religious offerings] and patronage of members of the *sangha* [monkhood]). In the process, the SPDC has challenged the spiritual integrity of Theravada Buddhism in Burma as it has sought to appropriate its beliefs, values and institutions, as well as its traditions, rituals and symbols, as a means of legitimating its political power and authority. The SPDC has encouraged the Buddhist laity to participate in state-sponsored Theravada Buddhist merit-making rituals as it represents such rituals as joint acts of merit and seeks to convey a sense of national solidarity between the Burmese people, the *sangha* and the military government. Such state-sponsored rituals help to foster and create a sense of belonging and sense of national identity and enjoins the Burmese people to feel a part of the 'imagined community' of the Burmese State.

Benedict Anderson in *Imagined Communities: Reflections on the Origin and Spread of Nationalism* (1983), provides an insight into how identity has been constructed around the notion of the nation state. Nationalism is centred on emotional sentiments and a sense of belonging, and as a result, its power to mobilize political activity for the purposes of nation-building, is unsurpassed. Nationalism is essentially about creating cultural conceptions of the Self and the Other, and territorial boundaries of inclusion and exclusion reinforce this dichotomy, as the nation is conceived as an 'imagined political community' (Anderson 1983: 15). While the SPDC has sought to create feelings of 'community' based on Theravada Buddhist beliefs in order to assist it in its nation-building ambitions, as Kong (2001: 221) argues, such feelings are not necessarily engendered, or shared, by those brought together in this way. In Burma, the Buddhist laity and the military leaders may congregate together at state-sponsored Theravada Buddhist sites and the SPDC may represent merit-making rituals as joint acts of merit, but this does not necessarily imply any sense of 'community'.

Cultural diversity

Three main approaches to Burma's ethnic and religious minority groups have been adopted by the SPDC, all of which erase cultural diversity, and

Figure 6.1 The *Tatmadaw* (Burmese army) and the 'united national people', joined together by the Burmese State, are depicted as working together in nation-building tasks, marching towards a 'new peaceful and prosperous modern developed nation' (*The New Light of Myanmar* 5 October 2000).

deny such groups their own sense of the past and their own sense of identity, as the SPDC seeks to affirm a Burman Buddhist national identity and achieve its goal of national unity. The first approach involves the promotion of the ethos of 'unity in diversity', which allows minority groups to express cultural diversity, but only where this does not contest 'national' identity. The second approach involves the destruction of cultural heritage such that minority groups have been denied the right to assert their own cultural particularity, that is, their own cultural heritage and cultural identity. The third approach involves the assimilation of minority groups into a cohesive 'national' cultural identity with their cultural heritage appropriated and redefined as 'national' heritage.

Unity in diversity: the Union National Races Village

The Union National Races Village was developed as a tourist attraction by the Ministry for the Progress of Border Areas and National Races and Development Affairs in Yangon in 2002. The village was established, according to the state-sponsored newspaper, *The New Light of Myanmar* (29 December 2002), 'with the aim of understanding the good foundations of culture, customs and traditions of national races and further strengthening of Union Spirit and national solidarity'. The village includes traditional houses of the eight main national ethnic groups (Burman, Kachin, Shan, Kayah, Kayin, Mon, Arakan and Chin), as well as miniature replicas of prominent national attractions in each state (for example, Kyaiktiyo Pagoda in Mon State, Inle Lake in Shan State). People from each of the ethnic groups, dressed in traditional costume, are located at the village, so 'that tourists can study their traditions and customs' (*Myanmar Times*, 6–12 January 2003). The Union National Races Village exemplifies the way in which the SPDC has taken the cultural heritage of the ethnic minority groups out of their cultural contexts and represented Burma as a culturally rich country where diverse ethnic groups live harmoniously together. But as Hafstein (2004) suggests, such traditional cultural practices are alienated, objectified and commodified, and as a consequence, far from contributing to their vitality and viability, it empties such cultural practices of their authenticity.

Destruction of ethnic cultural heritage: the Mon city of Bago

Cultural heritage that testifies to a country's cultural diversity has also been deliberately destroyed or allowed to deteriorate. In Burma, cultural heritage sites in Bago (Hanthawaddy) in Mon State, such as the Kanbawzathadi Palace, have been reconstructed by the SPDC as sites that glorify the Burman king, King Bayinnaung (r.1551–1581), who established the Second Burmese Empire. Only the palace's brick foundations and a few teak stumps (now displayed in a recently built museum at the palace site) were evident before the palace was completely reconstructed. In comparison, nearby *Oktha-myo*, a Mon cultural heritage site, has been allowed to deteriorate, denying not only the artistic and architectural contribution of the Mon to Burmese culture, but also a place in Burmese history, as dominant historical narratives are privileged over others. Ashworth (1995) terms this notion 'disinheritance', whereby certain non-powerful groups are written out of history for ideological or political reasons. The history of Bago, as the centre of the Mon Kingdom up until 1539, has been all but erased, as Burma's symbolic landscapes are reconstructed to revive and reinforce a particular version of Burmese history, one where the Burman ethnic group is dominant. (Bago ancient city is on the tentative list drawn up by the Department of Archaeology in Burma for World Heritage Listing) (Aung Kyuing 2001).

As Gamboni (2001) suggests, the symbolic values of cultural heritage, while leading to protection by those who share those values, may also lead to destruction by those who reject those values. The destruction of the fifth-century Buddhas of Bamiyan in Afghanistan was an act widely condemned by international institutions, and subsequently led to the UNESCO *Declaration Concerning the Intentional Destruction of Cultural Heritage* (2003). The Declaration recognizes that 'cultural heritage is an important component of the cultural identity of communities, groups and individuals, and of social cohesion, so that its intentional destruction may have adverse consequences on human dignity and human rights' (www.unesco.org).

The assimilation of cultural heritage: hti-hoisting traditions

One of the most important traditional cultural practices in Burma is the *hti*-hoisting ceremony. In the past, the king, as part of his inauguration, placed the finial, or *hti*, on the royal *stupa* (Moore 1999). The *hti* was symbolic of the king's crown, a sign of glory and power, and also indicated celestial power with the tiers representing the ascending realms of the heavens (Aasen 1998: 20; Gravers 1993). The styles of the *hti* of different ethnic groups were distinctive and were used to assert dominance over other ethnic groups and indicate territorial authority. For instance, when a Mon king invaded Burman-dominated territory, he put a *hti* like his own crown on top of each pagoda in the newly conquered land. Similarly, when a Burman king reconquered the land, he replaced the *hti* with a *hti* like his own crown, in a similar symbolic gesture of dominance (Moore 1999). Today, for the Burman-dominated military regime to assert its power and authority by placing

Figure 6.2 Lieutenant General Khin Nyunt hoists the *hti* on the twelfth-century Sulamani Pagoda in Bagan. The SPDC's military leaders claim such merit-making rituals as personal acts of merit as they seek to revive Burmese cultural traditions that legitimate their political power and authority (*The New Light of Myanmar* 1 October 1997).

a *hti* on pagodas throughout Burma, is a well-established cultural tradition that dates back to the monarchical period.

Since the SPDC assumed power, it has conducted many *hti*-hoisting ceremonies on pagodas in ethnic minority regions in a symbolic assertion of both Burman dominance and of central authority over outlying districts and provinces. For instance, the Shwemadaw Pagoda in Bago is a particularly important Buddhist pilgrimage site because this pagoda is believed to contain two of the Buddha's hair relics. Two *hti* were erected by the SPDC, with the second, the Burman *hti*, above the Mon *hti*, to symbolize Burman dominance over the Mon (Moore 1999).

Landscapes of power

The SPDC has also emulated monarchical traditions by constructing new Theravada Buddhist monuments in an attempt to create symbolic sites of religious and political power in Burma's landscape. Mindhamma Hill in Yangon is one such site as the SPDC maps out the sacred geography of its 'kingdom'.

The Lawka Chantha Abhaya Labha Muni Image is a Buddha image that was carved from a large marble block found in the mountains near Mandalay. Four similar marble Buddha images were carved during the rule of Burma's monarchs and are enshrined in the ancient cities of Sagaing, Innwa, Amarapura and Mandalay (*The New Light of Myanmar* 13 September 2000). (These ancient cities are all on the tentative list drawn up by the Department of Archaeology in Burma for World Heritage Listing.)

The construction of the Lawka Chantha Abhaya Labha Muni Image, under the auspices of the SPDC, exemplifies the way in which traditional monarchical rituals have been appropriated by the SPDC. Several state-sponsored Buddhist traditional ceremonies and merit-making rituals were undertaken. For instance, the marble block was conveyed by ceremonial barge and wagon from Mandalay to Yangon in August 2000; a stake-driving ceremony was held for the Gandakuti Kyaungdawgyi in September 2000, where the Buddha image is now enshrined; ceremonies were held to start carving the Buddha image; and the consecration ceremony of the completed Buddha image was held in February 2002.

Three white elephants, traditional symbols of royal legitimacy, emerged from the forest in Arakan State and their appearance was seen as an auspicious omen as it is believed that the white elephant brings peace, stability and prosperity to the nation. The legitimation of political power and authority in Burma is deeply influenced by traditional Theravada Buddhist beliefs in the king as *kammaraja*, where the holding of political power was seen as the *karmic* reward for merit attained in previous lives (Aung-Thwin 1983).

Once again, traditional ritual processions by float and truck on which four white umbrellas, symbols of the monarchy, were mounted, saw the white

Figure 6.3 Lawka Chantha Abhaya Labha Muni Image under construction on Mindhamma Hill (*The New Light of Myanmar* 6 September 2000).

elephants conveyed from Sittwe to Yangon (*The New Light of Myanmar* 15 November 2001). Another ceremony was held to hoist the *shwehtidaw* atop the elephant house. But significantly, a further ceremony to name the third white elephant, Rati Malar, was held on Union Day on 12 February 2003, an important national day that commemorates the signing of the Panglong Agreement. The SPDC's commemoration of this national day of significance extends the memory back to the British colonial period and the national independence struggle. The Panglong Agreement was formulated in 1947 with the intent to form a federation of ethnic states that would receive equal status with the Burman ethnic group based on the principles of self-determination, political autonomy and social equality (Joint Standing Committee on Foreign Affairs, Defence and Trade 1995: 66). But the Panglong Agreement failed to secure the support of a number of ethnic minority groups, and, as a consequence, was never implemented. The SPDC has expressed a renewed interest in reviving the spirit of the Panglong Agreement to counter the ongoing dissent over the status of Burma's ethnic minority groups that underlies much of the political unrest that characterizes Burma today.

In contemporary Burma, the political and the cultural have become intertwined and the boundaries between the secular and the sacred have become blurred as the secular political activities of nation-building have been conflated with sacred Theravada Buddhist rituals of merit-making.

Cultural heritage conservation in Burma today

In Burma, the Ministry of Culture is the sole designated authority with decision-making powers for the protection of cultural heritage, with delegation to the Department of Archaeology. The Myanmar Cultural Heritage Preservation and Protection Central Committee was established in 1993 for the purpose of defining, listing and preserving cultural heritage sites in Burma as the SPDC saw it as 'a national duty to protect and preserve Myanmar cultural heritage' (Ministry of Information 1999: 79).

The activities of the Myanmar Cultural Heritage Preservation and Protection Central Committee are as follows: the preparation and drafting of the *Protection and Preservation of Cultural Heritage Regions Law*; formation of State/Division/District/Township Cultural Heritage Protection Committees; publication of the *Inventory of Bagan Ancient Monuments*; preparation of the *Bagan Master Plan*; nomination of Bagan for the inclusion in the World Heritage List; excavation of ancient mounds and restoration of ancient monuments in Bagan; and construction of the new Bagan Archaeological Museum (Ministry of Information 1999).

The *Protection and Preservation of Cultural Heritage Regions Law* (1998) was predicated on the rationale of protecting, by legislation, the cultural heritage of Burma, but is a law that greatly restricts the independent building and renovation of Buddhist structures and precludes either individuals or organizations, other than the government, of potential power and influence, from undertaking merit-making rituals. As a result, according to Houtman (1999: 182), the construction of pagodas, temples, monasteries and so forth, have become the exclusive prerogative of the SPDC.

A more extensive list of Burma's cultural heritage sites was presented at the UNESCO *Sub Regional Global Strategy Meeting for Southeast Asian Cultural Heritage and Periodic Monitoring of World Cultural Heritage Sites* held in April 2001. This is the tentative list required by the World Heritage Committee that indicates the Member State's intentions for future submission and allows the Committee to evaluate each nomination when it is made in the context of the broader national plan. Cultural Heritage Sites in Burma proposed for future World Heritage Listing are: Bagan Archaeological Area and Monuments; Pyu cities: Beikthano-Myo, Halin, Tharay-Khit-taya (Sri Ksetra); Wooden Monasteries of Konbaung Period: Ohn Don, Sala, Pakhangyi, Pakhannge, Legaing, Sagu, Shwe-Kyaung (Mandalay); Badh-lin and associated caves; Ancient cities of Upper Myanmar: Innwa, Amarapura, Sagaing, Mingun, Mandalay; Myauk-U Archaeological Area and Monuments; Inle Lake; and Mon cities: Bago, Hanthawaddy (Aung Kyuing 2001).

Bagan Archaeological Zone

The Bagan Archaeological Zone is a site of immense importance because the Burmese State was established here with the introduction of Theravada Buddhism by King Anawrahta in the eleventh century AD. Located on the banks of the Irrawaddy River, the Bagan Archaeological Zone is a rich cultural heritage site where more than 2,000 monuments cover a vast plain of 50 square kilometres. The SPDC has sought to revive and deepen the glories of the Burmese monarchy at Bagan through the reconstruction and renovation of its ancient monuments, and, in particular, the many temples and pagodas that attest to the merit-making traditions of the monarchy from 1044 up until the invasion by the Mongol armies of Kublai Khan in 1287. It would seem that the SPDC is motivated, not only by the Theravada Buddhist concept of merit-making and the political legitimacy that this confers, but also by the desire to reconstruct this area as a memorial to Burma's past monarchs and the glory of the Burmese Empire as the SPDC seeks to create a sense of cultural continuity with those traditions, rituals and customs which have a history in both Theravada Buddhism and monarchical rule.

A nomination form for World Heritage status was submitted by the Burmese government in 1995 for the Bagan Archaeological Zone, but it was reported by U. Aung Kyuing (2001) that a comprehensive Management Plan had not yet been submitted to UNESCO's World Heritage Centre and this situation remained the case in 2008. A Master Plan for Bagan was completed in 1996 with the assistance of the Japanese Trust Fund, which included plans for the protection of the historical area, for the conservation and restoration of the monuments, and for cultural tourism and economic development (www.unesco.org).

Cultural heritage protection undertaken, however, has been on an ad hoc basis and has not conformed to the criteria and guidelines necessary for recognition and designation as a World Heritage site. UNESCO/UNDP was involved in cultural heritage protection in Bagan in the 1980s, providing assistance with institutional building, conservation work and restoration of mural paintings, but since then, conflicts and tensions between the SPDC and international organizations have been prohibitive to further collaborative work. Many pagodas and temples in the Bagan Archaeological Zone have undergone reconstruction and restoration work that would fail to meet the 'test of authenticity in design, material or workmanship' as defined in the *Operational Guidelines for the Implementation of the World Heritage Convention* (www.unesco.org). Even under a more expansive definition of 'authenticity' that recognizes approaches that are appropriate to local cultural contexts and consistent with local cultural traditions as first proposed in the *Nara Document on Authenticity*, and subsequently incorporated into the more recent Conventions, that recognize that the significance of a place resides primarily in its continued spiritual meaning and symbolic value related to everyday use and renewal rather than the built fabric, the work undertaken at Bagan is unlikely to meet the standards necessary for World Heritage status.

Development of the Bagan Archaeological Zone continues apace as the SPDC seeks to increase foreign exchange earnings from international tourism. Despite advice from Richard Engelhardt, UNESCO's Advisor for Culture in Asia and the Pacific, who expressed his concerns with 'any plans to develop any kinds of new infrastructure within a protected area' (Agence France Presse in *BurmaNet News* 9 May 2003), in the spirit of UNESCO's aim to monitor and mitigate potentially destructive effects of tourism on the conservation of cultural heritage, the SPDC proceeded with the construction of a 60-metre viewing tower, modelled on the watchtowers that were erected in palace precincts during the monarchical period, the establishment of the Bagan Golf Club, and the development of an extensive road network in the Bagan Archaeological Zone.

Cultural heritage policies and human rights: the difficulties in the Burmese context

Burma is a Member State of UNESCO and in 1994 ratified the *Convention Concerning the Protection of the World Cultural and Natural Heritage* (1972), but it has not ratified the *Convention for the Safeguarding of the Intangible Cultural Heritage* (2003), nor the *Convention on the Protection and Promotion of the Diversity of Cultural Expressions* (2005) which followed the adoption of the *Universal Declaration on Cultural Diversity* (2001) which sought to raise cultural diversity to the level of 'the common heritage of humanity'.[3]

Cultural rights and human rights

Cultural rights are acknowledged as fundamental human rights in the *Universal Declaration of Human Rights* (1948) and in the *International Covenant on Economic, Social and Cultural Rights* (1966). Both of the new Conventions also state the inseparability of cultural rights and human rights: '[C]onsideration will be given solely to such intangible cultural heritage as is compatible with existing international human rights instruments (Article 2)' (*Convention for the Safeguarding of the Intangible Cultural Heritage* (2003)). '[C]ultural diversity can be protected and promoted only if human rights and fundamental freedoms, such as freedom of expression, information and communication, as well as the ability of individuals to choose cultural expressions, are guaranteed (Article 2)' (*Convention on the Protection and Promotion of the Diversity of Cultural Expressions* (2005)). Human rights, however, have been much debated by the political leadership of Asian countries and in 1993 Asian delegates met to review the *Universal Declaration of Human Rights* (1948). The outcome was *The Bangkok Declaration*, which undertook to:

> [r]eaffirm their commitment to principles contained in the Charter of the United Nations and the *Universal Declaration of Human Rights* (Article 1). Emphasize the principles of respect for national sovereignty and territorial integrity as well as non-interference in the internal affairs of States ... (Article 5).[4] Recognize that while human rights are universal in nature, they must bear in mind the significance of national and regional particularities and various historical, cultural and religious backgrounds (Article 8).

Both of the recent Conventions also maintain the principles of nation state sovereignty. For instance, Article 2 of the *Convention on the Protection and Promotion of the Diversity of Cultural Expressions* (2005) reads: 'States have, in accordance with the Charter of the United Nations and the principles of international law, the sovereign right to adopt policies and measures to protect and promote the diversity of cultural expressions within their territory.' However, the Convention also states that: 'the protection and promotion of the diversity of cultural expressions presuppose the recognition of equal dignity of and respect for all cultures, including the cultures of persons belonging to minorities and indigenous peoples' (Article 2).

Brown (2005) argues that the predominantly authoritarian bent of most South-east Asian governments has been reflected in their depictions of the nation state as an artefact of colonialism, forged through nationalist struggle, whose identity must be defended against external threats and against internal ethnic rivalries. In Burma, perceived threats to national sovereignty and national identity have been engendered by the SPDC, together with the fear that Burma will lose its cultural identity as a consequence of globalization. Comparisons are made by the SPDC between past British colonial powers and contemporary Western 'neo-colonial' powers. Moreover, a connection is made between the Burmese democracy movement, in particular Aung San Suu Kyi and the National League for Democracy, and Western 'neo-colonial' powers, as the SPDC seeks to distinguish Burmese political culture and its authoritarian military political system from Western political culture and its democratic political system.

More specifically relating to human rights, the SPDC has shown a concern to preserve its Burmese cultural identity and has argued that internationally accepted notions of human rights encompass Western concepts that are alien to traditional 'Asian' values, and therefore, have no applicability to Burma's contemporary political, cultural and economic realities. Burma's Foreign Minister has been critical of Western concepts of human rights, stating that they represented 'Western attempts of imposing its values on ASEAN' (*Straits Times* 20 July 1996). Senior-General Than Shwe, furthermore, stated that: 'Our concept of human rights is based on our own values, traditions and cultures' (*The New Light of Myanmar* 25 October 1998). However, de Varennes (2006: 67) strongly contests such arguments, stating that 'the moral and philosophical underpinnings of international human rights are closely linked to Asian traditions and not intrinsically alien to them'.

The concept of 'Asian' values has been used by the SPDC in response to criticisms by the international community of human rights abuses in Burma. More specifically as they relate to cultural heritage, human rights abuses have included the use of forced labour in the restoration and reconstruction of Theravada Buddhist monuments. The SPDC, however, has consistently denied allegations of human rights abuses, describing the undertaking of such work as part of Burmese culture and traditional Theravada Buddhist concepts of merit-making – an historical legacy dating to monarchical rule whereby the king provided the opportunity for the Buddhist laity to acquire merit (Houtman 1999). Such cultural practices, nevertheless, may be seen to contravene international instruments such as the *Universal Declaration of Human Rights* (1948), Article 4 of which states: 'No one shall be held in slavery or servitude; slavery and the slave trade shall be prohibited in all their forms.' It is these aspects relating to Burma's cultural heritage conservation practices that pose some of the greatest challenges in the Burmese context.

Community participation

Recent Conventions also recognize that 'communities play an important role in the production, safeguarding, maintenance and recreation of the intangible culture heritage' (Preamble *Convention for the Safeguarding of the Intangible Cultural Heritage* 2003). Similarly, the *Convention on the Protection and Promotion of the Diversity of Cultural Expressions* (2005) acknowledges the fundamental role of civil society in protecting and promoting the diversity of cultural expressions by encouraging the active participation of civil society. This important recognition and inclusion in the Conventions is, not surprisingly, problematic for an authoritarian military regime like the SPDC in Burma which has made no attempt to encourage local community participation in cultural heritage conservation.

Cultural heritage approaches in Bagan have focused on those monumental structures, temples and pagodas, which signify the status of this area as one of the most significant seats of power and authority in Burmese history. Humble dwellings, though socially significant, are not recognized as part of Burma's cultural heritage. Historically, the Bagan area consisted of pagodas and temples intermingled with housing and work places as the people lived within the walled area of the ancient city, usually in differentiated residential sections defined by occupation. The residences of the people were thus enmeshed in the cultural and built fabric of the landscape (Philp and Mercer 1999: 33). But with the establishment of the Bagan Archaeological Zone, local communities were forcibly removed from the area, resulting in a rupture in the traditional connection between the Buddhist laity and these sites of worship. The SPDC have shown no concern whatsoever for maintaining the integrity or authenticity of these sites in terms of their function either in the broader social context today or their significance in the historical past. While the rationale provided for the relocation of residents into new townships was to provide better housing, facilities and services, by confining people and their activities to a manageable and clearly delineated area, it may be argued that the SPDC seeks to exert a greater capacity for surveillance, control and repression. Thus, not only have the broader concepts of the cultural landscape been ignored, but priorities for cultural heritage conservation do not necessarily reflect the local community's own sense of its past and its own sense of identity.

Conclusion

International heritage policy and the conventions and declarations relating to cultural heritage provide a framework in which to examine cultural and human rights and how they relate to the tangible and intangible cultural heritage. Understanding the key concepts involved (for example, cultural rights, cultural diversity, human rights and so forth) is essential if innovative theoretical and practical approaches to cultural heritage conservation are able to be formulated, applied and achieve desirable outcomes. Culture and cultural diversity have been increasingly recognized as key components of sustainable development as safeguarding cultural heritage enables sustainable social, economic, cultural and environmental advancement (www.unescobkk.org).

The SPDC assumed power on 18 September 1988 and it was only then that the country emerged from its former position of self-imposed isolation from the rest of the world. Despite Burma's greater integration into the global economy since then, a strong anti-Western stance remains evident in the military regime's political discourses. The SPDC is unlikely, therefore, in the near future, to defer to international cultural heritage instruments in the identification, safeguarding, conservation and management of Burma's cultural heritage, even though cultural heritage protection philosophies, principles and practices have adopted culturally relativist approaches, more consistent with local cultural traditions, that have addressed the Eurocentric paradigms that characterized earlier approaches. De Varennes (2006) suggests that many international standards take into account cultural and societal particularities without affecting their universal application.

Burma's entry into the Association of South-East Asian Nations (ASEAN) in 1997 has seen the military regime form closer alliances with the international community, albeit primarily its Asian neighbours. In 2000, the *ASEAN Declaration on Cultural Heritage* was formulated in recognition of the need to protect, preserve and promote the vitality and integrity of the vast cultural resources and rich heritage of civilizations, ideas and value systems of ASEAN countries. This Declaration also acknowledges that cultural traditions are an effective means of bringing together ASEAN peoples to recognize their deeply shared history and regional identity. One of the rationales behind the Declaration was that the promotion of a programme of regional cooperation based on perceived Asian values was seen as offering the best possibility for achieving the protection and promotion of ASEAN cultural heritage and cultural rights (www.aseansec.org). More recently, in November 2007, the ten member states of ASEAN signed the ASEAN Charter which lists the key principles and purposes of ASEAN. The ASEAN Charter pledged to establish an ASEAN human rights body that 'reflected the will of the ASEAN peoples to adhere to the principles of democracy, the rule of law and good governance and to respect human rights and fundamental freedoms'. The UN Human Rights Council, in December 2007, also suggested that 'ASEAN could play an important role in promoting the national reconciliation and political reform that had been long awaited by the vast majority of Burmese society' (www.un.org A/HRC/6/SR.29).

Burma's tangible and intangible cultural heritage has a historical legacy dating back to the rule of the monarchs in pre-colonial Burma. Traditional cultural practices have been appropriated as powerful political tools to support the SPDC's domination of ethnic and religious minority groups. Complex challenges, therefore, face conservation professionals seeking to identify, safeguard, revitalize and protect Burma's cultural heritage. Cultural rights and human rights need to be at the forefront of cultural heritage conservation approaches if cultural diversity is to be protected and promoted. In the case of Burma, the cultural traditions of ethnic and religious minority groups need to be recognized as part of the country's rich cultural diversity.

UNESCO's role in standard-setting, awareness-raising and capacity-building in cultural heritage conservation provides a base from which perhaps regional bodies working in the field of cultural heritage such as UNESCO Bangkok[5]; approaches encompassed in UNESCO's LEAP (Local Effort and Preservation) Scheme[6]; UNESCO's 'Cultural Survival and Revival in the Buddhist *Sangha'* project[7]; the Asia-Pacific Cultural Centre for UNESCO[8]; and the Asian Academy of Heritage Management (UNESCO/ ICCROM),[9] may provide the best possible opportunities for cultural heritage preservation and sustainable development in the current political climate in Burma for the principal reason that they explicitly recognize the traditions, values and meanings of cultural heritage in the Asian context. The strengthening of international cooperation and solidarity has been recognized as an important means by which developing countries may incorporate culture into sustainable development.

While the SPDC seeks to gain the support of the Burmese people as modern political activities of nation-building are conflated with traditional cultural merit-making rituals and practices, covert coercion and overt systematic use of violence, consistent with authoritarian military rule, are key factors that have contributed to the SPDC's hold on political power and authority in contemporary Burma. Yet the Burmese people continue to contest the SPDC's hegemonic domination. While the SPDC has appropriated Burma's cultural heritage for political purposes, strong resistance has been made to the state's nationalist policies by those ethnic and religious minority groups whom it seeks to assimilate. Covertly, cultural heritage sites have been appropriated by the Burmese people to oppose the SPDC's attempts at hegemonic domination as a politics of dissent and a culture of resistance have emerged. Political opposition has been expressed and inscribed in the landscape at specific sites of contestation and Burmese traditional culture has been appropriated in symbolic ways and invested with alternative meanings by religious and ethnic minority groups in Burma (Philp and Mercer 2002). Overtly, the Burmese people have demonstrated enormous courage in demonstrating their opposition to the worsening socioeconomic hardships and declining standard of living that they are experiencing today. This was most recently seen in September 2007, when video footage and media reports, broadcast across the globe, showed the Burmese military regime's violent repression of anti-government, pro-democracy protestors who staged peaceful demonstrations.

The promise of a political transition to a democratic political system has become a key element in the SPDC's political ideology with the military regime consistently reiterating its goal of implementing the 'Seven-Step Road Map towards a peaceful, modern, developed and disciplined-flourishing democratic state' (*The New Light of Myanmar* 13 October 2007) and announcing that 'multi-party democracy general elections will be held in 2010' (*The New Light of Myanmar* 11 February 2008). But any optimism concerning the possibility of political reform is perhaps more an idealistic dream than a political reality as long as Burma's military regime pursues a political transition to 'disciplined democracy', and as long as its flagrant human rights abuses, which include intimidation, harassment, torture and imprisonment, continue.

Notes

1 Theravada Buddhism holds that to achieve *nirvana*, each individual is responsible for his or her own salvation. Mahayana Buddhism holds that each individual should forego the opportunity to achieve *nirvana* until all humankind is ready for salvation.
2 Melford Spiro's *Buddhism and Society: A Great Tradition and its Burmese Vicissitudes* (1982) provides an important contribution to understanding Theravada Buddhism in the Burmese context. Spiro's research on Theravada Buddhism and indigenous beliefs and practices has continuing relevance in Burma today, in contrast to other South-East Asian nations, for instance, Vietnam, Laos and Thailand, where Theravada Buddhism has undergone profound reconceptualizations.
3 Conventions are legally binding and subject to ratification by states; they define rules with which states undertake to comply. Recommendations and declarations formulate principles and norms that UNESCO invites states to adopt in national legislation and are intended to influence the development of national practices.
4 De Varennes (2006) argues that the philosophical principle of absolute state sovereignty is not only the main obstacle to the application of human rights, but is more traditionally a construct of Western political thought than of Asian traditions.
5 UNESCO has developed six regional strategies for the Asia-Pacific region to guide programme development tailored towards the region's cultural diversity and deeply rooted cultural traditions.
    The Global Strategic Objectives and Asia-Pacific Strategic Pillars comprise:

- Promoting the drafting and implementation of standard-setting instruments in the field of culture;
- Extending international protection to endangered, vulnerable and minority cultures and expressions;
- Localization and empowerment of the culture profession to develop and implement standards.

Protecting cultural diversity and encouraging pluralism and dialogue between cultures and civilizations:

- Grass-roots mobilization for indigenous, sustainable management of cultural resources;
- Capacity-building in structuring arbitration for culture conflict resolution.

Enhancing the linkages between culture and development through capacity-building and sharing of knowledge:

- Engendering a paradigm shift in tourism in favour of culture and nature conservation;
- Stimulating creative enterprises and cultural industries in the poorest communities.

(www.unescobkk.org)

6 LEAP is a regional initiative that fosters local community stewardship over the heritage resources of Asia and the Pacific. The LEAP programme aims to encour-

age local community action for heritage conservation within existing legal frameworks and under the supervision of conservation professionals. LEAP project activities seek to assist people living within or near heritage sites to take a leading role in site management and conservation, providing local communities with the opportunity to benefit both economically and socially from conservation of their community's heritage.

7 UNESCO's 'Cultural Survival and Revival in the Buddhist *Sangha*' project's principal objective is to 'build local capacity in the conservation of the tangible and intangible heritage via revitalization of traditional artisan skills ... in particular amongst the religious communities such as the Buddhist *sangha*'. Such initiatives perhaps have the best chance of facilitating the traditional transmissions of knowledge and skills in the Burmese context. Sites in Mandalay in Shan State have been identified by UNESCO in its strategy for regional expansion throughout Buddhist countries in Asia (www.unescobkk.org).

8 The Asia-Pacific Cultural Centre for UNESCO is a non-profit organization, with the principles of UNESCO, working for the promotion of mutual understanding and cultural cooperation among peoples in the region.

9 The Asian Academy of Heritage Management is a network of institutions throughout Asia and the Pacific that offers professional training in cultural heritage management under the guidance of UNESCO and ICCROM. Its mission is to transfer technology and knowledge with a specific focus on heritage policy-making, management and implementation.

References

Aasen, C. (1998) *Architecture of Siam. A Cultural History Interpretation*. Kuala Lumpur: Oxford University Press.

Anderson, B. R. O'G. (1983) *Imagined Communities: Reflections on the Origin and Spread of Nationalism*, London: Verso.

Ashworth, G. J. (1995) 'Heritage, Tourism and Europe: a European Future for a European Past?' In D. T. Herbert (ed.) *Heritage, Tourism and Society*, London: Mansell, pp. 68–74.

Aung Kyuing, U. Department of Archaeology (2001) *Protection of Cultural Heritage in Myanmar*, Yangon, Union of Myanmar.

Aung-Thwin, M. (1983) 'Divinity, Spirit, and Human: Conceptions of Classical Burmese Kingship,' in Gesick, L. (ed.) *Centers, Symbols and Hierarchies: Essays on the Classical States of Southeast Asia*, New Haven: Yale University Press, pp. 45–85.

Brown, D. (2005) *Contending Nationalisms in Southeast Asia*. Asia Research Centre, Murdoch University, Working Paper No. 117, 21 pp.

de Varennes, F. (2006) 'The Fallacies in the "Universalism versus Cultural Relativism" Debate in Human Rights Law,' *Asia-Pacific Journal on Human Rights and the Law* (1): 67–84.

Gamboni, D. (2001) 'World Heritage: Shield or Target?' *The Getty Conservation Institute Newsletter*. Available at www.getty.edu/conservation/institute.

Gravers, M. (1993) *Nationalism as Political Paranoia in Burma. An Essay on the Historical Practice of Power*, Surrey, England: Curzon.

Hafstein, V. (2004) 'The Making of Intangible Cultural Heritage: Tradition and Authenticity, Community and Humanity,' PhD thesis (unpublished), University of California, Berkeley.

Hobsbawm, E. and Ranger, T. (1983) *The Invention of Tradition*, Cambridge: Cambridge University Press.

Houtman, G. (1999) *Mental Culture in Burmese Crisis Politics. Aung San Suu Kyi and the National League for Democracy*, Tokyo: Institute for the Study of Languages and Cultures of Asia and Africa, Tokyo University of Foreign Studies.

Joint Standing Committee on Foreign Affairs, Defence and Trade. The Parliament of the Commonwealth of Australia (1995) *A Report on Human Rights and the Lack of Progress Towards Democracy in Burma (Myanmar)*, Canberra: Australian Government Publishing Service.

Kong, L. (2001) 'Mapping "New" Geographies of Religion: Politics and Poetics in Modernity,' *Progress in Human Geography* 25 (2): 211–33.

Ministry of Information (1999) *Nation-Building Endeavours. Volume III. Historic Records of Endeavours made by the State Law and Order Restoration Council*, Yangon, Myanmar: Printing and Publishing Sub-Committee.

Moore, E. (1999) 'Ritual Continuity and Stylistic Change in Pagoda Consecration and Renovation,' *Myanmar Two Millennia Conference*, Universities Historical Research Centre, Yangon, 15–17 December.

Philp, J. and Mercer, D. (1999) 'Commodification of Buddhism in Contemporary Burma,' *Annals of Tourism Research* 26 (1): 21–54.

Philp, J. and Mercer, D. (2002) 'Politicised Pagodas and Veiled Resistance: Contested Urban Space in Burma,' *Urban Studies* 39: 1587–610.

Spiro, M. E. (1982) *Buddhism and Society. A Great Tradition and its Burmese Vicissitudes*, Berkeley: University of California Press.

UNESCO (1972) *Convention Concerning the Protection of the World Cultural and Natural Heritage.*

UNESCO (2001) *Universal Declaration on Cultural Diversity.*

UNESCO (2003) *Convention for the Safeguarding of the Intangible Cultural Heritage.*

UNESCO (2005) *Convention on the Protection and Promotion of the Diversity of Cultural Expressions.*

United Nations (1948) *Universal Declaration of Human Rights.*

Newspapers and magazines

BurmaNet News
Straits Times
The New Light of Myanmar

Websites

www.aseansec.org ASEAN Website.
www.burmanet.org BurmaNet News.
www.unesco.org UNESCO Website.
www.un.org United Nations Website.

Chapter 7

'Elasticity' of heritage, from conservation to human rights

A saga of development and resistance in Penang, Malaysia

Judith Nagata

Over the half century following the end of colonialism in 1957, Malaysia's political and economic policies have been driven largely by ethnic, racial and religious politics, whose divisiveness and lack of common purpose gave the country the character of a classic 'plural' society. References to 'cultural heritage' in this context have invariably served to reinforce these identities and to entrench their distinct claims and entitlements. At the same time, the national state has promoted a programme of aggressive economic development and the creation of a privileged economic elite which has increasingly put at risk the existence and quality of life of communities of all cultural backgrounds, particularly in urban areas. One response, over the past two decades, has been the mobilization of new movements focusing on cultural rights aligned with more extensive social, environmental, housing and human rights causes, united in a critique of promiscuous and politically abetted over-development. This is the context in which a more evolved notion of 'heritage' began to gain currency among a wide swathe of citizens, partly sustained and informed by an international heritage network, in what may be seen as a new variant of identity politics and management. This chapter chronicles the rise of heritage ideology and action as a resistance to the politics of irresponsible development in the Malaysian city of Penang.

The place of 'heritage' in contemporary development politics

The common English word 'heritage' has lately acquired more specialized meanings in response to changing social conditions, a trend also observed in other societies and languages. Thus the French term *'patrimoine'* has evolved into a major national cultural enterprise, involving collaboration beween anthropologists, historians and the Centre d'Ethnologie Française and the Mission du Patrimoine Ethnologique funded by the Ministry of Culture. For one French commentator, they are concerned with 'local constructions of identity, and stereotypes ... generated in a context dominated by processes of globalization' (Braudel 1986). For others, *patrimoine* is located in 'kinship, ethnic, ritual and industrial cultures as *lieux de mémoire* (sites of memory) (Abélès 1999: 401). In Canada, *patrimoine* has a profoundly political role in the politics of Québécois identity and the ongoing stakes of a culturally distinct society. In the rest of Europe, heritage awareness has surged as a consequence of industrialization, and in response to claims for recognition by communities culturally, economically and politically submerged by the seemingly all-encompassing European Union. Finally, in Asia, a wave of heritage awareness has swept across the region in such countries as Japan, Vietnam, Hong Kong, Malaysia and Indonesia, as well as in Australia.

In most Asian languages the concept of heritage is expressed through the adaptation of an existing quotidian term to the more specialized meaning of the English equivalent. Thus in Malay and Indonesian, the word customarily used for a family 'heir' or 'will', *warisan*, has been appropriated for the purpose. In written Japanese and Chinese, two characters, representing generalized notions of culture and inheritance have been combined as a new compound (pronounced as '*bunka issan*'), to convey a now internationally accepted idea.

Heritage and rights

Insofar as heritage is widely associated with culture in general, it can claim the benefits that 'rights to culture' enjoy in international conventions, including UNESCO. Article 27 of the 1948 *Declaration of Human Rights*, enshrined 'rights to freely participate in the cultural life of a community … to the protection of moral and material interests…'. An updated version, expressed in Article 15 of the *International Covenant of Economic, Social and Cultural Rights* of 1966 made the above legally binding on states who have ratified the convention. In 1985, provision was made for monitoring of violations of economic, social and cultural rights, by several subsequent subcommittees. UNESCO's 1972 convention was designed to oversee the protection of global cultural and natural heritage, and still establishes international standards. Notwithstanding, there remains a substantial range of interpretation within and between countries as to the implications and enforcement of the 'rights' dimension.

In once colonized zones, debates have been animated by issues of representation or preservation of colonial and other immigrant (such as Southeast Asian Chinese) cultures, as postcolonial societies engage in processes of history production appropriate to their changing national image. The politics of heritage thus begins with the right of inclusion: whose heritage is worthy of representation and conservation? Indonesian Chinese, for example, at least until the post-Suharto policy revisions after 2000, had no official cultural identity or heritage; also excised was most of the Dutch colonial heritage, and this was reflected in historical restoration and museum policies.[1] Where there are differences of opinion between national and local interpretations, heritage activities may take the form of citizens' and subaltern resistance movements, as a 'weapon of the weak' (Scott 1985), whether in opposition to disputed traditions, or against unwanted predatory development of the received heritage tradition. In construction-obsessed Hong Kong, residents' groups have mobilized in defence of historic 'heritage' fishing communities (Cody and Chang 2001). Heritage in Asia runs the gamut from material and architectural issues, as promoted by the Asia West Pacific Network for Urban Conservation (AWPNUC), to intangibles of culture and identity, or the products of living artists and craftspeople, sometimes called in Japan, 'living national treasures'.

Although in a generic sense, 'heritage' is a disarmingly benign and non-threatening idea, in recent years, as will be described below, the scope of the concept has expanded to include partnerships with environmental, health, civil society, good governance, housing and even human rights movements, as part of an evolving trend in social activism, hovering on the brink between social progressiveness and political irritant. Unquestionably, local and national politics have a bearing on who or what qualifies for heritage recognition: preoccupation with identity and rights is common in immigrant and multicultural as well as postcolonial societies. The process of selection itself is the story of the construction of heritage in particular societies. Regular communication and conferences between international heritage organizations such as the AWPNUC and UNESCO, however, serve to establish points of convergence and reference for heritage status and rights across regions.

The application of a 'human rights' dimension to cultural and heritage activities is a relatively recent trend, used opportunistically in some heritage contexts, to reinforce some of the adjunct claims in the social–political realm. But 'human rights' is a rather elastic concept, and often lacks specific charter references for particular local situations. What, for example, would some Asian cultures make of the 'self-evident' right of Americans to 'life, liberty and happiness', or in the case of the Canadian constitution, to 'rest'? Worse, 'human rights' may even be invoked by individuals more frivolously, to justify such claims as the 'right' to refuse blood transfusions, to live in a noise-free environment, to keep a pet, and so on, by any disaffected person, to the point of meaninglessness.

In the following, I explore the changing uses and meanings to which heritage has been harnessed in the multi-ethnic, multi-religious Malaysian city of Penang. Once the property of particular identity groups, heritage today has acquired newer, value-added connotations, in alliance with common environmental, good governance, consumers' causes and rights to housing, as part of a broader critique of irresponsible and aggressive development.

Penang: from cultural capital to market development

The colonization of the island of Penang began in 1786, as the last outpost of the British East India Company (EIC) east of Calcutta, under a treaty with the Sultan of the adjacent mainland state of Kedah. Terms and circumstances of the treaty have been retrospectively mired in successive colonial and nationalist revisions, but relations and trade with Siam were an issue for both parties. After 1867, Penang became, along with Singapore and Malacca, a British Crown Colony and Straits Settlement, administered independently from the neighbouring royal Malay states (Emerson 1964; Steinberg *et al.* 1987). From the late eighteenth to the early twentieth centuries Penang was a flourishing cosmopolitan entrepôt to immigrants and traders of diverse ethnic and religious origins, many of whom lived mobile, multi-sited lives between Penang and numerous ports from the Arabian Hadhramaut to India, China, Sumatra, Java and the rest of the Dutch East Indies of the day. The first official colonial census of 1881 enumerated 15 distinct ethnic communities, which in successive years have been reduced to today's constitutionally recognized trinity of Malays, Indians and Chinese. But then, as now, censuses failed to capture the exuberant cultural diversity lived on the ground, independent of national classifications.

Under EIC and colonial administrations, local lands and resources were strategically allocated to the non-European immigrants, who were managed, taxed and policed in day-to-day affairs by their own headmen or Kapitans and Penghulus in semi-autonomous communities, in a form of local indirect rule. Until the present, each community maintained its own schools, unions, chambers of commerce and religious associations. Substantial swathes of land were gazetted for Malay and Indian mosques and Muslim *waqf*[2] endowments, which permitted the emergence of an incipient immigrant Muslim hierarchy. *Waqf* land went frequently to a colonially favoured prominent Muslim leader (often an Arab or wealthy South Indian Tamil merchant), who was able to use it for personal philanthropy and patronage, in a form of competitive religious piety. One of the most impressive mosques in Penang today, the Masjid Kapitan Kling, was built on land granted in 1803 by the EIC to a Tamil Indian trader, Cauder Mohiddeen, whose family and clients benefited for several subsequent generations. Among the *waqf* services provided for ordinary Muslims were schools, markets, cemeteries, even facilities for organizing the pilgrimage (*haj*) trade to Mecca.

In the mid-nineteenth century, similar endowments of land were made in the Burmese, Thai and Ceylonese Buddhist communities, for Hindu temples and for Chinese clan (*kongsi*) enterprises. All these grants were strictly non-commercial, non-negotiable and not for resale, 'made in perpetuity for religious purposes'. Additional lands were also ceded to the Catholic and Anglican church dioceses on similar terms. All such grants were theoretically independent of secular law and land codes: religious and symbolic capital was never intended to be converted into market commodities.

Many of these religious and ethnic land endowments were simultaneously residential enclaves, called urban *kampungs*, enabling their inhabitants to live, work, pray, play and be buried in their community. In the inner city of George Town, poorer families were able to enjoy protected rents and tenancy rights, relatively immune from market forces. These were mixed-use residential areas, though often identified with specific ethnic occupations, crafts and services, and their distinctive vernacular architectural habitats. These rights lasted until well into the postcolonial era,[3] under the support of a rent control act (RCA) put in place by a progressive, socially conscious locally elected city council in 1966, which explicitly proscribed the destruction of historic 'heritage' properties, and kept them affordable as dwellings. Malaysian cities were run by their own elected municipal governments until 1969, when local government was abolished, leaving citizens in the hands of remote state and federal administrations and a Ministry of Housing. Religious lands remained nominally under their own elites, while the Muslim *waqf* properties came under the control of a new bureaucratic Council of Muslim Religious Affairs (Majlis Agama Pulau Pinang, or MAIPP).

Since Malayan independence[4] in 1957, the state of Penang has been subject to the national constitution and policies. The Chinese have remained numerically a large ethnic minority ever since, collectively approaching almost 50 per cent of the national population, and as late as 1970, the Malay political majority was only 53.2 per cent of the total (Department of Statistics 1972). In George Town, the principal urban area of Penang state, non-Malays (Chinese, Indians, Thais) remain demographically dominant today, accounting for almost 70 per cent of the population, while the dynamics of ethnic identity politics have long animated the local scene. Until recently, local heritage was always the perquisite of particular groups, which divided rather than united (see note 4).

The decades following the 1980s were marked by a frenzy of nationally promoted economic growth, which left George Town vulnerable to unplanned, random predatory development and a growing market for real estate. The eventual repeal of the Rent Control Act, however, had been planned by the federal government, and yet no preparation for its consequences had been anticipated by local authorities. When the date finally arrived, on 31 December 1999, as many as 12,000 once protected premises, accommodating over 60,000 residents, were affected. Most of these were small family business enterprises, such as Chinese and Indian shophouses, which were thereafter threatened variously with demolition, eviction or rent increases of several hundred per cent. This precipitated the largest single mass exodus ever recorded from the central city core, and destroyed in one blow a century-old intricate network of micro-commercial relationships, family and neighbourhood reciprocities, impossible to duplicate or recreate elsewhere. The displaced residents were decanted to ill-prepared suburbs, while their 'living heritage' disappeared irretrievably.

In the decade leading up to the RCA repeal, however, other once-pro-tected neighbourhoods and endowed lands were steadily succumbing to market pressures, at first without publicity. An early victim in 1990 was the kampung community of Eurasian Catholics (known as Serani), who had occupied at minimal rent diocesan land attached to their parish church for over a century. Against their wishes, the bishop[5] had negotiated a deal for a large income-generating high-rise apartment complex on the site, with a Chinese development company (Goh Beng Lan 2002). Members of the com-munity were forced to scatter across Penang Island. But loss of community generated a revival of Serani consciousness, accompanied by curiosity and a surge of research into their diverse genealogical roots. A few persistent Serani managed eventually to negotiate the right to a small corner of the new complex for a 'Eurasian heritage museum': today there is no sign of artefacts, but a lively little café has taken over, serving 'Serani cuisine'. For the Serani, 'heritage' was a response to dislocation, an *ex post facto* discourse of rights, and as evictions proceeded, rode on a wave of public sympathy. It was an idea whose time had come.

During the same period, religious leaders in some of the land-rich Bud-dhist temples began to be aware of their development potential. The largest and arguably wealthiest Thai temple, Wat Chaiyamangalaram, a magnet on most tourist maps, had long been the host to a substantial community of ethnic Thai tenants paying rents of a few *ringgit* (the equivalent of $3–4) per month. Many were engaged in small businesses or jobs which depended on location, and one was running a Thai language school on the premises. In addition, the temple owns a row of houses on an adjacent street, also rented far below market price. The tenants perform small services for the temple and monks, and take care of the grounds and cemetery, as acts of reciprocity. In the early 1990s, the chief monk, allegedly with the connivance of the Penang Thai consulate, tried to raise the rents to 'market' rates, and at the same time entered into negotiations with Chinese companies for income-generating developments. One of the affected tenants, a retired civil servant with the Penang Land Office, claims to have documentary evidence of illicit deals con-travening the terms of the original Buddhist land grant (personal communi-cation). In his concern for historical fidelity and as self-assigned protector of temple rights, the aggrieved civil servant always carried with him a briefcase of relevant documents 'for protection'. His awareness of public events and the George Town land scene enabled him to frame the Thai Buddhist situation along the lines of similar debates over heritage lands, and even used the term, 'Buddhist *waqf*' to make his point. Following the Serani case, ideas about heritage and rights in a broader public context were beginning to take off.

At the same time, in other Thai and Chinese temples, business-minded religious authorities were beginning to see market opportunities for their domains, and to put them to more 'productive use'. The committee of one of the largest Chinese *kongsi* (clan) associations started to evict kin[6] and other long-term tenants to make way for tourist complexes. Internal division and resentment was pervasive but lacked any viable strategy of resistance.

In the Muslim community for decades *waqf* and other religious lands had been gradually and quietly deflected from their original purpose without fanfare. The first to draw public attention (Nagata 1974; 1979) occurred in the late 1970s, when one centrally located urban kampung was blatantly targeted for a 'redevelopment' project by perpetrators at first unknown, though assumed by local cultural logic, to be Chinese. The proposal was for a high-rise apartment building to replace the single family wooden Malay-style houses and hawkers' stalls, and the installation of a petrol station by the road. Of course, the rents would escalate, and the Malay character of the kampung be destroyed. After much dissension,[7] and investigation, it emerged that the project had been secretly hatched by the Muslim Religious Council (MAIPP), through intermediaries and Chinese business colleagues, as a profit-making scheme for the benefit of rich Muslims, some connected to the Malay Chamber of Commerce. Following these revelations, the project went no further. But later, in the 1990s, such developments became more numerous and brazen and the justifications framed with greater political correctness. Thereafter they were announced to 'promote the improvement of living conditions for indigent Muslims', 'to help the Malay community modernize and engage in business' (relative to the unspoken comparison with the Chinese). Following the logic of business and the mantra of progress, the MAIPP embarked on a series of highly visible rezoning and commercial redevelopment of several prominent historic *waqf* properties around the iconic Masjid Kapitan Kling and in the Arab kampung attached to the *waqf* land of the Acheen Street Mosque (Nagata 2001). By then it was evident that the MAIPP was more in the business of development than religion or the protection of Islam and Malay culture. Further, these decisions were made in conjunction with UMNO federal political elites,[8] and the active participation of the Malay and Indian (Muslim) Chambers of Commerce in Penang, who solicited the capital and expertise of Chinese business partners. Malay and Muslim heritage was for sale on the market by its own heirs. Sympathetic non-Muslims and Muslims alike saw such actions as an infringement of the cultural and religious rights of a powerless community of poorer Muslims. Heritage as an inalienable attachment to traditional identity groups, was being taken into public protective custody, as the responsibility of the entire community. At the same time, new lines of cleavage were appearing. Concern for the rights of the poor and displaced in all the affected communities ran counter to ethnic and religious solidarity. These responses clearly raised issues of social class, although in Penang the class term has never been used in public discourse.

An issue whose time had come: the Penang Heritage Trust

Beginning in the late 1980s, and swelling in the 1990s, was a wave of public awareness and concern over unplanned and uncontrolled development. At first, the only voices came from professional and somewhat idealist middle-class (cf. Low 1994) professionals of all religious and ethnic backgrounds, and at first, the concerns were more about the aesthetics of the built and architectural heritage. Conservationists preoccupied with vernacular architecture and authenticity of history and tradition, strongly influenced by their connections with Australian, Japanese and German foreign experts, led the pack. This was the constituency responsible for the eventual launching of the Penang Heritage Trust (PHT), which in its Malay form (Badan Warisan Pulau Pinang), redeployed the everyday Malay word *warisan*, meaning 'heir', to convey a composite idea of cultural heritage and entitlement and project it on a wider social scene. Initially the PHT was engaged in campaigns against what were regarded as illegal and/or unethical demolitions of historic properties, for infringing land and rent controls. It is noteworthy here that the Malaysian national Heritage Association, located in the Culture, Arts and Heritage Ministry in Kuala Lumpur, not only refrained from offering support or help to the PHT, but refused to act on appeals, following egregious destructions of historic Penang sites and buildings (*Penang Heritage Trust Newsletter*, 19 December 2006). To PHT members, this indifference reflects the political chasm between the elites in the federal capital and the marginal 'Chinese' city of Penang.

Once the idea of heritage was in the public domain, it rapidly became a gravitational point for a growing range of interests. Old and new issues took on new meanings and urgency, from matters of land use, title and occupancy, housing, consumers' rights, quality of life, environmental sustainability, public transport, local governance, political accountability to sustainable tourism. Eponymous organizations, such as the Consumers' Association of Penang (CAP), Malaysian Nature Society (environment), and even some disaffected municipal officials, lawyers, doctors and academics, brought their professional influence and connections to bear on the problems of a city sinking into uncontrolled and disastrous chaos, at the hands of a distant and hostile federal elite.[9] Many of these same professionals contributed their expertise to an unending series of conferences and public forums on topics of transparency, efficient and clean government and other responsibilities, but ended up speaking largely to the already converted. In a city where social, political and material conditions were seen as out of control, a uniting theme was sought in the 'diversionary potential of heritage'. The protagonists were intent on serious reform, as they took on fundamental issues of local governance and civil rights, tenants' and housing rights, promotion of equitable and transparent rules on land utilization, environmental measures against pollution and traffic control, a 'health watch' programme, all kinds of workers' and women's rights, and finally, reform of the (unelected) city council. In effect, they operated like an informal shadow cabinet. For these activists, heritage was a continuing 'charter for political struggle' and more significant, one with more positive, less divisive connotations than those of traditional ethnic and religious community interests, hence less easily assailable by detractors. The reformers counted members from all ethnic and religious backgrounds; their distinctiveness lay in their disproportionately upper-middle-class ('elite') status, and their strong international connections. But subaltern discourses of social class, in the absence of any significant left-oriented political parties, have little currency, save among intellectuals, and the epithets with resonance are usually about culture and cultural group identities.

One notable event bringing many of the above interests together was the so-called SOS (Save Our Selves) protest movement, in fact an NGO created opportunistically in response to the devastating housing crisis following the repeal of the RCA, in early 2000. This was led, among others, by a young Chinese graduate from an Australian university, whose student colleagues from Malaysia included the man who was later to launch the most influential opposition political Internet service (Malaysiakini) for Malaysians, and another who became an important Malaysian labour leader. The SOS leader runs an organic farm and café in Penang as a hobby, and as such embodies several of the qualities and attributes of the elastic/ever-expanding scope of the heritage movement. It was under his advice that the decision was made to claim 'housing as a human right', partly as an experiment to test the responsiveness of Malaysia's newly ratified human rights commission (SUHAKAM), in April 2000. SOS claimed the distinction of filing the first ever human rights appeal in Malaysia, but that too got lost amid the bureaucracy. In principle, it no doubt faced the conviction, widely held in Malaysian official circles, that Western ideas of human rights are often inflated and unsuitable for the very different Asian context (cf. Acharya *et al.* 2001). Undoubtedly Penang's heritage movement would qualify as too 'Western'.

From local to world heritage

For all its unsuccessful confrontations with government, PHT and its partners did manage to shift the focus of heritage away from historic traditions, invented or otherwise, to more universal issues beyond ancient ethnic and religious identity lines, and the elite/subaltern confrontation implicit in the growing disaffection against out-of-control developers became more evident. Individuals and groups from all backgrounds were persuaded to unite for broader common public purposes, and to see themselves as stakeholders in a larger and more diverse community. In this spirit, the supporters of public heritage decided to make an ambitious international move. Largely inspired and implemented by two freelance historians and writers, a Muslim couple, one of Indonesian descent, the other a Chinese convert, scion of an illustrious Chinese clan, both were founder-members of PHT, and had accumulated wide experience and connections with heritage organizations outside Malaysia. Long active in the conservation and restoration of endangered buildings and less tangible cultural activities, they had been awarded contracts by the MAIPP to produce written histories of some of the most emblematic of Penang's heritage sites and communities, including the principal mosques and *waqf* properties. Members of some wealthy Indian Muslim families had commissioned family histories, as part of what was to become a more expanded 'Penang Story'. This was the theme and title of a series of conferences held in George Town beginning in 1998. Another effort, sponsored by the PHT and the Malaysian Interfaith Network, was the Penang Global Ethic Project, whose sub-theme was 'world religions and universal peace', an appropriate celebration of Penang's religious diversity and harmony. This marked a shift in focus from particular religious heritages to one over-arching spirit of co-operation and understanding, for which PHT promoted 'world religion walks', in the form of tours of Penang religious sites.

During this time, a more ambitious goal was being hatched to shoot for the most coveted and elusive prize of all: recognition of Penang as a UNESCO World Heritage Site. This was the supreme test of Penang citizens' capacity to pull together as 'stakeholders' in a common enterprise and identity, as UNESCO's regional cultural adviser, Richard Engelhart (1998) phrased it. Beyond the production of written histories, demonstration of the continuity of viable culture and crafts in vibrant communities, and the existence of adequate tourist sites and services, was the requirement of solid government support at all levels. It was this last that was most difficult to secure in the Malaysian political climate, and the factor responsible for a delay of several years between the initial 'Penang Story' conference and proposal to UNESCO, and the first tentative responses. In the meantime, PHT had been successful in attracting funds from a number of global agencies, including American Express. Penang also succeeded in being listed by World Monuments Watch as 'one of the 100 most endangered sites'. It then secured a preliminary UNESCO Local Effort and Preservation (LEAP) award for its youth projects concerned with revival of traditional music and dance forms, of local markets' dying crafts. However, the greatest challenge was to graduate from 'endangered' to full recognition, and this would involve serious commitment from national and local leaders. Unsurprisingly, many entrenched business, development and religious elites[10] were uncomfortable at the prospect of enforced stringent UNESCO standards over their activities, or of unwanted surveillance. In this respect, any joint enterprise between a World Heritage Site candidate nation and UNESCO is a form of international political relations and entails binding political contracts. The contract invariably comes with conditions, which may impose transparency requirements about the status and rights of particular communities, minorities and cultures, beyond material conservation. In the Penang case, the first submission was made subject to one substantial amendment by the UNESCO committee. Given the many historical and cultural parallels between the two ex-Straits Settlements of Penang and Malacca, and the presence of an important heritage movement in the latter, the evaluators proposed a joint World Heritage project between the two sites. By expanding the scope beyond Penang, more decisions devolved to national authorities, who in the eyes of PHT and its supporters, were responsible for the stalling which followed. However, at higher levels of government, misgivings about externally imposed conditions and quality control were balanced in some measure by the prospects of external funding to be added to municipal and national troughs and to their tourism budgets. The immediate instinct was to treat management of heritage as a bargaining chip, as symbolic capital in a game of cultural politics. In the event, the fact that no serious concessions were offered by political leaders at any level, remains a major obstacle to the entire venture.

For the stakeholders of world heritage, to carry forward the SOS idea of linking it to human rights, as briefly considered, would have made transparent the fragility of such rights in the Malaysian context, and possibly killed off the entire project. The fact that Malaysia was very late (April 2000) in signing and then ratifying the international charter of human rights, and that its first Human Rights Commission (SUHAKAM) was staffed by political appointees, is an indication of its low priority. The ratification marked a long process of acrimonious debates in Malaysian political and civil society circles as to the relevance of a Western concept such as 'human rights' in an Asian society. In the 1990s, Malaysia's Prime Minister Mahathir, following the lead of Singapore Senior Minister Lee Kwan Yew, was intent upon enhancing the country's symbolic ideological and political autonomy vis-à-vis the West (Acharya *et al.* 2001). Human rights (together with civil liberties, such as the status of NGOs, freedom of group assembly and so on), were associated a priori with social and political instability, and other dissident attitudes. In international public relations discourse, these attitudes were justified in the language of 'Asian values', where the idea of 'rights' is seen as too dogmatic and inflexible for Asian contexts. In this view, Asians are 'naturally' more oriented towards community values where individual human rights have little relevance. The individualism of rights conflicts by this logic does not sit well with group interests, seen as central to 'Asian' societies.[11] Whatever the merits of these self-defined, even contradictory, cultural analyses, they have played a large role in public policy and in Malaysia's sense of obligation towards international rights charters. This helps to explain how the idea of human rights surfaced at all in the Penang context, where heritage activities and civil mobilization against the development elite were in large part conceptualized and presented by a middle-class constituency with international (and Western) connections. Yet it is not easy to dissect the logic of Malaysian authorities in such matters. For the 'rights' proposed by SOS in the housing crisis were clearly a case of group action for common purpose, in this instance, the 'stakeholders' of a heritage community on the verge of a terminal loss. It can only be concluded that, in evaluating the human rights claim, SUHAKAM dutifully followed a political mandate rather than a more detached legal process.

The political interpretation is most plausible in light of succeeding events. In 2006, the Malaysian Culture, Arts and Heritage Minister wondered aloud if UNESCO conditions for World Heritage status were too difficult for Asian societies to meet, indeed, if the Penang submission, in conjunction with one by Malacca, might not be so important after all (*Penang Heritage Trust Newsletter* No. 89, January 2007). It was with resignation, but little surprise therefore, when in 2007, the above Ministry announced its planned construction of a 'viewing tower' to be planted in the historic centre of old Malacca, the better to see what is left of its heritage. There was no provision, however, for any of the conservation projects originally requested by the heritage groups. George Town was equally devastated by a proposal from a consortium of leading national politicians and developers (known locally as 'crony capitalists'), to impose their own latest vision of a modern Penang, in the form of a mega-forest of 40-storey concrete towers, rooted in what was once green space or occupied by inconveniently located old buildings, and once again showing scant awareness of its potential impact on the lived or natural environment. This 'Penang Global City Plan' was imposed without consultation with local groups or interests, and risks substantial erosion of what is left of George Town's heritage status (*Penang Heritage Trust Newsletter* No. 91, September 2007). Understandably, this plan has mobilized thousands of citizens beyond the PHT, and in early 2008 construction had not yet begun. The 2007 progress report by the UNESCO evaluator, mentioned 'mistakes of the past' (unregulated demolitions or change to buildings), and their impact on the city's 'vista'. However, he was impressed with Penang's continuing commitment, and noted that 'although some of George Town's built heritage had been lost, there was still much left' (*Penang Heritage Trust Newsletter*, ibid). National political commitment, however, remains uncertain.[12]

Conclusions

The idea of heritage and movements under its cover are flourishing across the world, in many cultures and languages. Heritage activists are increasingly linked in international networks of mutual support and exchange, but given the differences in local social and cultural environments, the parameters of 'heritage' are not necessarily constant from place to place. What is clear is the concept's elasticity and apparent capacity to appropriate under its benign image an ever-expanding range of other public civil, social, cultural and even rights causes beyond the material or built environment. In many instances, heritage is becoming profoundly political, a weapon of the weak (Scott 1985), as it unavoidably confronts the fallout from unbridled and often hostile development projects, often aligned with higher-level national and political interests. Even UNESCO World Heritage contracts are not immune to such issues.

In some countries too, such as Malaysia, more conventional notions of heritage, attached to specific (and sometimes divisive) communal ethnic and religious sub-groups, originally enshrined in basic constitutional, political and popular charters of identity, have been pressed into service for public issues of solidarity and supra-communal purposes, although without erasing more traditional attachments. Penang's experiences oversaw the rise of a stronger sense of Penang civic identity, an incipient citizenship super-imposed on existing communities. Heritage therefore inevitably is a polysemic concept, which is its weakness and its strength. Never, however, was social class made a public issue in the Malaysian situation, or proposed as an ideological alternative, even though observers may independently make that interpretation.

The question of human rights in Malaysia emerges as more elusive and fluid than appears in legal charters. Assuming that a specific country has signed and ratified international rights agreements, and given that there is a political will to apply them equitably (both variable), there still remain problems of local interpretation. Thus in certain Asian regimes, including Malaysia, the relativist philosophy of seeing human rights in its proper context is a matter of doctrine. This is inseparable from the political discourse of distancing 'Western' from 'Asian values', and the promotion of national versions of culture. Such were the ideological justifications behind the footdragging of the Malaysian Ministry of Arts and Cultures and other national leaders over the UNESCO proposal, and the apparent impotence of the government-appointed SUHAKAM human rights appeals committee. Within the heritage movement itself, however, with its infusion of 'Western values' and internationally connected participants, different perceptions prevailed, and an ideological clash was inevitable.

Notes

1 These were among the fiercely debated issues by the fledgling Sumatra heritage movement (Badan Warisan Sumatera Utara) in Medan in 1998: there was resistance to restoration of buildings from the colonial period (described retroactively as an era of *penjajahan*, or 'domination'), while at the time, the Indonesian Chinese minority were still subject to numerous forms of social and political discrimination, and were forced to keep a low cultural profile.

2 At its broadest, *waqf* refers to land or other material resources, donated by a pious Muslim for the benefit of the broader Muslim community, in perpetuity. This normally takes the form of mosques, schools, burial grounds and sometimes, orphanages or markets. As a charitable trust, *waqf* may not be sold, mortgaged or otherwise alienated, nor should it revert to the family of the original donor, and is managed by trustees, or today, by the Muslim Religious Affairs Council. In practice, disputes over terms and dispositions of *waqf* occurred in subsequent generations and by secular authorities.

3 Independent Malaya came into existence in 1957, becoming Malaysia in 1963, following the addition of the Borneo territories of Sarawak and Sabah, as East Malaysia. By this union the sultans of all the original Malay states, together with the Straits Settlements, were subordinated to a national parliament, constitution and legal system under a system of rotating kingship. After independence, the myriad ethnic communities of previous eras were reduced to three, constitutionally recognized and defined 'immigrant' groups, as citizens of the new national state.

4 Enshrined in the independence agreement was the recognition of the Malays as the senior political community, from whom the prime minister and a certain proportion of high civil servants and professionals must be drawn. After a particularly disturbing series of ethnic riots in the 1960s, the Malay-dominated emergency government in 1972 introduced a New Economic Policy (NEP), whereby Malays were entitled to an array of special rights educational, occupational and funding benefits, while Malay became the national language, and Islam the official religion, though not in the form of an Islamic state. The goal of the NEP (continued under newer labels until the present), was to enable the Malays to rise to the challenge of Chinese dominance and an opportunity to 'catch up'. Each of the three constitutionally recognized ethnic communities (Malays, Chinese and Indians), runs at least one communal political party, and most electoral politics and public policy follow ethnic lines. The senior Malay party, which has dominated government since independence, is UMNO (United Malays National Organization), in a coalition with other ethnic parties, such as the Malaysian Chinese Association (MCA), and the Malaysian Indian Congress (MIC).

5 Since these events, the same bishop has been responsible for the sale for redevelopment of numerous diocesan endowment lands, once considered 'sacred', including a historic cemetery and other rentable properties.

6 Chinese clans typically comprise several lineages, and can run to several thousand members. Kinship 'solidarity' therefore is commonly diluted by substantial economic inequality, and relative powerlessness on the part of the more indigent kin.

7 I have written extensively elsewhere about these debates and their impact on internal kampung relations, particularly chronicling the divisions between the politically well-connected and wealthier residents versus those with little political or economic influence.

8 One prominent UMNO politician implicated in the development of *waqf* and mosque lands in the mid-1990s was the then deputy prime minister and one-time Muslim youth leader, with a holier-than-thou public reputation for religious integrity. This was Anwar Ibrahim, subsequently disgraced (for other reasons), following a power conflict with the prime minister.

9 The most recent (2007) example of this attitude was the unilateral imposition, without consultation, by a consortium of politically connected developers of all ethnic backgrounds in Kuala Lumpur, of a plan to gut what remains of the hori-

zontal skyline of George Town, to construct a forest of vertical concrete towers, without provision for wind, traffic, transit or pedestrian patterns in the living city below. This has galvanized massive demonstrations, to little avail, but suggests that, for all its efforts, the causes championed by PHT have not been advanced by much, and that the situation has everything to do with money politics and clientelism, and the wilful infringement of citizens' rights by politicians at all levels. In April 2008, following an unprecedented election defeat in the state of Penang, when the office of Chief Minister was taken over by an opposition party, it was discovered, in the files of the Land Office, that enormous sums of money and resources had been illegally appropriated by UMNO officials and allies during their term, a relic of years of corruption at Penang's expense.

10 At one stage, the Muslim religious council (MAIPP) attempted to appropriate the UNESCO project and divert it in the direction of 'Muslim Heritage Site', which failed to appeal to the UNESCO evaluation team.

11 This critique of rights as an ideology of Western individualism is not unique to Asian societies, but can also be found in Western scholarship. It is most developed in the literature on indigenous peoples, and the weakness of current human rights norms and practice in relation to communal ownership and other group assets.

12 The March 2008 national elections brought a number of unpredicted changes, including the control by an opposition party in the state of Penang. Several key decision-makers in Kuala Lumpur also lost their posts, and more importantly, an unexpected wave of popular rejection of many past government policies was set in motion. The fallout is still occurring at the time of writing, but there may yet be room for optimism on the heritage front.

Bibliography

Abélès, Marc (1999) 'How the Anthropology of France has Changed Anthropology: Assessing New Directions in The Field,' *Cultural Anthropology* 14: 403–8

Acharya, Amitav, Frolic, B. Michael and Stubbs, Richard (eds) (2001) *Democracy, Human Rights and Civil Society in South East Asia*, Toronto: Joint Centre for Asia Pacific Studies.

Braudel, Fernand (1986) 'Espace et Histoire,' *L'Identité dela France*, Arthaud, Flammarion, Vol. 1.

Cody, Jeffrey and Chang Wallace (2001) 'Hong Kong's Tai O: A Significant Drop in the Ocean of Mass Tourism,' paper presented at the American Asian Studies Association.

Department of Statistics (1972) *1970 Population and Housing Census of Malaysia: Community Groups*, Kuala Lumpur: Government Printer.

Emerson, Rupert (1964) *Malaysia: A Study in Direct and Indirect Rule*, Kuala Lumpur: University of Malaysia Press.

Engelhart, Richard, Regional Advisor for Cultures in Asia and the Pacific (1998) Address to Penang Story Conference, *AWPNUC Newsletter* 4: 33.

Goh Beng Lan (2002) *Modern Dreams: A Enquiry into Power, Cultural Production and the Cityscape in Contemporary Penang, Malaysia*, Ithaca: Cornell University Press (Southern Asia Publications).

Goh Beng Lan (2001) 'Rethinking Urbanism in Malaysia: Space, Power and Identity,' in Maznah Mohamad and Wong Soak Koon (eds) *Risking Malaysia: Culture, Politics and Identity*, Bangi, Malaysia: Penerbit Universiti Kebangsaan.

Hobsbawm, Eric and Ranger, Terence (1983) (eds) *The Invention of Tradition*, Cambridge University Press.

Khoo Salma Nasution (1998) 'The Kapitan Keling Mosque and the South Indian Muslim Community in Penang,' Penang Heritage Trust.

Liow, Benny Woo Khin (1989) 'Buddhist Temples and Associations in Penang, 1845–1948, Part I,' *Journal of the Malaysian Branch of the Royal Asiatic Society* 62: 57–85

Low, Setha (1974) 'Cultural Conservation of Place,' in Mary Hufford (ed.) *Conserving Culture: A New Discourse on Heritage*, Urbana and Chicago: University of Illinois Press, 66–77.

Nagata, Judith (1974) 'What is a Malay? Situational Selection of Malay Identity in a Plural Society,' *American Ethnologist* 1 (2): 331–50.

Nagata, Judith (1979) *Malaysian Mosaic: Perspectives from a Poly-ethnic Society*, Vancouver: University of British Columbia Press.

Nagata, Judith (2001) 'Heritage as a Site of Resistance: from Architecture to Political Activism in Urban Penang,' in Maznah Mohamad and Wong Soak Koon (eds) *Risking Malaysia: Culture, Politics and Identity*, Bangi, Malaysia: Penerbit Universiti Kebangsaan, 170–201.

Penang Heritage Trust Newsletter, issues from 1998–2007.

Scott, James (1985) *Weapons of the Weak: Everyday Forms of Peasant Resistance*, New Haven: Yale University Press.

Steinberg, David *et al.* (eds) (1987) *In Search of Southeast Asia: A Modern History*, Honolulu: University of Hawaii Press.

Chapter 8

Rendered invisible

Urban planning, cultural heritage and human rights

Graeme Bristol

The Pom Mahakan community in Bangkok is one of thousands of urban communities around the world under threat of eviction as a result of a number of development pressures common to city life. What makes their story much less common is the range of issues their fight brought forward. This was not just about tenure or lack of compensation for relocation. Those issues were certainly among the first raised over the many years this fight went on. Other fundamental conflicts surfaced about planning, about culture, history and rights. These differing understandings gave rise to conflicts about the methods and intentions of planning, about the arbiters of culture and history and how both affected the rights of this and other communities in the area. For many years, the people of Pom Mahakan have had an intimate relationship with the material history of the area. However, their fate rests with the planners and politicians who, with very few exceptions, refuse to recognize the community perspective of their part in the history of Rattanakosin. They are just poor. And the poor should be, in every sense, on the margins of the city and the society. They should be invisible.

To unravel these conflicts the story must first be told. (Pom Mahakan)

Background

Rattanakosin Island, where King Rama I established the Royal Palace in 1782, was created by the digging of a defensive canal/moat which joined with the Chao Phraya River at the north and south and encircled the royal settlement. A wall was built around the perimeter about 50 metres back from the water's edge with a series of 16 defensive towers at regular intervals. One of the two remaining towers or forts, Pom Mahakan, faces the San Saab canal which runs east through the city. The residents live on that 50 by 150 metre piece of land between the wall and the canal next to Pom Mahakan at the north end and Wat Saket or the Golden Mount across the moat to the east. One of the last remaining pieces of the original wall of the city runs south from the Fort enclosing the western side of the community (Figure 8.1).

In the early 1800s this land was divided into three parts. The north and south parts were given to two courtiers of the king. The middle portion was given to the temple, Wat Ratchanadda, across Mahachai Road from the old wall. By the mid-1800s ancestors of some of the current residents had settled on all three parcels of this land.

I first met the people of Pom Mahakan in November of 2002. They had been fighting Bangkok Metropolitan Administration (BMA) and their various eviction threats since 1994. Some residents had accepted a compensation package and moved out of the north parcel of land and by the time I arrived there it had been turned into a parking lot of city vehicles.

I had come there with seven architecture students to work with the residents of Pom Mahakan for a semester in developing a set of proposals for improvements to their community. At the end of this participatory process the students would hand over a report to the community leaders. That report – the result of three months of data gathering and design with the community – was to be a feasibility study to identify and create budgets for improvement projects the community could undertake themselves or with the support of the city.

The community and the architecture students identified a number of projects related to infrastructure – improved fire safety, waste removal, elec-

Figure 8.1 Pom Mahakan. The Golden Mount (Wat Saket) beyond to the east. The old wall of the city is in the lower right of the image (Graeme Bristol).

trical and water distribution – as well as improvements to the canal edge and the physical relationship to the old wall of the city. Their central concern, though, was community economic development. They wanted to capture some part of the huge tourist trade of Rattanakosin Island. In that, their aims were no different from those of the BMA.

The residents of Pom Mahakan saw other people in the area making a good living from tourism and they drew the natural conclusion that, since many of these tourists went by their front door, they should try to capture some of that market. They did not have a specific business plan in mind but they knew they needed to do something visible to attract that trade. They believed they had something to sell and they could develop more. There was a history to this area, not only protected structures such as the fort and the wall, but in a number of the old teak houses still occupied by residents. One of these teak houses had been turned into a community museum – a repository of papers, photographs and crafts that represented the history of the community. In addition there were other current crafts including one of the last remaining makers of the elaborate Thai bird cages. The community was convinced they had something to offer. They just needed a means to create a market or retail space that would attract tourists not simply to walk through the space but to stop and take part in the local culture of the community. Part of the architectural programme for the students' designs, then, was to create that 'storefront' for the community.

After collecting data, doing interviews with the residents, holding public meetings and developing some preliminary design ideas, the students arranged to make a presentation of the proposed design for comment by the community in late January 2003.

In the afternoon of the previous day, BMA officials had come into the community and posted eviction notices on the front door of every house. They were served notice that they had three months to leave. The students still had to make their presentation but there was an atmosphere in the community that the proposals the students were presenting were now without much value. When the presentation was finished the community leaders turned on the television set up in the square. Along with about 100 residents we watched the five-minute news piece on ITV which gave a sympathetic presentation of the plight of the Pom Mahakan community. Indeed, the fact that the newscast devoted so much time to this news was a clear recognition that this eviction was more than a typical relocation of some 300 people. It had to do with the overall city plans and this eviction, if successful, would have repercussions for many of the other 200,000 people that live and work in Rattanakosin. This was the first step in the implementation of the city's Rattanakosin Master Plan.

The Rattanakosin Master Plan

Many plans for the area had been developed over the years (Bristol 2007). One of the more enlightened of these was sponsored by the BMA, the French Embassy in Thailand and UNESCO. The 'Humanize Bangkok' plan proposed a number of small-scale interventions along the riverfront and the klongs of Rattanakosin. Dr Bhichit Rattakul, then the Governor of Bangkok, proposed to use this joint project to

> initiate the process of consulting the local inhabitants through public exhibitions, on new urban projects in accordance with the principles of democratic consultations and transparency, to demonstrate a break from the past when mega-infrastructural projects entailing significant public debts were decided upon with no prior public consultations.
>
> (UNESCO 1998)

At the same time, one of Governor Bhichit's advisers, Manop Bongsadadt, then the chairman of Housing Development at Chulalongkorn University, said: 'My dream is to turn these areas [Rattanakosin and Thonburi] into an open museum, to make them as handsome as Paris' (*The Nation* 1997). Paris, of course, continues to be considered as having the sine qua non of urban culture.

BMA was hiring consulting planners and architects to develop the Rattanakosin Master Plan at this time. However, this would not involve, as Governor Bhichit had hoped, any consultation with the public. By the time the plan was ratified by BMA in 2001, few people outside the officials and their consultants knew what the plan proposed. It was clear, though, to many of the residents of the 22 communities in Rattanakosin that Pom Mahakan was where the city would begin the implementation of the plan. As a result they were all watching the fate of the Pom Mahakan residents and many were prepared to support them because they knew what failure here implied.

'The Master Plan for Land Development: Ratchadamnoern Road and Surrounding Area' of the National Economic and Social Development Board (NESDB) was a beautification scheme motivated, in large part, by tourism prospects. After the 1997 economic crash tourism became an ever more critical part of the economy. BMA wanted to be able to keep tourists in the Rattanakosin area for longer than a one-day tour before they headed down to the beaches of Phuket and elsewhere. The beautification was planned to help keep tourists in the area. The plan, supported by then Prime Minister Thaksin, called for a number of features. Among them were:

- Making Ratchadamnoern Road the Champs-Elysées of the East.
- Turning the Klong Lod (Lod Canal) into a Thai-style Li Jia (a watertown in China), later referred to as 'un petit Montmartre à Bangkok' (Queffélec 2006).

- Dramatically increasing the park land in the area, particularly around existing monuments such as the Golden Mount (Wat Saket). While park land in the area is scarce, this increase was motivated more by aesthetic intentions (to provide clear viewing points to monuments) than by environmental considerations. Since Pom Mahakan is directly opposite the klong from Wat Saket, this was one of the reasons for the eviction – to provide tourists with a clear view of the Golden Mount.

At the time of the ratification of the Master Plan, Governor Samak Sundaravej was eager to get this plan underway. He had many plans for beautification and the first phase of the Master Plan was to begin by the eviction of the Pom Mahakan community. It was through this eviction action that the nature of the plan became more widely known and its implications understood.

Preservation of culture (large and small)

The city planners were intent on this image-driven approach to planning. While Bangkok's canals made it the 'Venice of the East', the planners were pursuing the Parisian image for Rattanakosin. Underneath these superficial images, though, the residents of the Pom Mahakan community certainly noticed the neglect of some aspects of the city's heritage in their community – the wall of the old city and the abandoned gate house alongside the klong. The wall had been maintained poorly by the city and the Pom residents had begun to do some basic maintenance work on it. Indeed, at one point in the negotiations about their eviction, the community leaders offered to take complete responsibility for the care and maintenance of the wall. They considered it an integral part of their community in any case. The city, of course, refused this offer. After all, the care of such heritage must be left to professionals.

The city planned to tear down the old gate house. In a report in the *Bangkok Post* (2003), 'Mystery of old building explained', it was left to a Pom resident to explain to the city officials and the Committee for Conservation and Development of Rattanakosin City the actual history of this building:

> Chalermsak Ramkomut, a senior resident of Mahakan Fort community, says the building was once a pier for court officials wanting to take a boat trip to Sra Pathum Palace, residence of Her Majesty Somdej Phra Phanwassa (Queen Sawang Vadhana). Mr Chalermsak, now in his 80s, said the pier was built by a senior official at the Agriculture Ministry.
>
> An official on the committee of experts working on conservation and development of historical sites under the Fine Arts Department said the pier theory seems valid. 'It must have been a grandiose pier,' said the official, who asked not to be named.
>
> (*Bangkok Post* 2003)

It is hardly surprising that the official would ask to remain anonymous. The local residents knew more about the history of the place than the experts did.

In addition to their greater understanding of these aspects of Thai architectural heritage, the community also wished to restore the old teak houses including the one that had been converted to the community museum.

They also agreed with BMA about having a park. They just did not want to have to move to create it. One of the steps they took in 2004 to make that point is that they built their own community park in the BMA parking lot that was left from the eviction of residents years before. They saw this as an opportunity to make improvements to this piece of land that, even as a BMA parking lot, had been sadly neglected.

The battle

At the end of the student presentation in January 2003, it was agreed that we would use the information and the design itself as an argument about why they should stay. It was certainly possible to design housing in the middle of a series of mini parks.

Along with the design, the arguments concerned:

- History – the destruction of this community, we argued, would destroy an important part of the urban history of Rattanakosin. This was certainly made evident by the lack of knowledge of the history of the gate house on the part of officials.
- Development – who are the beneficiaries of development and who pays the cost? In this case, the intended beneficiaries seemed to be tourists and the tourist market rather than citizens.
- Parks – the city planners had a very narrow concept of 'parks'. According to their design plans for the area this meant an expanse of grass with isolated trees dotting the site. It was our contention that, if one accepted Jane Jacobs's advice about parks (Jacobs 1992: 89–111), there was little chance for the BMA design of the park to be a success (Herzfeld 2003: 116). The community design for the area with the housing included would work better.
- Gentrification – who is included and who is excluded from economic development? It was clear that the working poor of Pom Mahakan – citizens who would benefit most from economic development – were to be excluded.
- Culture – whose culture matters? Who defines it? Is their history part of the heritage of the city? We argued that people should be as much a part of that living heritage as monuments.
- Land – their connection to this particular piece of land was also an important aspect of their right to be there. Their length of tenure was

stated in terms often heard in traditional communities. 'My grandfather/ great-grandfather planted that tree.' Their connection to the trees as well as to the wall and the klong were all important parts of their community heritage. These were more than reified objects. They were integral parts of their history and ongoing lives. They know where they are and they know it is not Paris or Venice.

The students handed over the final document to the community leaders by the second week of February. Time was running out for the people of Pom Mahakan. The document in hand, the community leaders went straight to the BMA planners and said, 'We have an alternative plan.' Not surprisingly, the planners had no interest in any alternatives. After all, these people were not professionals. Their plan could have no relevance to their overall designs to turn Rattanakosin into Paris.

The Pom leaders were not ready to resign themselves to the dictates of the experts. They went instead to the National Human Rights Commission (NHRC) and argued that their right to housing was being abridged. A meeting was held in early March with the Chairman of the NHRC, representatives of the National Housing Authority, the Governor's office and the BMA planning department, and, in the back row, the community leaders and four of the KMUTT architecture students.

The argument about cultural rights was not made but partway through the two-hour meeting one of the KMUTT students was asked to present the proposed plan. At the end of her short presentation, the NHRC chairman said that he found the alternative plan reasonable and could not understand why the city officials did not. He requested that the city cease their eviction action until such time as the NHRC had the opportunity to further review the alternative plan and resolve this ongoing conflict.

Although the NHRC has little legal authority to back up its requests, it had the moral authority to press the authorities to comply. This gave the Pom community the breathing room to develop further strategies to fight the eviction. Along with finding support in the academic community both locally and internationally and in other communities in the area, the Centre on Housing Rights and Evictions (COHRE) also provided international support by helping the community leaders draft a letter to the UN High Commission for Human Rights pointing out lapses at all levels of the Thai government in their protection of housing rights.

It also meant that the BMA had further opportunities to pressure the community into coming to the 'right' decision and leave. In 2004 there were two actions against the community that were meant to create enough anguish that it might break their resolve. The first was the destruction of the community park and the second was the removal of the old teak community museum. The BMA, as the landlord, sold the building to a contractor who came in and dismantled it for resale. The community leaders offered to buy it back from him before he dismantled it but the offer was refused. BMA deliberately removed the cultural heart of the community. This was not just about housing rights.

Rights

What of cultural rights? Should the community leaders have pursued this avenue of argument? Clearly there was a problem with this pursuit – justiciability. With the ambiguity in the concept of culture (Stamatopoulou 2007: 5) and, generally, the progressive nature of economic, social and cultural rights, there has long been a reluctance on the part of the courts to consider these rights. Often these are referred back to the parliamentary process as policy issues rather than legal issues. Hence, raising cultural rights as a strategy for gaining some protection from the courts was hardly a strong suit for the community. Still, the Pom Mahakan battle was certainly, in part, a cultural battle. Is there some form of protection in international law?

It is worth taking a brief look at some of these international instruments to address that question. In addition to the UN Charter (1945) which recognized the need for a specialized agency (UNESCO) to deal with these broad issues, the *Universal Declaration of Human* Rights (1948) which first recognized cultural rights and the *International Covenant on Economic, Social and Cultural Rights* (1966) which broadened the concept of cultural rights to better recognize minority cultural rights, there are a number of other more recent documents.

Convention concerning the Protection of the World Cultural and Natural Heritage (1972)

As its name suggests, the 1972 World Heritage Convention seeks to protect natural and cultural heritage places 'which are of outstanding universal value' (Article 1). Defined narrowly in the Convention as monuments, groups of buildings and sites, the inscribed cultural heritage places have been identified by the Member State and by the World Heritage Committee as being 'so important we want to pass them on to the generations to come' (Logan 2007: 34). In Thailand, for example, the World Heritage List includes the Historic City of Ayuthaya and the Historic Town of Sukhothai and Associated Towns. The definition of the cultural heritage values that make places significant has widened since 1972 and greater importance is placed on local communities in the attribution of significance and in the identification and management process. Nevertheless, none of the monuments of Rattanakosin are included and certainly not the Pom Mahakan community.

Despite that, the heart of the old city is a repository of the culture of Thailand – the official culture, the marketed culture. For the State the wall and the fort were a small part of that culture and they wished to maintain them both. The gate house and the community itself were considered expendable with respect to their understanding of heritage. This is not what they wanted to see passed on to future generations. In fact, they would prefer that future generations could be rid of both the gate house and the community.

While the community leaders made the argument that the Pom community contributed to the culture of the city and the country – indeed, they 'emphasized that Thainess [was] the basis of their rights' (Herzfeld 2003: 110) – there was no point in arguing that this constituted world heritage of 'outstanding universal value'.

The *Nara Document on Authenticity* (1994)

The Nara document addressed the issue of universality that was evident in the Venice Charter of 1964 and the World Heritage Convention of 1972. It stated that it is 'not possible to base judgments of values and authenticity within fixed criteria. On the contrary, the respect due to all cultures requires that heritage properties must [be] considered and judged within the cultural contexts to which they belong' (Article 11). In this way, instead of the Western emphasis on the static materiality of heritage value, 'other cultures might place value on the significance of a site, the ritual associated with it, or the periodic renewal or replenishment of its architectural fabric' (Silverman and Ruggles 2007: 4). Ritual uses of land 'including honouring the burial sites of ancestors are examples of spiritual use of land and of land-based religions' (Stamatopoulou 2007: 142). The Pom Mahakan community regularly emphasized their relationship to the wall and this small strip of land on which they lived and nurtured the trees their ancestors had planted. While this could hardly be considered a religious use of the land, the community certainly saw a deeper significance in the place they lived than did the city planners who wanted to turn the site into a park.

Nevertheless, the community could not really bring the Nara position to their argument. Whether of universal value or of relative cultural value, this community did not meet these broad criteria. In addition, it needs to be emphasized, they did not see themselves as distinct. They sought to be seen as part of the majority Thai culture, not as a potentially protected minority within it. The State simply did not see their relation to the wall as having any significance to that culture. This is not the way they wanted Thai culture to be presented to the public. Their concern was much more for the control of that image for the purposes of marketing it for tourism.

UNESCO *Universal Declaration on Cultural Diversity* (2001)

As Koïchiro Matsuura, UNESCO's Director-General stated in the preface to this document: 'It raises cultural diversity to the level of "the common heritage of humanity", "as necessary for humankind as biodiversity is for nature" and makes its defence an "ethical imperative indissociable from respect of the individual"'. The recognition that diversity is a universal value addresses the conflict between universality and relativism. While affirming diversity and moving well beyond the concept of culture as monuments or tangible heritage, the Declaration in its broader and more anthropological definition of culture, still refers to 'distinctive spiritual, material, intellectual and emotional features of society or a social group'. The 300 people of Pom Mahakan hardly constitute a distinctive society. And, once again, they did not want to be considered as 'distinctive' as such but recognized as part of the majority culture.

Convention for the Safeguarding of the Intangible Cultural Heritage (2003)

Given the direction of the *Universal Declaration on Cultural Diversity*, the recognition of intangible heritage was the next logical step. Certainly for the Pom Mahakan community their relationship to the wall, the land and the trees was a part of their intangible heritage. But was their heritage worthy of recognition by the State? Was it worth protecting as representative of Thai culture? Obviously the State thought otherwise. They were simply poor people once again in the way of development.

What protection?

The *Maastricht Guidelines on Violations of Economic, Social and Cultural Rights* points out that important among those groups that 'suffer disproportionate harm' in the violation of cultural rights are low-income groups. The obligations of the State with regard to the respect, protection and fulfilment of these rights have been justiciable, particularly in the areas of minority languages and harassment by non-state actors (Stamatopoulou 2007: 162). In much the same way that COHRE helped the community draft a letter to the UN High Commission for Human Rights concerning evictions and housing rights, a similar presentation could be made about the infringement of cultural rights – if those rights can be identified as such.

The basic problem for the Pom Mahakan community here is that what makes them distinctive, certainly in the eyes of the BMA planning department, is the fact that they are poor.

In her book on cultural rights, Elsa Stamatopoulou makes reference to 'special groups'. While mainly focused on minorities and indigenous peoples, she also refers to other groups including women, children and youth, persons with disabilities, migrant workers, refugees and other non-citizens, and the poor. With women and persons with disabilities, the focus has been on the principle of non-discrimination in terms of their enjoyment of cultural rights. With youth and the poor, the focus is more on access and education in the arts. Stamatopoulou points out: 'Poverty, some would say, creates its own culture, the marginalized culture of the poor...' (2007: 242). Nevertheless, this is not to say that one wants to protect this culture of poverty in order to encourage the art that is produced out of such cultures. Poverty, she says,

> ... imposes human indignity, marginalization and invisibility, exclusion from participating in the cultural life of the rest of society. They [sic] poor are viewed as the 'non-public' and they do not enjoy the means to culture understood as the generality of intellectual and artistic perspectives open to members of a certain elite, of 'cultured' people.
>
> (Stamatopoulou 2007: 243)

The planning authorities of the BMA were certainly trying to render the Pom Mahakan community invisible in two significant ways – they wanted to evict them so they were not just invisible but not there at all; and, through the destruction of their park and their community museum BMA was trying not just to ignore this community's local history and heritage, it was intent on erasing it.

Stamatopoulou's recommendations for positive measures by the State to fulfil its obligations for the progressive implementation of cultural rights of the poor include: 'free access to museums or other public institutions of culture, scholarships for students of art schools, subsidies to publications to ensure their economic affordability to the poor and others' (2007: 244). Clearly, such recommendations are of little value in the protection of this community's relationship to the land and the wall. Further, these public institutions of culture are part of the problem for the Pom Mahakan community. It is the public institutions of culture that have decided what is included in that culture and what is outside it. One of those public institutions is the planning department and their architectural consultants. These are the arbiters of culture. In that respect, the Pom Mahakan community is truly outside the wall of the city.

Urban culture

Pom Mahakan represents something broader than the conflict between the community and BMA. This is about the culture of cities and the culture of planning, not just for Bangkok but for the future of urban development in general. Cities are repositories of the monuments of official/sanctioned culture but they are also the place where the majority of the planet's population lives, works and plays. Along with rapid urbanization the growth of slums is expected to double from its present one billion people to two billion by 2030 (UN-Habitat 2003). Given such statistics, conflicts between basic housing/poverty and culture will worsen. Some land invaded for the purposes of housing will be archaeological sites (Silverman and Ruggles 2007: 16) or sites of similar significance to the land the Pom Mahakan community occupies. The official argument taken by BMA is similar to those taken elsewhere. The greater good is served by protecting these monuments for all rather than diminishing them or, in some cases, destroying them for the purposes of housing the poor. '[E]thically the sites do more good for the public welfare in terms of tourist revenue and archaeological significance than is to be derived from permitting squatter settlements' (Silverman and Ruggles 2007: 16). Sometimes, as in the case of Pom Mahakan, this becomes a conflict between the public welfare, who defines it and how it is defined, and the rights of the residents to their past. BMA was intent on resolving that conflict by erasing their past.

There are a number of issues that arise out of this conflict. Here I will briefly consider two of them – the problem in exclusion and the problem of planning culture.

Exclusion and cosmopolitanism

Cultural rights emphasize diversity – the right to be different (Lewis-Anthony 1998: 334). Beyond that diversity is a greater sense of commonwealth – the wealth we share, knowledge, art, or all those monuments and sites on the World Heritage List. These connect us all (Appiah 2006: 135).

Cities, by their nature, tend towards some form of cosmopolitanism. Different skills, perceptions and memories arrive in the city and, if only because of proximity, these are shared. Often, though, it is much more than proximity – it is some sense of shared memories and perceptions of what the city is and what it offers. Appiah points out that there are two intertwining strands of the concept of cosmopolitanism: the obligations we have to others and taking 'seriously the value not just of human life but of particular human lives, which means taking an interest in the practices and beliefs that lend them significance' (2006: xv). This means taking an interest in the culture of those particular human lives, in this case the particular lives of a community of some 300 Thai people who happen to be the working poor and who, as a consequence of their relative poverty, were to be excluded from the city by its planners.

Who belongs in the city? Derrida expanded on that sense of the other in his call for 'cities of refuge' (Derrida 2001: 4). Such cities depend upon the original concept of hospitality, the duty of it and the right to it. This is directly related to the right to asylum and the concept of sanctuary (Derrida 2001: 18). It is also related to the recognition of the other – their identities and their culture.

Bangkok may be, for some, a city of refuge but that is not the case for the residents of Pom Mahakan and so many others under threat of eviction as a result of the Rattanakosin Master Plan – up to 150,000 according to one report (Poonyarat 2002). It would appear, if the planners of BMA had their way, the people who belong in the city would not include the poor.

Planning culture

For whom, then, do the planners plan? Given the Parisian fantasies of the BMA planners and their consultants, it would be in order to take a glance in the direction of Baron von Haussmann and the development of modern Paris beginning in the 1850s. It might be said that Haussmann gave birth to modern city planning, particularly with his design of these broad new boulevards such as the Champs-Elysées which were widened through the sacrifice of working-class housing. Acting on behalf of Napoleon III, Haussmann 'pushed broad easily policed streets through pockets of working-class resistance' (John Rennie Short quoted in Miles 2007: 54).

Le Corbusier followed Haussmann's penchant for the rationalization of the streets and housing of Paris with his Plan Voison which superimposed a rational grid over the existing plan of Paris. 'This was to be the new style of planning, liberated from the past, from history' (Sandercock 1998: 23). It was a style that needed a new kind of planner: 'technocrat, engineer, "surgeon" incorruptible and autocratic' (Sandercock 1998: 23). This also was a good description of Haussmann, something of a mentor for the modern planner – a model that held sway until the 1960s. The rational here must be viewed as a form of protection from the forces of the irrational in the city where the irrational is seen as the other – migrants, the poor, women – monstrous and beyond predictability (Ruddick 2004). The rational planner domesticates these monsters of difference. They become 'acts of safe consumption in ethnic restaurants or neighbourhoods' (Ruddick 2004: 36). As Herzfeld put it:

> The struggle at Pom Mahakan can therefore in some sense be seen as a struggle over whether the margins should be defined as polluting a clean image of Thainess (*khwaampenthai*) or as the hallowed survivor of massive foreign assaults on essential Thai identity.
>
> (Herzfeld 2003: 109)

The planners of BMA had defined these people as a polluting influence. This neither supports the concept of cosmopolitanism nor of cultural rights.

The culture of the modernist planner is still alive and all too well in Bangkok and most major cities. This is the world of the Master Plan as the rational text that domesticates the other and, with that, history. History can be erased (as with the destruction of the Pom Mahakan community museum) and it can be made anew. Bangkok can become Venice or, even more ambitiously, Paris. The modern planner then, is intent on producing the City of Spectacle (Boyer 1996: 47) – a city solely of superficial historical images.

These historical styles need be no more than superficial. In fact it is better that they are devoid of the messy attachments of actual history. Turning Ratchadamnoern Road into the Champs-Elysées would otherwise have some sinister implications in the memory of the many students who were killed in the demonstrations in 1973, 1976 and 1992. This might lead one to ask if the BMA planners shared Haussmann's design motivations – the maintenance of order, the ease of military movement and the clearing out of working-class housing. However, in the City of Spectacle, history has no such depth or meaning. It is a commodity to be marketed by the Tourism Authority of Thailand.

The city of the future, however, must be more than a Las Vegas or Disneyland pastiche of history. In real cities the 'other' becomes visible. How can that visibility be supported?

Rendering visible

One of those consequences of rapid urbanization and globalization is multiculturalism. 'They are part of the landscape of postmodernity, which is a landscape marked by difference' (Sandercock 1998: 16). This is a place where universalist principles can no longer dominate. 'Planning practices based on this perspective have failed in a number of instances to respond to the needs of a multicultural society with ethnic and cultural minorities whose worldview differs from that of the dominant culture' (Burayidi 2000: 37). These universalist principles were central to the modern movement in architecture and planning as was the authority of Western knowledge.

Now we are thrust into the multicultural city that no longer can be perceived in the same way. In January 2003, with its Pom Mahakan eviction notice, the BMA was working under the universalist top-down assumptions that seem invariably to come with the modern city. As such, the implementation of the Rattanakosin Master Plan should simply proceed according to their schedule. In the real city, the plan, in due course, is likely to be abandoned. Those unpredictable and irrational social and political variables have already moved beyond the static rationality of the Master Plan. In this case, BMA and other authorities were firmly fixed in hierarchical authority. Pom Mahakan and its network of academics, NGOs and other communities had a power of resistance that was completely unpredicted by the hierarchy. Information moves too slowly (if at all) through to the top of hierarchical organizations and the response to rapidly changing circumstances is equally slow. 'In those flatter, more network-like organizations, people won't be merely information transmitters – they will be empowered assets, acting independently' (Rischard 2002: 43). On the other side, BMA was committed to the emasculating protection of knowledge just as they were intractable in ignoring the value of the knowledge the community had about planning, about the history of the area and about their rights. Lorraine Code pointed out that: 'There is no more effective way to create epistemic dependence than systematically to withhold acknowledgement; no more effective way of maintaining structures of epistemic privilege and vulnerability than evincing a persistent distrust in someone's claims to cognitive authority...' (in Sandercock 1998: 75).

As effective as that withholding can be, this was not the case for the Pom Mahakan community. When, for example, BMA refused to acknowledge the alternative plan, the Pom leaders did not accept that 'epistemic privilege'. They went on to the National Human Rights Commission.

The relative value of these two differing views is clearly indicated by the fact that the Rattanakosin Master Plan has not been implemented. A world view is changing and city officials have yet to catch up to or understand the implications of these changes. 'The future multicultural city – cosmopolis – cannot be imagined without an acknowledgement of the politics of difference (which insurgent planning histories embody); a belief in inclusive democracy; and the diversity of social justice claims of the disempowered communities in our existing cities' (Sandercock 1998: 44).

In the politics of difference there are layers of history and layers of perception that must be recognized. This is not something that can be done on a drawing board alone. It may be done by communities in conjunction with the technical support of planners and architects.

There are a number of stumbling blocks to better realizing the cosmopolis and rendering visible those who have been marginalized, in part, by the culture of modern planning. I will raise two related issues here – democratization and governance.

Democratization of planning

One of the implications of the multicultural cosmopolis is that it is more dynamic and responsive to the multiplicity of needs from a wide variety of actors. An outcome of that dynamism is that the static quality of Master Plans is ineffective.

> [I]n most cases it would be a waste of resources to put forward a masterplan. This is certainly the case where rapid urbanization is taking place ... The days of the 'Masterplan' hanging on the wall behind the desk of the proud Mayor or Governor must be numbered.
>
> (Rowland 1996: 78)

The city can no more be centrally planned than an economy. Both the marketplace and the city are too dynamic, layered and nuanced for that.

In addition, the shift from comprehensive planning has started to mean planning practice is now (or should be) 'more involved with individual development projects and the day-to-day managing of land use and zoning' (Burayidi 2000: 54). This is evident in the different approaches to the Rattanakosin area represented by the Humanize Bangkok plan and the Rattanakosin Master Plan.

Governance

Participatory planning processes must be institutionalized in urban governance. In the first place it is, after all, a right. Second, the voices of the marginalized have far greater difficulty being heard without such a process. The voices of the Pom Mahakan community were heard in the end but this was a result of the unique circumstances of their struggle – strong and inventive community leaders, support of academics and NGOs, and the support of other communities who were aware of the threat they faced if the Pom Mahakan community lost their argument. This set of favourable circumstances can not be expected in every instance. However, the State does have the responsibility to stand by their international agreements and implement improved methods for all citizens to have a voice. If their voices are loud enough, there is even some possibility they might be heard. A participatory process certainly does not guarantee that anyone with the money, power and authority to get things done will actually listen to those voices. The withholding of acknowledgement and the disregard of other ways of knowing, even in an ostensibly participatory process, is a common trait of professionals.

With every confrontation with the authorities the Pom Mahakan community was insistent that they too were Thai people. They were demanding recognition not as a minority but as part of the majority culture. While the instruments of cultural rights are, as noted above, focused more on the recognition of difference, the opposite can be equally valid where there is a refusal by authority to recognize commonalities. In the case of the Pom community, the city saw only poverty and difference. As such they could not fit into the marketable image of Thai culture for tourism. Nevertheless, nearly six years after their eviction notices were posted in the community in January of 2003, the community still has not moved and they continue to be resolute in their conviction that they too are Thai people.

Bibliography

Appiah, Kwame Anthony (2006) *Cosmopolitanism: Ethics in a World of Strangers*, New York: W. W. Norton.
Bangkok Post (2003) 'Mystery of Old Building explained,' 21 July.
Beauregard, Robert B. (2000) 'Neither Embedded nor Embodied: Critical Pragmatism and Identity Politics,' in Michael Burayidi (ed.) *Urban Planning in a Multicultural Society*, London: Praeger, pp. 53–66.

Boyer, M. Christine (1996) *The City of Collective Memory: Its Historical Imagery and Architectural Entertainments*, Cambridge, MA: MIT Press.

Bristol, Graeme (2007) 'Strategies for Survival: Security of Tenure in Bangkok,' in *Enhancing Urban Safety and Security: UN-Habitat Global Report on Human Settlements*. Case Study available at www.unhabitat.org/grhs/2007.

Burayidi, Michael A. (2000) 'Tracking the Planning Profession: From Monastic Planning to Holistic Planning for a Multicultural Society,' in Michael Buryadi (ed.) *Urban Planning in a Multicultural Society*, London: Praeger, pp. 37–52.

Crinson, Mark (2005) 'Urban Memory – an Introduction,' in Mark Crinson (ed.) *Urban Memory: History and Amnesia in the Modern City*, New York: Routledge, pp. xi–xxiii.

Derrida, Jacques (2001) *On Cosmopolitanism and Forgiveness*. Translated by Mark Dooley and Michael Hughes, London: Routledge.

Herzfeld, Michael (2003) 'Pom Mahakan: Humanity and Order in the Historic Center of Bangkok.' in *Thailand Human Rights Journal* 1: 101–19.

Jacobs, Jane (1992) *The Death and Life of Great American Cities*, New York: Vintage Books, [1961].

Lewis-Anthony, Sian (1998) 'Autonomy and the Council of Europe – With Special Reference to the Application of Article 3 of the First Protocol of the European Convention on Human Rights,' in Markku Suski (ed.) *Autonomy: Applications and Implications*. The Hague: Kluwer Law International, pp. 317–42.

Logan, William S. (2007) 'Closing Pandora's Box: Human Rights Conundrums in Cultural Heritage Protection,' in H. Silverman and D. F. Ruggles (eds) *Cultural Heritage and Human Rights*, New York: Springer, pp. 33–52.

Miles, Malcolm (2007) *Cities and Culture*, London: Routledge.

(The) Nation (1997) 'Ambitious Planner Hopes to Turn City into Utopian Wonder,' 30 December. Available at www.2bangkok.com/2bangkok/MassTransit/ratt.shtml.

Poonyarat, Chayanit (2002) 'Thai Community Fears Being Driven Out For Tourist Dollars,' *Asheville Global Report*, No. 191, 12–18 September 2002. Available at www.theglobalreport.org/issues/191/culture.html.

Pyburn, K. Anne (2007) 'Archeology as Activism,' in Helaine Silverman and D. Fairchild Ruggles (eds) *Cultural Heritage and Human Rights*, New York: Springer, pp. 172–183.

Queffélec, Pierre (2006) 'CULTURE – Klong Lod, un petit Montmartre à Bangkok,' 31 August. Available at www.lepetitjournal.com/content/view/7849/1013/.

Rischard, J. F. (2002) *High Noon: Twenty Global Issues, Twenty Years to Solve Them*, New York: Basic Books.

Rowland, Jon (1996) 'Being a Partner: Educating for Planning Practice,' in Nabeel Hamdi (ed.) *Educating For Real: The Training of Professionals for Development Practice*, London: Intermediate Technology Publications, pp. 77–86.

Ruddick, Susan (2004) 'Domesticating Monsters: Cartographies of Difference and the Emancipatory City,' in Loretta Lees (ed.) *The Emancipatory City? Paradoxes and Possibilities*, London: SAGE Publications, pp. 23–39.

Sandercock, Leonie (1998) *Towards Cosmopolis: Planning for Multicultural Cities*, New York: John Wiley & Sons.

'Secretary General's visit to Kibera, Nairobi 30–31 January, 2007.' Available at www.unhabitat.org/downloads/docs/Press_SG_visit_Kibera07/SG%205.pdf.

Silverman, Helaine and Ruggles, D. Fairchild (2007) 'Cultural Heritage and Human Rights,' in Helaine Silverman and D. Fairchild Ruggles, *Cultural Heritage and Human Rights*, New York: Springer, pp. 3–22.

Smith, Laurajane (2007) 'Empty Gestures? Heritage and the Politics of Recognition,' in Helaine Silverman and D. Fairchild Ruggles, *Cultural Heritage and Human Rights*, New York: Springer, pp. 159–71.

Stamatopoulou, Elsa (2007) *Cultural Rights in International Law: Article 27 of the Universal Declaration of Human Rights and Beyond*, Leiden: Martinus Nijhoff.

UNESCO (1998) 22nd Session of the World Heritage Committee, Kyoto, Japan, 30 November–5 December, 1998. Available at http://whc.unesco.org/archive/1998/whc-98-conf203-inf12e.pdf.

UNESCO (2001) *Universal Declaration on Cultural Diversity*. Available at http://unesdoc.unesco.org/images/0012/001271/127160m.pdf.

UN-Habitat (2003) 'Slum Dwellers to Double by 2030: Millennium Development Goal Could Fall Short,' in *The Challenge of Slums*. Available at ww2.unhabitat.org/mediacentre/documents/whd/GRHSPR1.pdf.

Chapter 9

'Indigenous peoples are not multicultural minorities'

Cultural diversity, heritage and Indigenous human rights in Australia

Michele Langfield

Despite the existence of international instruments to safeguard fundamental human rights, specific rights of Indigenous peoples worldwide remain inadequately protected. Governments have practised enforced assimilation and varying degrees of ethnocide and genocide, including massacres, child removal, and eradication of culture, spirituality and languages (Havemann 1999a: 2–6; Tickner 2001: 2). Indigenous peoples are still severely disadvantaged according to social indicators such as detention rates, homelessness, unemployment, health, life expectancy, alcohol and substance abuse, domestic violence, discrimination and exploitation (University of Minnesota 2003).

This chapter interrogates these issues in the Australian indigenous setting focusing on interconnections between cultural diversity, heritage and human rights. The first section addresses the terminology. The second provides a brief comparative background on British settler societies. The international human rights context for Indigenous peoples is then charted, before the discussion moves to the Australian experience, especially since the 1970s. Finally, it examines Australia's response to the *United Nations Declaration on the Rights of Indigenous Peoples*, adopted by the General Assembly in September 2007. Arguably, the change of national government in Australia in November 2007 ushered in a period of qualitatively different relations between Indigenous and non-Indigenous Australians.

Defining indigeneity

Multiple descriptors (Indigenous 'people', 'peoples', 'populations' and 'First Nations') evoke different responses, including government fears of secession and 'nations within'. Confusion exists about who can legitimately claim indigeneity, who is accepted, and who can speak for whom. While there is no single definition, there are particular criteria by which Indigenous peoples are identified. The International Labour Organization (ILO) Convention no. 169 considers people as Indigenous either because they are descendants of those who inhabited the area before colonization or have maintained their own social, economic, cultural and political institutions since colonization and the establishment of new states (IWGIA 2008).

In the Martinéz-Cobo *Report to the UN Sub-Commission on the Prevention of Discrimination of Minorities* (1986), Indigenous communities, peoples and nations are identified as those which

> having a historical continuity with pre-invasion and pre-colonial societies that developed on their territories, consider themselves distinct from other sectors of the societies now prevailing in those territories, or parts of them. They form at present non-dominant sectors of society and are determined to preserve, develop and transmit to future generations their ancestral territories, and their ethnic identity, as the basis of their continued existence as peoples, in accordance with their own cultural patterns, social institutions and legal systems.
>
> (IWGIA 2008; Fletcher 1999: 337)

This is the generally accepted 'working definition' of Indigenous peoples. Self-identification and acceptance by the group are crucial, as in the ILO Convention.

Another approach by Erica-Irene Daes, Chairperson, UN Working Group on Indigenous Populations, is also widely used. Daes identifies peoples as Indigenous:

1   because they are descendants of groups already in the country when other ethnic or cultural groups arrived there;
2   because of their isolation from other segments of the population, they have preserved almost intact the customs and traditions of their ancestors; and
3   because they are, even if only formally, placed under a state structure which incorporates national, social and cultural characteristics alien to theirs (IWGIA 2008).

Indigenous peoples share a history of injustice where colonization has removed their dignity, identity and fundamental rights to self-determination. According to Augie Fleras:

> Indigeneity, as principle and practice, is concerned ultimately with restructuring the contractual basis of indigenous–State relations. It moves away from the colonization of the past towards recognition of First Peoples as distinct societies whose collective and inherent rights to jurisdictional self-determination over land, identity and political voice have never been extinguished but serve as grounds for entitlement and engagement with the state. The politicization of this indigeneity is inextricably linked with its manifestation in indigenous ethno-politics.
>
> (Fleras 1999: 192)

This chapter adopts the meaning of indigeneity as discourse and in its recently politicized form.

Indigenous peoples in British settler societies

There are 350 to 500 million Indigenous individuals worldwide, divided into 5,000 peoples, constituting 80 per cent of the world's cultural and biological diversity, and occupying 20 per cent of its land (University of Minnesota 2003). Australia, Canada and New Zealand all have histories of migration superimposed on pre-existing Indigenous populations which share the experience of 'subjugation, marginalization, dispossession, exclusion and discrimination by the dominant society' (Havemann 1999a: 5–6). Early British settlers were relatively homogeneous compared with the cultural diversity of those displaced. Nation building was based on racism and capitalism, contrasting with traditional Indigenous subsistence practices of sustainability and close spiritual relationships with the land.

Australian Aborigines and Torres Strait Islanders represent 500 communities, speak 170 languages and have their own flags. They number approximately 450,000, 2 per cent of Australia's population of 20 million (ABS 2006). Inuit, Indian and Métis are recognized as First Nations in Canada. Ten language groups and 40 tribes exist, comprising some 1.3 million people, 4.4 per cent of the population (Statistics Canada, Aboriginal Peoples of Canada 2001). In New Zealand, English and Māori share official language status. Māori number approximately 500,000, 15 per cent of New Zealand's population, with 40 distinct tribal groups (Havemann 1999a: 2–6; Statistics New Zealand 2006). Although these Indigenous populations are increasing faster than non-Indigenous, they remain greatly outnumbered.

Factors affecting race relations and human rights in settler societies include the density, distribution and comparative isolation of Indigenous peoples; their leadership structures and degree of diversity; the timing and nature of European settlement; the imposition of Western notions of citizenship and sovereignty; the ability of traditional societies to resist or adapt; the influence of Christian missionaries; the existence of treaties; and the effects of 'dispersion', segregation, 'protection' and assimilation. In all three countries, Indigenous populations were reduced to dispossessed and underprivileged minorities by the late nineteenth century (Fisher 1980).

Since the 1970s, multiculturalism has underpinned public policy in Australia and Canada, whereas bi-culturalism prevails in New Zealand (Havemann 1999a: 10). This difference in the management of cultural diversity partly explains the less disadvantaged position of Māori compared with Australian Aborigines and Canadian Indians. Nonetheless, all three societies have a history of imposing monoculturalism through assimilation, marginalizing Indigenous peoples based on the ideology of scientific racism. From an Indigenous perspective, this is tantamount to cultural genocide.

Only recently has cultural diversity been managed by enabling limited self-determination and recognizing some 'way of life' and cultural rights (Havemann 1999c: 331).

International human rights and Indigenous peoples

Indigenous peoples' rights in international law have changed markedly over time. Since the 1970s, the emphasis has shifted from assimilation to greater recognition of their right to remain separate with their own distinctive identities. This shift is particularly relevant to the theme of this chapter, which argues that Indigenous peoples have *special* rights, over and above cultural minorities within nations in general. How has this evolution in international human rights law affected British settler societies, especially Australia? While these societies have many similarities, they also display differences affecting the manner and extent to which international developments are locally incorporated.

Traditionally, only states could be subjects of international law. By the nineteenth century, customs of natural law recognizing Indigenous peoples as deserving of rights were replaced by state-made laws, reducing their legal status. The principle of *terra nullius* held that Indigenous peoples had no land tenure or land law at the time of British settlement and consequently the Crown could claim sovereignty. 'Protection' policies aimed to assimilate Indigenous peoples who had no international legal status until the mid-twentieth century (Tickner 2001: 4). Human rights law gradually evolved, however, allowing Indigenous peoples at least to become *objects* of international concern, initially for their protection and later to promote self-determination. Awareness of their living conditions spread and international standards provided them with moral support to fight for their rights (Havemann 1999b: 183–4; Iorns Magallanes 1999: 236–7; Fletcher 1999: 339).

The UN *Universal Declaration of Human Rights* (1948) was the first international instrument to assert that all people were equal in dignity and rights (Article 1), irrespective of race, colour, sex, language, religion, political or other opinion, national or social origin, property, birth or other status (Article 2). The *Convention on the Prevention and Punishment of the Crime of Genocide* (1951) followed, defining genocide as acts intended to destroy, totally or partially, a national, racial or religious group, including the forcible transfer of children of one group to another. The first international agency to address Indigenous issues specifically was the ILO. In 1957 it adopted Convention No. 107 and Recommendation No. 104 'Concerning the Protection of Indigenous Populations within Independent Countries'. This reaffirmed that Indigenous peoples had different rights and needs from other minorities, but contained no guarantee that they could remain culturally distinct (Iorns Magallanes 1999: 237–8).

Human rights laws protecting minorities and individuals against discrimination within states were extended in the UN Declaration (1963) and International Convention (1965) on the *Elimination of all Forms of Racial Discrimination* (*ICERD*). The *ICERD*, signed in 1966 by Canada, New Zealand and Australia and ratified in 1970, 1972 and 1975 respectively, had significant domestic ramifications (Iorns Magallanes 1999: 238). Article 1 defines racial discrimination as 'any distinction, exclusion, restriction or preference based on race, colour, descent, or national or ethnic origin which has the purpose or effect of nullifying or impairing the recognition, enjoyment, exercise, on an equal footing, of human rights and fundamental freedoms in the political, economic, social, cultural or any other field of public life' (*ICERD*).

The *International Covenant on Economic, Social and Cultural Rights* (*ICESCR*) and the *International Covenant on Civil and Political Rights* (*ICCPR*) were adopted in 1966. The latter recognized the right to self-determination, becoming the 'charter' for post-imperial decolonization. Both protect individual and collective rights, the *ICCPR* specifically mentioning intangible cultural heritage. Ratified by Canada in 1976, New Zealand in 1978 and Australia in 1980, the *ICCPR* has affected domestic policies in all three nations, particularly the frequent use by Indigenous peoples of Article 27:

> In those states in which ethnic, religious or linguistic minorities exist, persons belonging to these minorities shall not be denied the right, in community with the other members of their group, to enjoy their own culture, to profess and practise their own religion, or to use their own language.
>
> (*ICCPR*)

Initially, states interpreted this as meaning not to undermine minority cultures but it now implies an obligation to support them (Iorns Magallanes 1999: 238). Although formally, the right to self-determination had no domestic applications, it became a means to assert indigeneity within these states. All ratified the Optional Protocol of the *ICCPR* allowing individual complaints against governments for breaches of the Covenant and the *ICERD*, important in Australia which has no Bill of Rights (Tickner 2001: 302).

The 1970s brought greater awareness of the legitimacy of Indigenous rights. This arose largely from Indigenous peoples themselves taking their concerns to the international arena which then influenced domestic laws. It was increasingly accepted that they be considered as distinct peoples rather than minorities, and legitimate *objects* of international law with clearly defined rights. Acknowledgement that they should participate in making decisions that affected them led to the establishment of a permanent UN forum (Iorns Magallanes 1999: 238–9). In 1972 a special Rapporteur was appointed on discrimination against Indigenous peoples and subsequent reports indicate that they were of separate international concern. The International Court of Justice in the 1975 Western Sahara case found that, under the laws of decolonization, Indigenous peoples were entitled to self-determination and the application of *terra nullius* was no longer appropriate (Havemann 1999b: 184). This indicated that they were being considered not only as legitimate *objects* of international law but also as *subjects* (Iorns Magallanes 1999: 239). It was not until the 1992 *Mabo* Judgment that the Australian High Court rejected *terra nullius* in the same way.

The establishment of the Working Group on Indigenous Populations (WGIP) by the UN Human Rights Commission in 1982 was particularly significant. States rejected the word 'peoples' (in favour of 'populations') fearing that it implied the right to self-determination. The Group's mandate was to review the situation of Indigenous peoples and draft guidelines for their protection. A Draft Declaration was prepared between 1985 and 1993, the objective being to present it to the General Assembly by 2004, the last year of the International Decade for the World's Indigenous Peoples. Wide consultation occurred and annual meetings became important platforms for Indigenous participation. States began to reject assimilation and accept the rights of Indigenous peoples to their *separate* culture and identity (Havemann 1999b: 185; Iorns Magallanes 1999: 239–40; Tickner 2001: 302–5).

Although these attitudinal shifts were reflected in international human rights instruments, the only legally binding document, the 1957 ILO Convention No. 107, remained assimilationist. Influenced by the WGIP, the ILO replaced Convention No. 107 with Convention No. 169 in 1989, recognizing Indigenous peoples' aspirations to cultural preservation and self-determination. Indigenous representatives, however, considered it had not gone far enough, giving Canada, Australia and New Zealand a convenient reason not to ratify or feel legally bound by it (Iorns Magallanes 1999: 240–1).

Nonetheless, Convention No. 169 confirmed international commitment to Indigenous cultural self-determination, participation in decision-making and rights to traditional lands. It facilitated further discussion of the Draft Declaration establishing a minimum set of rights on which it could build. The final version was submitted by the sub-Commission to its parent body, the Commission on Human Rights, in 1994. The Commission, however, failed to approve it owing to state concerns about the self-determination provisions and established its own Working Group on the *Draft Declaration on the Rights of Indigenous Peoples* (Iorns Magallanes 1999: 241–2; DUNDRIP 1994). This met annually in Geneva for another decade. Indigenous representatives from the settler societies consistently argued for a strong Declaration including 'the right of self determination' as stated in Article 1 of the International Covenants. Government representatives, however, opposed this as it could imply the right of secession. Australia later altered its view when it was accepted that secession was an unlikely outcome (Iorns Magallanes 1999: 242).

The work of the Human Rights Committee, which monitors compliance with the *ICCPR*, was particularly relevant for settler societies, making the following reaffirming recommendation in 1994:

> Culture manifests itself in many forms, including a particular way of life associated with the use of land and resources, especially in the case of Indigenous peoples. That right may include such traditional activities as fishing or hunting and the right to live in reserves protected by law. The enjoyment of these rights may require positive legal measures of protection to ensure the effective participation of members of minority communities and decisions which affect them.
>
> (Iorns Magallanes 1999: 243)

Meanwhile a UN *Permanent Forum on Indigenous Issues* was being considered, established in 2000 with eight Indigenous members. It was the first international UN body to have Indigenous representation and provided advice and recommendations to the Council. In 2001, a special Rapporteur on human rights and freedoms of Indigenous peoples was appointed (University of Minnesota 2003).

The *Declaration on the Rights of Indigenous Peoples* was finally adopted by the Human Rights Council on 29 June 2006, referred to the General Assembly and accepted by the UN on 13 September 2007. However, the three British-based settler societies (along with the United States) voted against it. Despite this rejection, these same societies have generally supported the concept of human rights as they have evolved internationally. All ratified the *ICERD*, the *ICCPR* and the Optional Protocol and use similar methods of incorporating them domestically. Although local practices vary, they are aware of their obligations. All have rejected assimilation and accepted a degree of self-determination (Iorns Magallanes 1999: 244–5, 264; Havemann 1999b: 185).

Australia

Historically, Australia's relations with its Indigenous peoples were based on the denial of citizenship, land rights and cultural heritage. Colonization meant dispossession with scant recognition of international human rights. Aborigines became state wards, confined to reserves and missions. Until the 1960s, assimilation underpinned Australian nationhood, exemplified by the white Australia policy. In 1951, as post-war immigration gathered momentum, assimilation was also adopted as official policy for Aborigines (Fletcher 1999: 341); unofficially it had existed for decades. Cultural integration was seen as the solution for non-British migrants and Aborigines alike. The consequences, however, were devastating. According to Michael (Mick) Dodson, human rights activist and member of the Yawuru peoples from the southern Kimberley region, Western Australia:

> Assimilation was and is a massive abuse of human rights ... human
> rights had no application to indigenous Australians in 1951 unless they
> were fully assimilated into the dominant culture. Despite the existence
> of international human rights instruments, indigenous rights did not
> inherently accrue to Aboriginal people but were, instead, a reward if
> they would renounce their Aboriginality and embrace the dominant
> status quo. It was equality based, not on respect for racial difference, but
> on the denial of your race.
>
> (cited in Fletcher 1999: 342)

While the aim was partly to improve living conditions, assimilation also
arose from government efforts to eliminate Aborigines as a distinctively different element in white Australia. As Christine Fletcher argues, governments
collaborated in situating Aborigines 'in a cultural vacuum' (missions, welfare
organizations and reserves), re-educating them as British (Fletcher 1999:
342). Until the 1960s, states and territories had different laws and practices.
Although Canada took over Indian affairs in 1867, and New Zealand
assumed power over Māori affairs in 1852, no coordinated central power over
Aborigines existed in Australia until 1967. Nonetheless, similar racist practices developed across the country (Havemann 1999c: 331).

In contrast to Canada and New Zealand, the Australian constitution does
not mention human rights. With federation, the Commonwealth gained
specific powers, all other powers remaining with the states. When the Commonwealth legislates 'with respect to' one of its powers, it overrides state
legislation (Iorns Magallanes 1999: 245–6). Aborigines only appeared in the
Constitution in ss.127 and 51 (xxvi), the first excluding them from the
national census, the second preventing the Commonwealth from making
laws concerning them. It was not until the 1967 Constitutional Referendum
that s.127 was removed and s.51 altered (Fletcher 1999: 340).

With its overwhelming 'yes' vote, the 1967 Referendum was a watershed
in the cultural and political freedoms of Aboriginal people, providing opportunities for change (Fletcher 1999: 335–6). Many individuals and organizations influenced this outcome, particularly the Federal Council for the
Advancement of Aborigines and Torres Strait Islanders (Taffe 2005; Tickner
2001: 5, 8–9). On Australia Day 1972, a 'tent embassy' was erected outside
old Parliament House, Canberra, flying the Aboriginal flag, a symbol of sovereignty reflecting the growing unity of Indigenous Australians in the struggle for their rights (Tickner 2001: 11; Wells 2000: 212). Multiculturalism
became official policy in 1973 followed by the 1975 Racial Discrimination
Act (RDA), signalling the end of legal discrimination on the basis of race.
The RDA established a 'non-negotiable foundation of human rights protection', giving effect to the *ICERD*. Without it, the *Mabo* decision might
never have happened since it requires that Aboriginal and non-Aboriginal
land rights are treated equally (Tickner 2001: 16, 83, 85).

The Indigenous population has since grown substantially, their leaders and spokespeople increasingly acknowledged. Living standards have improved but are still well below those of other Australians. There is no constitutional recognition of Aboriginal rights as First Peoples, so reforms of one government can be revoked by the next (Fletcher 1999: 341, 347–8). Australian states and territories have passed equal opportunity and anti-discrimination laws benefiting all, but Aborigines have relied primarily on the Commonwealth for justice (Tickner 2001: 5). Under its external affairs power, the Commonwealth has used international human rights law to gain recognition of specifically *Aboriginal* rights and enacted legislation particularly for Indigenous peoples, despite state opposition (Iorns Magallanes 1999: 246; Fletcher 1999: 340).

In the 1970s support grew for equal access to social services and limited self-determination for Indigenous communities (Markus 2001: 21). Self-determination was predicated on principles for decolonization identified by the UN, 'that all people have the right to cultural freedom, to exercise choice over their own lives and to be free from coercion'. This is reflected in Article 1 of the *ICCPR*: 'All people have the right to self-determination. By virtue of the right, they freely determine their political status and freely pursue their economic, social and cultural developments.' In Australia, self-determination implies solidarity, empowerment and enhanced life chances; its broader international connotation of self-governing autonomy is rejected (Fletcher 1999: 342–3). Nonetheless, increased recognition of Indigenous aspirations led to the first Aboriginal Land Rights (NT) legislation, initiated under the Whitlam government and enacted in 1976. The administration of Aboriginal affairs was reorganized under Whitlam who established the Commonwealth Department of Aboriginal Affairs in 1972; the House of Representatives Standing Committee on Aboriginal Affairs and National Aboriginal Consultative Committee in 1973; and the Aboriginal Land Fund Commission in 1975 (Fletcher 1999: 343–4; Tickner 2001: 13, 14, 27; Markus 2001: 22).

The Hawke and Keating Labor governments, 1983 to 1996, promoted social justice (Fletcher 1999: 336). The Community Development Employment Project, begun in 1977 under the Fraser government to provide work in remote communities, was expanded under Hawke (Tickner 2001: 18). Bob Hawke was committed to commercial land acquisition for dispossessed Aborigines and enhancing their rights, particularly to veto mining on their lands. Apart from South Australia, state governments failed to legislate adequately in this area. Clyde Holding, Minister of Aboriginal Affairs, enacted the first Commonwealth Aboriginal and Torres Strait Islander Heritage legislation in 1986. Uluru and Kata Tjuta, spectacular landscapes excised from Aboriginal reserves and incorporated into a national park, were returned to Aboriginal ownership in 1985 with future lease-back and joint management arrangements (Tickner 2001: 21–4).

Indigenous cultural heritage is intertwined with spirituality and place. Often it is secret, sacred and gender specific. Several conflicts between this largely intangible, mystical culture and industrial and commercial interests have led to misunderstandings and double standards, exemplified by the Hindmarsh Island Bridge case in South Australia (Tickner 2001: Ch.13). When, in the face of disagreement amongst local Indigenous women, the 1995 Hindmarsh Island Bridge Royal Commission found that Ngarrindjeri women's beliefs were fabricated, Dodson responded vehemently:

> The right to religious freedom and respect for spiritual beliefs lies at the heart of human rights. It is a right which all Australians are obliged to respect, and all Australians entitled to enjoy. And that principle holds irrespective of whose beliefs are at issue, or on what basis those beliefs are held. What we have in this Royal Commission is the abuse of human rights of Aboriginal people masquerading as a lofty legal procedure.
>
> (cited in Tickner 2001: 283)

On Australia Day, 1988, most Australians celebrated 200 years of European settlement while Aborigines protested with the slogan 'White Australia has a black history'. In June, Hawke was presented with the historic Barunga Statement requesting government support for an *International Declaration of Principles for Indigenous Rights*. In response, Hawke promised a treaty. While treaties exist elsewhere, in Australia there was concern that this would divide the nation. The idea was repeatedly raised but never seriously entertained by later governments (Tickner 2001: 25–6, 40–2; Markus 2001: 87).

Hawke responded actively to the Royal Commission into Aboriginal Deaths in Custody (RCADIC), appointing Dodson as Australia's first Aboriginal and Torres Strait Islander Social Justice Commissioner. He strengthened the capacity of the Human Rights and Equal Opportunity Commission (HREOC) to inform Indigenous communities about their rights and improved mechanisms for handling complaints under the first Optional Protocol to the *ICCPR* (Tickner 2001: ix, Ch. 4). These measures had little impact on the disadvantage underlying deaths in custody, a situation exacerbated in the 1990s by Western Australia's juvenile justice legislation and the NT's mandatory sentencing which contravened the recommendations of the RCADIC and violated the *Convention of the Rights of the Child* and the *ICCPR* (Tickner 2001: 79–80, 306; Markus 2001: 110–11; Wells 2000: 215).

In a clear move towards self-determination and in line with international developments in Indigenous human rights, Hawke created the Aboriginal and Torres Strait Islander Commission (ATSIC) in 1989, through which Indigenous Australians could participate in government processes affecting their lives. ATSIC had a distinctive structure for managing cultural difference through joint accountability (Havemann 1999c: 332) and was politically very significant (Tickner 2001: 49). It was to be the voice of Indigenous peoples: promoting self-determination by formulating, implementing and monitoring programmes; advising the Minister; developing policy; assisting and cooperating with communities; improving social conditions; protecting cultural material; conducting research; and empowering Aborigines through devolution and self-management (Fleras 1999: 216; Markus 2001: 36). It was given considerable resources and autonomy.

Throughout the 1990s, Australians were engaged in a national debate about their history, 'the history wars' (Macintyre and Clark 2003), especially the relationship between Indigenous Australians and European colonizers. The Hawke and Keating governments established a reconciliation process urging public acknowledgement of the legacy of invasion, dispossession and assimilation (Reynolds 1999: 129; Tickner 2001: 27–47). A Reconciliation Council was formed in 1991. For Robert Tickner, Minister in the Indigenous affairs portfolio, 1990–1996, its objectives were threefold: to educate non-Indigenous Australians about Indigenous history and culture and the need to address Indigenous disadvantage and human rights; to produce a formal document or agreement; and to actively address Indigenous aspirations, human rights and social justice. Tickner argued that advancing these objectives was a precondition of any celebration of Australian nationhood in 2001 (Tickner 2001: 29, 33, 45, 47). On 27 May 1992, the 25th anniversary of the 1967 referendum, parliament passed a motion supporting reconciliation and the government's response to RCADIC, including the principle of self-determination (Tickner 2001: 42). Paul Keating's landmark Redfern speech on 10 December 1992 was a public acknowledgement by the Prime Minister of Aboriginal human rights abuses, delivered at the Australian launch of the UN International Year of the World's Indigenous People in 1993:

If we can build a prosperous and remarkably harmonious multicultural society in Australia, surely we can find just solutions to the problems which beset the first Australians – the people to whom the most injustice has been done ... the starting point might be to recognise that the problem starts with us non-Aboriginal Australians. It begins, I think, with the act of recognition. Recognition that it was we who did the dispossessing. We took the traditional lands and smashed the traditional way of life. We brought the disasters. The alcohol. We committed the murders. We took the children from their mothers. We practised discrimination and exclusion. It was our ignorance and our prejudice.
(cited in Fletcher 1999: 336; Tickner 2001: 95; Markus 2001: 37)

Prominent conservatives, including Tim Fischer, National Party leader, John Stone, ex-National Party senator, and Hugh Morgan, Western Mining's Chief Executive Officer, publicly opposed Keating's stance (Tickner 2001:

97–9, 107–8; Markus 2001: Chs 3–4). John Howard, leader of the Liberal–National Party Coalition, rejected the notion that Australia had a racist past and denounced the 'black armband version' of Australia's history (Reynolds 1999: 129). In 1996, Howard proclaimed:

> I sympathise fundamentally with Australians who are insulted when they are told that we have a racist bigoted past. . . . Now, of course, we treated Aborigines very, very badly in the past . . . but to tell children whose parents were no part of that maltreatment . . . who themselves have been no part of it, that we're all a part of a, sort of, racist bigoted history, is something that Australians reject.
>
> (cited in Fletcher 1999: 336; Markus 2001: 86)

Henry Reynolds (1999: 129) identifies the *Mabo* judgment as the main cause of the 'history wars'. Similarly Augie Fleras (1999: 213) describes *Mabo* as a 'defining moment' in Aboriginal ethno-politics. After wide consultation with Indigenous representatives and much political wrangling with state and Territory governments and the mining industry, the Keating government passed the 1993 *Native Title Act*, acknowledging Aboriginal title as common law where not explicitly extinguished by crown or law (Tickner 2001: Chs 7 and 8). In 1995, a Land Fund was established for the 95 per cent of Indigenous Australians unable to prove possession of, or continuous connection with land (Reynolds 1999: 129–39; Fleras 1999: 213; Tickner 2001: Ch.11; Markus 2001: 39). Other policy responses to *Mabo* followed, promoting fairness, equality and better access to government systems. The 1996 High Court *Wik* decision determined that native title could coexist with existing pastoral leases where previously it was extinguished (Tickner 2001: Chs 7 and 8; Markus 2001: 42). In response, Howard released his 10-Point Plan, arguing: 'The fact is that the *Wik* decision pushed the pendulum too far in the Aboriginal direction. The 10-point plan will return the pendulum to the centre' (Australian Politics.com). Tickner considered this a new attack on Indigenous human rights (Tickner 2001: 308).

Mabo's significance is disputed as it simply recognized a pre-existing legal right based on Indigenous customs and occupancy. Placing the onus of proof on Aborigines, continuing to see land ownership from a Eurocentric perspective rather than a holistic Indigenous one, and the widespread dismissal of the Act created obstacles. Dodson argues that Australian governments remain 'locked in a *terra nullius* mindset', unwilling to renegotiate Aboriginal–Crown relationships (cited in Fleras 1999: 213–15). Social inequities persist: staggering death rates, high unemployment, low standards of education, health and housing, and disproportionate incarceration rates. Indigenous identities, cultures and languages remain threatened and human rights discourse has shifted firmly towards self-determination, sovereignty and reconciliation.

Fleras (1999: 215–16) argues that Aboriginal ethno-politics have been relatively successful because Indigenous rights have been presented as human rights and Aboriginal socio-economic disadvantage linked with a national crisis requiring immediate attention. He attributes this to Indigenous activism that rejects inclusion in a multicultural society, favouring a conception of Aborigines as nations distinct from other Australians; the treatment of Aborigines in custody; international embarrassment over images of dispossessed Aborigines; and increasing awareness of past discrimination.

Such activism is exemplified in the push since the late 1980s, albeit unsuccessful, by Torres Strait Islanders for greater independence (Tickner 2001: Ch.12). While the Queensland and Commonwealth governments opposed this, Hawke established an Interdepartmental Committee to consider Torres Strait Islander grievances: loss of control over their future, disadvantage, and disregard for their cultural identity. In April 1993, an Island Coordinating Council document argued for self-determination by 2001:

> Many Australians do not understand that Indigenous autonomy is a recognized world standard for public policy. Indigenous peoples are not simply another group to be assimilated. Rather we are distinct cultures with a will to survive and thrive on our traditional territories. There is irony in the fact that in order to participate fully in the opportunities and life of Australia, we need more autonomy and self-government.... Our purpose is not to import or copy a foreign model but to recognise that practical models exist and that the dangers in Indigenous autonomy and self-government feared by some Australians have not occurred elsewhere.
>
> (Tickner 2001: 243–4)

Despite the establishment of the Torres Strait Regional Authority in 1994 and existing local models in Norfolk, Christmas and Cocos-Keeling Islands, Australian governments have rejected devolution of power to Torres Strait Islanders (Tickner 2001: 248).

Overall, the Hawke–Keating Labor governments effected considerable change in the relationship with Indigenous Australians, enhancing their human rights protection, initiating a path to reconciliation and launching the HREOC Enquiry into the 'stolen generations' in 1995 (Havemann 1999c: 332). In 1996, however, Labor lost power to the Liberal–National Coalition. Ambivalent towards Labor's Indigenous affairs policies, the Coalition withdrew its support, ignoring international human rights trends and confining Indigenous Australians to the status of other minorities within its multicultural society. It failed to follow the social justice agenda of the Reconciliation Council and abandoned Labor's third-stage response to the Native Title Act. It ignored Indigenous claims for differentiated citizenship, replacing the term 'self-determination' with 'self-management' or 'self-empowerment', which have no standing in national or international law (Havemann 1999c: 332; Tickner 2001: 45–7, 307; Wells 2000: 212). The 1997 Bringing Them Home Report recommendation for a government apology to the 'stolen generations' was rejected. Under mounting pressure in 1999, Howard expressed 'deep and sincere regret' but fell short of saying 'sorry' for fear of compensation claims (Tickner 2001: 56–7). This resulted in censure from both the UN Commission on Human Rights and the CERD in 2000.

The Howard government drastically reduced ATSIC's funding and autonomy, and community programmes were adversely affected by pressure for improved accountability. The Coalition was sceptical about Indigenous demands for inherent and collective rights with the Minister increasingly seen as indifferent. Indigenous participation in self-governance declined owing to increasing racial intolerance and impatience with political correctness (Fletcher 1999: 347). Pauline Hanson, leader of the ultra-conservative One Nation Party, promised to abolish special Indigenous rights during the 1996 election campaign. Her emphasis on equal rights for all, supported by Howard, alienated Indigenous Australians (Fleras 1999: 217; Markus 2001: 156, 193–4). Concern over the implications of *Mabo* and *Wik*, particularly any suggestion of an Aboriginal state, led to a steady erosion of post-*Mabo Native Title Act* rights. The pace of reconciliation was slow and Australia celebrated the centenary of federation with little progress, despite thousands of Australians symbolically walking over bridges the previous year. On 1 January 2001, the Council for Aboriginal Reconciliation ceased to exist (Tickner 2001: x; Markus 2001: 112).

While ATSIC promised much in terms of social justice, it was increasingly engulfed in scandal and litigation. Success was compromised by self-management policies which duplicated state and regional structures; lack of accountability; and charges of favouritism and paternalism. Howard established the Aboriginal and Torres Strait Islander Services (ATSIS), and during the 2004 election campaign announced plans to restructure Indigenous affairs and abolish ATSIC. Contrary to recommendations of a government review in 2002, ATSIC was formally abolished on 24 March 2005 (Pratt and Bennett: 2004–2005).

Fleras (1999: 218) argues that Australian ethno-political battles post-*Mabo* included a commitment to self-sufficiency and cultural survival within the context of self-determination. A comparison across the settler dominions led him to identify certain themes. Above all, he emphasizes that 'indigenous peoples are not multicultural minorities'. Their concerns are not those of newcomers, striving for equality and an end to discrimination within existing structures of host societies. Rather, as descendants of the original inhabitants, their inherent and collective rights to self-determination have never been extinguished and await reactivation as the basis for negotiating a new relationship with the state. Their claims *transcend* the socio-cultural concerns of immigrants and refugees. Unlike other minorities, they have a *special* relationship with the state and collective entitlements that flow from that relationship. They see themselves as 'peoples' or 'nations within' as described at the outset of this chapter, and their task as decolonization, demarginalization and self-determination (Fleras 1999: 196, 219–20).

Fleras's argument highlights the delicate balance in settler societies between preserving the heritage of different cultural groups, managing their diversity and recognizing Indigenous rights. Indigenous Australians clearly distinguish themselves from other minorities. Their inherent rights are essentially about self-determination, not necessarily confined to existing political frameworks. As Dodson explains:

> Policy makers must accept that indigenous people are not a special category of disadvantaged souls who require attention or even caring or gentleness. We are peoples with rights and imperatives of our own. Our principal right is to make the decisions that direct our present and our future.
>
> (cited in Fleras 1999: 196)

Settler nations manage their cultural diversity by encouraging minorities to coexist with a shared set of responsibilities and core values. They oppose the Indigenous agenda of self-determination for fear of threatening national integrity. They reject the idea of differentiated citizenship, preferring universal individual rights to the shared sovereignty and collective rights to which Indigenous peoples aspire. Their responses to international laws and conventions are strongly influenced by these prevailing views.

Conclusion

Despite gains in recent decades and the reconciliation agenda, little progress has been made in Australia on Indigenous human rights and disadvantage. Arguably, Australia has breached its obligations under the *CERD*, *ICCPR*, *ICESCR*, the *Convention against Torture* and the *Convention on the Rights of the Child* (Tickner 2001: 308–10). A critical issue since the establishment of the WGIP has been how far nations are prepared to accept the concept of self-determination. Increasingly contested in international law, this concept is one which Indigenous people consider central to the *Universal Declaration of the Rights of Indigenous Peoples* (Fleras 1999: 221–2; Tickner 2001: 306). The settler societies, however, are simply not endorsing it. At the UN General Assembly in September 2007, 144 nations voted for the Declaration, 11 abstained and only four voted against – the United States, Canada, New Zealand and Australia. In a public lecture in October 2007, Mick Dodson, by then Professor and Director of the Australian National University's Centre for Indigenous Studies, referred to the result as an amazing international consensus.

Settler societies are therefore clearly out of step, as in their non-ratification of other UN instruments such as the *Conventions for the Safeguarding of the Intangible Cultural Heritage* (2003), and *Protection and Promotion of the Diversity of Cultural Expressions* (2005). Admittedly, they are the nations most affected. Yet Dodson (2007) emphasized that the Declaration represents minimum standards for the treatment of Indigenous peoples. 'This is the floor not the ceiling.' Like other international instruments, it is 'not legally binding but aspirational, a call to good behaviour', replete with words such as 'consultation', 'cooperation' and 'partnerships'. Somewhat sarcastically, Dodson outlined Australia's stated objections, quoting Mal Brough, then Minister for Indigenous Affairs, who justified Australia's position as follows: 'It's not fair. It refers to specific groups and not others. It's outside what we Australians believe to be fair. We did this because of Australia's interest. We are all one under the national flag.' Dodson argues that the government feared the Declaration would again raise questions of compensation. Australia's objections relate specifically to Articles 25, 26 and 27, all of which concern the rights of Indigenous peoples to lands, territories, waters and other resources they have traditionally owned, occupied, used or acquired. Ironically, Australia was a leader in supporting the Draft Declaration for over two decades. Australian representatives were fully engaged in the deliberations of the WGIP with numerous opportunities to shape its final form. For over a decade, Dodson himself participated in its drafting. 'It is not as if there had been no chance to ensure that it was fair' (Dodson 2007).

More recent developments may influence future relations between Indigenous and non-Indigenous Australians. The first was the Howard government's emergency response to the NT Report 'Little Children are Sacred' on child sexual abuse (NT Government 2007). Legislation in August 2007 allowed comprehensive, compulsory intervention in 73 NT Aboriginal communities. This occurred with little consultation with the NT government or Indigenous leaders, disregarding the importance of Aboriginal input into decisions affecting their lives (Brennan 2007: 1). It is an issue which continued to be controversial under Kevin Rudd's Labor government which maintained the intervention.

The second was the first ever Indigenous opening of parliament under the new Rudd government on 13 February 2008 and the historic apology by the Prime Minister to the 'stolen generations' as his first parliamentary act (ABC 2008). Then on 3 April 2009, 16 months after taking power, Rudd acted upon Labor's election promise to endorse the UN *Declaration on the Rights of Indigenous Peoples*. Indigenous Affairs Minister Jenny Macklin declared this was an important symbolic step for building trust and 'resetting' black and white relations in Australia but she hastened to emphasize that it did not bestow any additional rights on Aboriginal Australians (*The Age*, 26 March, 3 April 2009). While these were long overdue positive gestures, they only partly address ongoing Indigenous aspirations for special rights and self-determination.

References

(The) Age, 26 March, 3 April 2009.

Australian Broadcasting Corporation (ABC) (2008) ABC News, The Apology. Available at www.abc.net.au/news/events/apology/text.htm.

Australian Bureau of Statistics (ABS) (2006) Available at www.abs.gov.au/ausstats/abs@.nsf/.

Australian Politics.com (1997) John Howard's Amended Wik 10-Point Plan, 8 May. Available at australianpolitics.com/issues/aborigines/amended-10-point-plan.shtml.

—— (1992) Paul Keating's Redfern Speech, 10 December. Available at http://australianpolitics.com/executive/keating/92–12–10redfern-speech.shtml.

Brennan, F. (2007) 'The Northern Territory Intervention,' Public Address with Fr Tony Doherty, University of Notre Dame Australia, Broome, 21 August. Available at www.acu.edu.au/__data/assets/pdf_file/0007/55879/NDA_Talk_Aug_2007.pdf.

Dodson, M. (2007) 'UN Declaration on the Rights of Indigenous People,' Public Lecture, Melbourne University Law School, 2 October.

(Draft) United Nations *Declaration on the Rights of Indigenous Peoples (DUNDRIP)* (1994). Available at www.unhchr.ch/huridocda/huridoca.nsf/(Symbol)/E.CN.4.SUB.2.RES.1994.45.En.

Fisher, R. (1980) 'The Impact of European Settlement on the Indigenous Peoples of Australia, New Zealand and British Colombia: Some Comparative Dimensions,' *Canadian Ethnic Studies* 12: 1–13.

Fleras, A. (1999) 'Indigenous Peoples' Rights, Politicising Indigeneity. Ethno-Politics in White Settler Societies,' in P. Havemann (ed.) *Indigenous Peoples' Rights in Australia, Canada & New Zealand*, Auckland: Oxford University Press, pp. 187–234.

Fletcher, C. (1999) 'Living Together but not Neighbours. Cultural Imperialism in Australia,' in P. Havemann (ed.) *Indigenous Peoples' Rights in Australia, Canada & New Zealand*, Auckland: Oxford University Press, pp. 335–50.

Havemann, P. (1999a) 'Introduction. Comparing Indigenous Peoples' Rights in Australia, Canada, and New Zealand. Some Signposts,' in P. Havemann (ed.) *Indigenous Peoples' Rights in Australia, Canada & New Zealand*, Auckland: Oxford University Press, pp. 1–12.

—— (1999b) 'Self-determination and the Paradigm Muddle,' in P. Havemann (ed.) *Indigenous Peoples' Rights in Australia, Canada & New Zealand*, Auckland: Oxford University Press, 183–6.

—— (1999c) 'Variations on a Theme?,' in P. Havemann (ed.) *Indigenous Peoples' Rights in Australia, Canada & New Zealand*, Auckland: Oxford University Press, pp. 331–4.

International Work Group for Indigenous Affairs (IWGIA) (2008) *Definitions of Indigenous Peoples*. Available at www.iwgia.org/sw641.asp.

Iorns Magallanes, C. J. (1999) 'International Human Rights and their Impact on Domestic Law on Indigenous Peoples' Rights in Australia, Canada and New Zealand,' in P. Havemann (ed.) *Indigenous Peoples' Rights in Australia, Canada & New Zealand*, Auckland: Oxford University Press.

Macintyre, S. and Clark, A. (2003) *The History Wars*, Melbourne: Melbourne University Press.

Markus, A. (2001) *Race. John Howard and the Remaking of Australia*, Sydney: Allen & Unwin.

Northern Territory Government Australia, Inquiry into the Protection of Aboriginal Children from Sexual Abuse, established 8 August 2006, reported 15 June 2007. Available at www.nt.gov.au/dcm/inquirysaac/.

Pratt, A. and Bennett, C. (2004–2005) 'The End of ATSIC and the Future Administration of Indigenous Affairs,' Current Issues Brief no. 4, Parliament of Australia, Parliamentary Library. Available at www.aph.gov.au/library/pubs/CIB/2004–05/05cib04.htm.

Reynolds, H. (1999) 'New Frontiers: Australia,' in P. Havemann (ed.) *Indigenous Peoples' Rights in Australia, Canada & New Zealand*, Auckland: Oxford University Press, pp. 129–40.

Statistics Canada (2001) Aboriginal Peoples of Canada. Available at www12.statcan.ca/english/census01.

Statistics New Zealand (2006). Available at www.stats.govt.nz/census/about-2006-census/default.htm.

Taffe, S. (2005) *Black and White Together: FCAATSI The Federal Council for the Advancement of Aborigines and Torres Strait Islanders 1958–1973*, St Lucia: University of Queensland Press.

Tickner, R. (2001) *Taking a Stand. Land Rights to Reconciliation*, Sydney: Allen & Unwin.

United Nations (1948) *Universal Declaration of Human Rights*. Available at www.un.org/Overview/rights.html.

United Nations High Commissioner for Human Rights, *Convention on the Prevention and Punishment of the Crime of Genocide*. Available at www.unhchr.ch/Huridocda/Huridoca.nsf/(Symbol)/E.CN.4.RES.2003.66.En?Opendocument.

United Nations, *International Convention on the Elimination of all Forms of Racial Discrimination*. Available at www.unhchr.ch/tbs/doc.nsf/0/042ab707ad4c08e4c1256a090050f911/$FILE/G0140615.pdf.

United Nations, Office of the High Commissioner for Human Rights, International Covenant on Civil and Political Rights. Available at www.unhchr.ch/html/menu3/b/a_ccpr.htm.

United Nations (2000) *Permanent Forum on Indigenous Issues*. Available at www.un.org/esa/socdev/unpfii/.

United Nations (2007) *Declaration on the Rights of Indigenous Peoples*. Available at www.un.org/esa/socdev/unpfii/en/declaration.html.

University of Minnesota Human Rights Library (2003) *The Rights of Indigenous Peoples*. Available at www1.umn.edu/humanrts/edumat/studyguides/indigenous.html.

Wells, P. (2000) 'Does Australia Have a Human Rights Diplomacy?' in M. Grattan (ed.) *Essays on Australian Reconciliation*, Melbourne: Black Inc.

All websites accessed 23 March 2008.

Chapter 10

A sung heritage

An ecological approach to rights and authority in intangible cultural heritage in Northern Australia

Fiona Magowan

'Doing' is akin to dancing, on stage. We live. We are seen. We breathe meaning and purpose. We are part of the ongoing creation process, if we so choose. Whose lives have we touched? Whose lives have touched us? Who have we become, after the 'dance'?

(Deborah Ruiz Wall, OAM, Order of Australia Medal, deborahruizwall.com/Ideas/Ideas/tabid/70/Default.aspx)

The 2008 Garma Festival Key Forum[1] held in north-east Arnhem Land, Australia, called for 'a new understanding of Indigenous law and governance' to prevent the loss of Indigenous knowledge and maximize the potential for cooperation over caring for country (see Figure 10.1). Two key themes focused on 'Indigenous art and performance in maintaining social cohesion, cultural identity and community wellbeing' and the 'involvement of: Indigenous people and their traditional ecological knowledge in ... sustainable economic development policies and actions' (Yothu Yindi Foundation n.d.). As Indigenous communities in Australia have been progressively disenfranchised by Western practices and agendas that measure, authorize and legitimate knowledge in domains that are not their own (Lee *et al.* 2006: 16), this has impacted upon Aboriginal rights in all aspects of culture and lifestyle. Consequently, Indigenous leaders are seeking ways of addressing disempowerment through dialogue and collaboration with governments and local and regional communities to consider the effects of disadvantage. As the 'most significant Indigenous cultural event in Australia for Indigenous Australians', Garma is one arena in which Aboriginal rights and cultural recognition is debated, performed and negotiated.

This chapter examines how 'a new understanding of Indigenous law and governance' over caring for country may be approached through two interrelated ways of viewing and experiencing the environment. First, I consider an 'environmental habitus' that emphasizes the political and economic effects of human actions in and on places, and second, an ecological habitus that is derived from the embodied presence and aesthetic awareness of places within

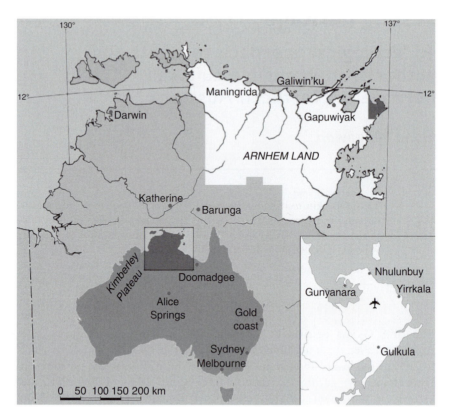

Figure 10.1 Arnhem Land, Northern Territory, Australia (Courtesy: Aaron Corn).

human relations.[2] These habitus are different kinds of orientations towards the natural world and may be held simultaneously but drawn upon to varying degrees depending upon context. I am not simply making cultural distinctions here between Indigenous and non-Indigenous knowledges as has been the case, for example, in development studies; I am also teasing out different types of habitus to show how people can amass their experiences of the world to generate capital and, in turn, influence systems of law and governance. It may be the case that within some cultures a particular habitus is emphasized more than others, while in other contexts, boundaries between them may be blurred. The extent to which different kinds of habitus fuse within and across cultures depends upon how effectively they serve social (and ritual) agendas, behavioural expectations and patterns of law, including state welfare and political issues.

Bourdieu's theory of habitus explains how varieties of enacted bodily practice based upon a structural form together make up social interaction (Acciaioli 1981: 37) that can take different forms. Habitus refers to an embodiment of the 'practical mastery of fundamental schemes' of 'hexis', or the body, that is shaped by individual dispositions and not simply a shared ideology about culture (Bourdieu 1977: 90). Intersubjective qualities of perception, practice and appreciation create 'a meaningful world, a world endowed with sense and value, in which it is worth investing one's energy' (Bourdieu and Wacquant 1992: 127). The interests, tastes and values of individuals shape their expectations of life and the extent to which they share similar kinds of expectations with others and, equally, alternative tastes and interests can distinguish one habitus from another. Different fields such as the market, religion or politics shape the habitus and, in turn, different expressions of habitus influence the way capital is generated within any given field. Fields are, however, not discrete, isolated entities. They are intimately related to one another and therefore social, cultural and economic capital may be exchanged between them.

Distinctions between different habitus occur through discontinuities of meaning and experience. These distinctions have implications for how legal fields are determined which become increasingly complex in terms of determining rights cross-culturally as can be evidenced in conflicts over 'property', 'ownership', 'obligation', 'profit' and 'leadership'. While Yolngu have come to understand to some extent how Western concepts of individual land ownership entail the protection of bounded, commercial rights over time, where land is a potentially alienable commodity, this Westernized view of the spatial and temporal quality of land management is fundamentally at odds with Yolngu notions of the cyclical continuity of Aboriginal stewardship of Arnhem Land (see Rose 1999). Yolngu ecological systems are communally held and cared for as areas that extend out from sacred sites (rather than being areas that are bound in) where rights over country are affirmed by presencing memories in performance rather than staking one's claim in a fence.

The Yolngu concept of 'country' (*wänga*) therefore differs from non-Indigenous ideas of land or landscape. *Country* refers to sentient ecological zones of various kinds, including rivers, coastal regions, seas and eucalyptus forest which may contain one or more sacred sites. Ian Gumbula commented:

> Our identity is in the soil, land, water, plants. In the large communities where we are on someone else's land we do not feel right. We have strong feelings when on our own land ... It is the land that gives us our songs, language and designs, it's through these that we recognize and reveal our identity to each other.
>
> (Gumbula quoted in Lee *et al.* 2006: 35)

Ecological habitus is more than vague feeling though, as Yolngu are concerned with the sustenance of the natural environment from which their spiritual and physical well-being comes and which is an extension of skin, breath, blood and flesh. Like a human body deprived of oxygen, water or food that cannot function, so Yolngu no longer are able to feel for country if they do not practise its presence in order to learn about it. Yingiya Guyula commented that:

> When children receive clan specific instruction from parents away from country the learning is abstract and divorced from the country from which they are receiving instruction. This is evident when children do not understand the connections between *manikay* (songs) and individual clan estates.
>
> (Guyula quoted in Lee *et al*. 2006: 35)

This symbiotic relationship with country was clearly recognized by Tom Calma, Aboriginal and Torres Strait Islander Social Justice and Race Discrimination Commissioner, at the 2008 Garma Festival Key Forum who remarked: 'The Indigenous population is the fastest growing sector of the Australian population. It's young and must not be disenfranchised from our land and our culture.' (See the 2008 Garma Festival Day 5 report. URL accessed at www.garma.telstra.com/2008/08d4.htm.)

Disenfranchisement takes many forms and the impact of Aboriginal dispossession is frequently debated in terms of poverty and financial loss. Scholars have noted particularly the effects of Aboriginal exclusion from the provisions of the Australian State up to the 1960s; low incomes leading to family poverty; problems of remote locations; and social impacts of large family households with higher economic burdens than other Australians (Taylor 1997). Yet, critical questions about how dispossession breaks the connection between tangible and intangible cultural heritages and generates inequalities by violating the essence of Aboriginal personhood are seldom argued out in government policies or in courts of law. For Yolngu, tangible and intangible cultural heritage are interdependent, based on an ontology of relational rights that are inseparably collective as well as mutually self-perpetuating. I will argue that the violation of relational rights most often stems from incompatibilities between environmental and ecological habitus. Second, I will demonstrate that these two kinds of habitus can co-exist within both Aboriginal and Australian worldviews when the protection of Indigenous cultural heritage and intellectual property rights are brought to the fore. I begin by locating these arguments more broadly within a critique of the environmental and development literature around the application of different knowledges in social change policies.

Environmental discourses around Indigenous knowledge

Within development studies, comparisons between Western and Indigenous knowledges have been debated for at least 25 years through competing, complementary or alternative models. Western knowledge has often been juxtaposed as rational, objective and verifiable in relation to Indigenous knowledge as emotional, local, unscientific and primitive (Agrawal 1995; Ellen and Harris 2000). Some have argued against generating a false division (Chambers 1979), while others have viewed Indigenous knowledge as having the potential to effect economic and social change (Escobar 1995; Chambers 1983), and offering solutions through nature rather than through abstracted technologies (Agrawal 1995: 414). Many development agendas have sought to garner Indigenous knowledge to generate sustainable habitats. When knowledge is transferred, Briggs (2005: 5) points out that 'its institutionalization casts it as an object that can be essentialized, archived and indeed transferred itself'. Transferring knowledge can detach information from practice and remove relational engagement with the land in search of practical outcomes (see Magowan 2007a). It is my contention that insufficient attention has been given to understanding the differences between ecological and environmental capital and their consequences for human rights.

Western discourses of public relationships to the environment have become more prominent owing to the current global crisis stemming from a disengaged habitus that has privileged visiting, taking from, altering and depleting resources. It has become evident that knowledge of environmental problems alone is insufficient to create balance and sustainability. Work by Justin Karol and Trevor Gale (2005: 8) considers the role of education in the production of a 'habitus of sustainability'. They suggest that people need to become 'acquainted with a variety of *action skills*' (cf. Fien 1993: 71) based on planning, deep thinking and decision making (Byrne 2000: 49), as well as an ecological awareness of human impact through activities such as recycling, tree planting and minimizing carbon emissions. Fien (Fien and Maclean 2000) has outlined a range of educational methods to teach students how to understand their impact upon the environment by working through representations and accounts of the land as well as their concerns.

Karol and Gale consider that the move towards a sustainable habitus will increase 'environmental capital'. However, solutions to address a disengaged habitus tend to be derived from Western epistemology beginning with the premise that humans are the primary source of agency changing the landscape, rather than perceiving a sentient landscape with its own subjectivity that can impact and influence human feeling and behaviour, as Aboriginal people do. While their approach to an environmental habitus is a useful tool to rethink how economic and political changes can be effected by altering actions upon the land, this habitus can operate alongside an 'ecological habitus' in which the land imprints itself upon personal experience, not because people are trying to change it per se, but because they are open to being changed by its natural effects. Recognizing these differences between habitus is critical for understanding how to formulate laws and governmental structures that facilitate and empower Aboriginal culture, recognition and respect.

An ecological approach to law and human rights

The basis of Yolngu law is an ecological ancestral system whereby the landscape holds ontological values that inscribe kin relations, concepts of exchange, group rights and spiritual identities that serve to differentiate certain groups whilst consolidating political connections with others. The landscape is involved in a continuous cycle of mutual obligation, respect and reciprocity with humans who nurture it through song, dance and ritual as its custodians. In turn, the spirits of the land reciprocally engage with human values such as deference, nurture, affirmation and respect as well as challenge, danger and defiance through the elements and the flora and fauna of sacred sites. Recognizing spiritual laws pertaining to the landscape, then, is a means of acknowledging that customary rights and identity politics emanate from and are embedded in a sentient landscape. For Yolngu, feelings and rights are integrally entwined in land. Singing the environment demonstrates rights of custodianship, reserved for Yolngu who have the authority to sing. However, an ecological approach to learning about law and authority is not always recognized in legal domains and practices of presencing are not necessarily accepted as evidence of land ownership. Instead, Western judicial discourses of economic exchange tend to subvert the ontological and performative dispositions of relational rights to land. In a recent land claim asserting rights based on a history of Macassan contact with Croker Island, Justice Olney did not recognize Aboriginal rights or interests in the land but only forms of trade (Langton *et al.* 2006: 12). Evidence for transactions between Macassans and Aboriginals on Croker were not considered to constitute rights in trading natural resources and so access to and use of resources were not recognized as engaging in a native title right.

As agents tend to act from their own knowledge bases, there is a potential to violate rights symbolically in rhetorics that talk about communicating or 'sharing' experiences of the environment without recognizing ontological differences. For example, in the Australian government's restructuring of Indigenous Coordination Centres,[3] 'solution brokers' are expected to understand all the Indigenous programmes under their remit as well as their impact on communities and how to adapt them to ensure better outcomes. Yet, the Aboriginal and Torres Strait Islander Social Justice Commissioner (2006) has noted his concern that 'recruitment practices ... do not sufficiently recognize that the ability to communicate effectively with Indigenous communities is an important and essential skill and an integral component of all merit based selection processes' (see also Aboriginal and Torres Strait Islander Social Justice Commissioner 2005). Even here, there is no analysis of what constitutes effective communication, how it can be achieved and how this stems from ontological differences. As Waitt *et al.* (2007: 253) have argued in the context of tourist interpretations at Uluru, rational engagement is viewed as reliable and trustworthy while embodied knowledge based on sensory appreciation 'derived from running, walking, smelling, listening or tasting the land' is to be distrusted. This disjuncture has implications for how the value of intangible cultural heritage as a relational expression of belonging and rights in the land is perceived by government and non-Indigenous visitors, especially in relation to land rights issues.

Similarly with regard to government 'interventionist' strategies in the Northern Territory, land leases have been imposed from an economic standpoint that assumes cognitive equivalences between socio-political gains from environment-related commodities, thereby subverting or ignoring Yolngu ecological capital. At Galiwin'ku, for example, Yolngu have been asked to sign away their rights to land for 99 years in return for around 50 houses which will only be granted if the community ascribes to full school attendance and a drug-free community policy. The government's underlying agenda is to facilitate the development of home ownership and businesses. Yet, the implicit coercion and inducement involved both in the offer and the way discussions have taken place with the community have been viewed as tantamount to a breach of human rights (Gray and Sanders 2006: 13). As there is a clear power imbalance, there is concern that this situation is approaching 'an expropriation of Indigenous land' (Gray and Sanders 2006: 13). However, it is far more than this. The potential for violating intimacy between body and land, gift and obligation, moral well-being and spiritual order is clear in these strategies which do not mention the effect that such leases could have on processes of authorization and the recognized exchange of ecological capital and rights through ritual performance.

Performing ecological capital

Ecological capital derived from *singing the land* means that clan leaders are able to legitimate their ritual status and authority; to sustain spiritual relationships with land; to control inappropriate behaviour; and to generate meaning and rights through family values across an extended kin and clan network. Songs are shared across the 36 clans of the region as a result of the crossing and meeting of different ancestral beings as they travelled across the landscape and meanings operate in a gender-restricted system of ritual knowledge and ceremonial practice in which all laws are embedded. Men and women share the same ancestral law (*maḏayin*) but only have rights to perform it in different ways. As songs convey relational principles between land and people, tangible and intangible cultural heritages are inextricably bound together. Those who have the right to sing for land also have rights over matrimonial exchange of women from that area since women are sacred belongings of the clan land whose essences travel with them when they are given to another clan's land in marriage. Those who are 'strangers' or are distantly related kin have no right to sing for another's land because they are not intimate with it or its spiritual essences that need to be controlled and appeased.

Authority to sing, to tell the stories of the songs, or even to show that one knows what the songs mean, depends upon which clan's songs are being discussed as well as the status and gender of the performer or narrator. Ritual authority is a process of recognition over a lifetime of demonstrating skill and ability first of all in dancing, assisting in ritual and eventually singing. Senior ritual leaders known as *dalkarra* for those in the Dhuwa moiety or *djirrikay* for those in the Yirritja moiety hold the deepest inside knowledge of the ancestral law.[4] These men have the authority to sing of the sacred names of ancestral beings who formed the landscape and still reflect the spiritual essences of deceased clanspeople.

Dispossession as disjunctive habitus

Historically, Western perceptions of the environment have not served Indigenous people well and much myth-making has existed in the Australian imaginary, classifying Aboriginal environments as 'wilderness', denying intimate Aboriginal involvement with it and perpetuating environmental racism (Langton, Epworth and Sinnamon 2000: 15–20).[5] Part of the Western misconstrual of Indigenous land use is due to divorcing resources from the politics of identity and resource use from the aesthetics of personhood, especially the significance of rights in song and dance. This can be seen in government legislation that separates tangible heritage laws that protect sacred sites from laws that govern the performance of intangible cultural heritage. Yet, Yolngu control of country entails an integration of cultural property with resource rights as well as intellectual property rights over performance. It has been noted that this complement needs to be recognized legally if environmental racism is to be tackled. As Janke (1998: 156, 7) notes, 'There is a need for greater protection for Indigenous heritage particularly in relation to the protection of knowledge and the intangible aspects of a site or place.'[6] Singing the land is a practice of intimacy, opening the self spiritually through listening and presencing 'country'. Yet, these practices of presencing require translation when they are used to engage with non-Indigenous people who bring other environmental perspectives with them in contexts such as cultural tourism programmes. The last part of this chapter asks how do tourists perceive their relationships to the environment in a cultural tourism programme; how are Yolngu (re)educating tourists about ecological relationships in song and dance; and how much is misrecognized in this exchange?

Exchanging recognition

The Garma Festival is an award-winning example of a cultural tourism programme that is reorienting visitors' perceptions of ecological engagement. It is also repositioning a colonial past of dispossession and welfare dependency as one of interdependency in which tourists finance the possibility of cultural engagement on Yolngu terms. Some scholars have argued in other contexts, that tourists come because they want to validate a pre-existing narrative about their perceptions of heritage (cf. Edensor 1998). However, in the context of Garma, the majority of tourists I spoke to had little preconception of what the area, the people or the tourism programme would be like. The Garma Festival ground is situated in a large clearing at Gulkula that accommodates a conference forum located under a large awning on the escarpment. A range of stalls, such as the Alcan Mine Corporation and Dhimurru Land Management Corporation display local employment opportunities[7] on the fringes of the eucalyptus clearing, and a cultural tourism programme operates during the day with its participants attending evening performances.

The philosophy of educating tourists stems from the concept of 'two ways' learning developed in Arnhem Land in the 1970s. This concept was derived originally from government support for bilingual programmes to teach Yolngu in their own language as the Australian Federal Government moved from assimilation to integration. Yet, with the decline of funds for bilingual schools in the 1980s, the programme petered out in 1998, only to be reinstated more strongly in 2000 due to pressure from communities and various human rights organizations (Lee *et al.* 2006: 11). The term, 'two ways' or 'both ways' education is intended to capture the spirit of learning as an holistic educational experience. As Galarrwuy Yunupingu notes about Garma, 'It's about unity, it's about learning from each other' (Yothu Yindi Foundation n.d.). Participants in the cultural tourism programme at Garma took part in a range of activities. Women could learn to paint, make baskets and mats, gather berries, honey, look for yams, make damper and hear women singing in the morning, while men were taken hunting, taught to make spears, collect turtle eggs and fish along the coast and told about some of the ancestral stories of the area. It is notable that performance education takes place through dance not song for a number of reasons: as songs are based on an esoteric language not all clans have the right to sing other clans' songs and even if songs could be shared, tourists would not necessarily be able to follow either the words or the melody. Songs then remain part of spectacle rather than tourist practice. Instead, instruction about the ancestral law takes place through dance. One woman from Sydney said:

> Dancing was great – it made me realise how uncoordinated I am. Dancing goanna, emu, dolphin, brolga. It was hilarious. I realise it's a country full of these creatures that they not only know are there, but they know how they move and look and behave.

Legitimizing tourists' recognition of Yolngu rights in ritual

Many of the tourists in the Garma cultural tourism programme have never engaged with Aboriginal people before and are not necessarily cognizant of the field of relational rights that constitutes the ancestral law. Handler and Saxton (1988: 242) argue that participants/actors in events such as 'living history' projects experience the past as present, but Garma tourists cannot experience a past which relates to a habitus foreign to their own and of which they have limited comprehension. At the beginning of the programme, tourists reflected upon their response to Yolngu dancing, many reading their participation as entertainment, even if they were aware of some notion of its ritual function. As one female tourist commented:

> [I didn't understand] the ceremonial connection with people's expecta-tions, that while they might be working in the Land Council or with Dhimurru, they are still on call as ceremonial participants and have a role to play in ritual, and that should be seen. That was very impressive and very strong, and I didn't understand that that was what was going on when R's husband was dancing her daughter...

Some dance scholars argue that tourist dance aims to capture 'authenticity' based on '*anonymous* authorship and skill or accuracy in the replication of something used functionally by members of a given society' (Daniel 1996: 782, my emphasis).[8] However, this understanding of tourist participation does not sufficiently express what Yolngu are trying to do by allowing tour-ists to participate. As dancing generates various movements of ancestral animals in their habitats, a co-presencing of the environment and the moral and legal rights held within it are manifest. It 'is a way of presencing ecology which does not separate experience from thinking and analysis from a sense of social commitment and responsibility' (Tamisari 2005a: 177). As Tamisari notes:

> If dancing is one of the most effective ways of claiming, affirming and legitimizing one's knowledge and authority in ceremonial contexts, the effectiveness of these 'dancing statements' cannot be realized merely through acquiring the technical skills required for their flawless execu-tion nor through an explanation of their complex symbolism. More importantly, Australian Indigenous dance in local and intercultural con-texts, needs to be understood in terms of intersubjective relationships.
>
> (Tamisari 2005b: 50)

Although tourists may not fully appreciate the complexity of rights in the dances they join in with, Yolngu are offering them the opportunity to trans-form their sense of connection with the landscape and each other through the humility and vulnerability of observing, doing, being seen, receiving instruction and by being positively supported by the leaders in dancing. Tourists then validate their participation, not simply by taking part in a 'staged authenticity' (MacCannell 1973) but on the depth of personal experience achieved in their movements and partly on the legitimation afforded by the right to participate and explore cultural difference intersubjectively.

Conflicting habitus in performance

Some tourists who were open to trying to understand the landscape as co-presencing people-as-nature, became cognizant of a disjuncture between forms of environmental and ecological habitus. A nurse from Darwin told me:

> I would read the land scientifically or environmentally as a very clean environment. As a result of being at Garma I realize the importance of absolutely everything. When we were with the women in the morning they were singing the silence and the different birds would be sung in and certain people would cry in their singing for these birds and things and then they pointed out the importance of the escarpment, and I started to see it as they saw it and could imagine and feel how they might have lived in it.

Prior to Garma, this nurse perceived herself reading or acting upon the landscape in a personally detached manner, while her description of an ecological habitus of self-awakening through the landscape was transformative of the landscape altering her sense of relationship to it. Similarly, other tourists understood that through witnessing the performance of ecological relations they were also privy to the effects of place-presences within themselves. A female artist from Sydney commented:

> I've understood that the land has been made by the ancestors but coming here you actually see it in action and people talking about it as a living thing as a three dimensional experience of the relationship people have.

In contrast, a medical doctor from Central Australia whose spirituality was based on new age philosophies, perceived that his own habitus had always been ecological. He expressed an alternative yet interrelated disposition to that of Yolngu, stemming from his personalized affinity with nature.

> I ascribe to the idea through Garma and sitting with men in the Central Desert – that it's *gaya* I suppose, that it's all one organism, that's my religion if you want to call it that. You breathe in, you breathe out, your mouth blows out carbon dioxide and that tree grabs it and it goes into

that tree, so there is no difference between me and the land and we're all part of the same organism. If you subscribe to that philosophy then you don't bother raping the land and you don't buggerise it up too much mining and all that.

Of course, it has also been recognized that the projection of alternative spiritualities onto Aboriginal culture and landscape can distort, romanticize and decontextualize indigenous issues (see Neuenfeldt 1994). Even though this medical participant embodied both scientific and ecological habitus, the combination does not always translate across cultural systems with the potential for a lack of understanding around rights and ethics of appropriation, representation and intellectual property.

Unequal rights in the exchange of capital

The institutionalization of expressive culture in the marketplace and its translation within a cultural tourism programme creates a commoditization of experience that some tourists consider an economic right. Furthermore, as aesthetic experiences and aesthetic resources are differentially weighted in the marketplace, how audiences receive intangible cultural heritage is subject to alternative modes of evaluation. Those tourists who understood their participation as a right of economic exchange were keen that cultural knowledge be translated into a definable product beyond display, that could be sampled and bought. Listening to performances was not always seen as a valid currency of exchange. One man commented:

> There's been a showcasing of culture, not a sharing of culture ... Three days, for seventeen fifty, [$1750] this is a sizeable investment and you would expect the opportunity for dialogue and interaction but that's what Garma [the festival's] been a bit like too – the total separation of Yolngu as performers and non-Aboriginal people and Aboriginal visitors from elsewhere, as observers and respecters. That's our role and it would be an unusual experience to enter into cultural dialogue or interaction or reconciliation ...

For the most part, the success of Garma operates through the 'misrecognition' of what Yolngu intangible cultural heritage is and tourists' roles in sustaining it. In Bourdieu's terms of misrecognition (*méconnaissance*), some tourists choose to view their experiences as a 'gift' from Yolngu (in spite of financial exchange) and in doing so have more to gain by valuing the rules and experiences they are being offered because they allow the *'agent to put himself in the right'* (Bourdieu 1977: 22) by participating. Some tourists consider they have gained symbolic prestige and respect which can be shared by relating their experiences at home with others. As one man explained:

It's about privilege, either white insiders who are in the Aboriginal industry or rich cultural tourists who have the resources to be able to buy a slice of Aboriginal culture and consume it so we can feel better and go off again, which is okay...

Expanding ecological competencies as a human rights strategy

The ways in which performing and consuming performances are viewed by Yolngu and tourists have economic, political and social implications for how they understand their relationships to one another. Tourists who viewed their experiences as economic transactions expected these rights to be fulfilled in products rather than appreciating simply being with Yolngu as an exchange process and gift of ecological capital.

For Yolngu, what Sklar (1994) refers to as 'kinesthetic empathy' creates engagement with others through a sensual register as an inherent part of cultural competency. Yet, when bodily aesthetics are seen as resources in and of themselves, this can be misconstrued by some tourists as unwillingness to 'share' culture or as a lack of interest in dialogue or not equivalent to financial exchange. As the key characteristic of an ecological habitus is relational, based on giving and receiving through 'co-presencing' (see Tamisari 2000, 2005), kinesthetic empathy can take the participant beyond discourse, allowing meaning to be created in and through practice. In dancing, there is the possibility to show respect and care by giving and receiving in a mediated and transformative relationship that opens up emotional expression. As Bourdieu (1977: 94) notes:

> Nothing seems more ineffable, more incommunicable, more inimitable, and, therefore, more precious, than the values given body, *made* body by the transubstantiation achieved by the hidden persuasion of an implicit pedagogy, capable of instilling a whole cosmology, an ethic, a metaphysic, a political philosophy...

However, Western notions of 'sharing' suggest a habitus of describing, detailing, revealing, interrogating, inquiring, all of which are contrary to Yolngu modes of education which operate on the basis of what an elder considers a learner needs to know rather than what one wants to know. In addition, an expectation of understanding does not always require talk and neither does talking guarantee listening, especially if the wrong kinds of questions are asked (see Harris 1980). Somewhat ironically, tourists' experiences of Yolngu teaching and learning through silence rather than explanation are, in part, products of colonialism and white authority.

For Yolngu, the authorization of knowledge and its exchange is an embodied skill that is never reduced only to intellectual debate. Yolngu feel there is a need for relevant custodians to control and teach ecological capital as appropriate to non-Indigenous participants and agents (see also Langton *et al.* 2000: 53) whilst recognizing disjunctures between communication, meaning and intent: '...outsiders [need] to spend the time learning how to listen and work with Indigenous people, not zipping in and out at whim or speaking over Indigenous voices whilst pretending to consult' (Lee, Martin and Wurm 2006: 48).

Some steps are being made by mining companies who are undertaking 'cultural competency' training and assessment to improve the conditions of the mine site to enable more sustainable Indigenous employment (Lee *et al.* 2006: 36). Given the centrality of an ecological habitus to Yolngu life and its divergence from Western ecological and environmental forms of habitus, there may be a role for intangible cultural heritage to play in mediating this exchange by teaching how songs carry Yolngu rights to land and water (see Magowan 2001).

I have drawn upon the Garma cultural programmes to illustrate how differences in habitus shape contrasting expectations around religious, political and economic capital, both within and between cultures. What is the potential then for embodied practice and kinesthetic empathy to enhance cultural heritage legislation and government practice? Too often in native title determinations and other government contexts, it is considered that 'owning' land gives one the right to perform instead of appreciating that people can sing for land because it breathes life into them. In legislation, there is a tendency to overlook Aboriginal concepts of ecological relationality and how they operate in decision-making processes and laws, as we have seen in the government's handling of intervention policies noted earlier. Instead of delivering detached policy advice, there is a need for meaningful participation by all involved in the creation of acts that affect how rights are established through traditional customs and laws (Kerwin and Leon 2002). To develop cross-cultural competency, a decentring of self-sufficiency is required in order to allow the continuous transformation of feeling for and belief in mutually supportive engagement. If those involved in legislation and its implementation are willing to challenge and critique their assumptions about how they relate intersubjectively in the systems and processes that generate their ways of feeling and thinking, there could be a more empathetic appreciation of intangible cultural heritage as part of the land and people. By deconstructing terms such as sharing and respect between value systems, it may be possible to develop a greater appreciation of through-otherness and trust about the ways in which Indigenous knowledge is differentially exchanged. This process would have the potential to empower Yolngu by recognizing and respecting systems of Indigenous rights in law and governance. What appears to be needed in translating rights through law and cultural heritage between cultures is a transformation of attitudes, behaviours and appreciation in which social and material relations are understood as continuous practices of co-presencing.

Notes

1 The Yolngu expression *bungguldumurr*, literally 'dancelarge/great' is used to refer to a person who shows interest in dancing and performs assiduously (see Tamisari 2000: 280).
2 The festival is organized by the Yothu Yindi Foundation at Gulkula. The 2008 key forum was entitled 'Indigenous Knowledge: Caring for Country'.
3 'Environmental capital' has been examined by Justin Karol and Trevor Gale (2005) and Karol (n.d) from a Bourdieuian perspective to argue that it can form the foundation of a 'sustainable habitus'. I draw upon their arguments, developing them in relation to cross-cultural environmental perception.
4 ICCs as they are called now replace the former regional ATSIC offices.
5 Ancestral law divides Yolngu society into two patrilineal moieties known as Dhuwa and Yirritja into which people are born and take their identities.
6 In a parallel vein elsewhere in the eighteenth century, English gentry separated aesthetic value from social capital in the form of landscape painting and sculpture, thereby naturalizing economic power and obfuscating class inequalities. They benefited from this subversion of control by aesthetic value through the laws they implemented over land ownership (Davis 1997: 31).
7 The report also notes that control is an issue in performance and recommends that, 'legislation covering performers' rights should be amended to give Indigenous communities the right to control any subsequent reproduction of cultural activities such as ceremonies, dances and songs. Control must be defined from an Indigenous point of view; control to include authorization of a particular Indigenous community, the learning and sharing of their cultural activities with non-Indigenous people for non-commercial or profit purposes' (Janke 1998: 130).
8 Dhimurru oversee environmental impacts in north-east Arnhem Land by applying Yolngu knowledge in sustainable and culturally appropriate ways.
9 Authenticity has been analysed in two ways, as an external judgement upon the visual arts by observers or analysts and one that is an 'experiential' authenticity (Handler and Saxton 1988: 242–60).

Bibliography

Aboriginal and Torres Strait Islander Social Justice Commissioner (2005) *Social Justice Report 2005*, Sydney: HREOC, pp. 166–9.

Aboriginal and Torres Strait Islander Social Justice Commissioner (2006) *Social Justice Report 2006*, Sydney: HREOC. URL accessed on 5 June 2008. Available at www.humanrights.gov.au/social_justice/sj_report/sjreport06/chap2.html.

Acciaioli, G. (1981) 'Knowing What You're Doing: A Review of Pierre Bourdieu's Outline of a Theory of Practice,' *Canberra Anthropology*, IV (1): 23–51.

Agrawal, A. (1995) 'Dismantling the Divide between Indigenous and Scientific Knowledge,' *Development and Change* 26: 413–39.

Bourdieu, P. (1977) *Outline of a Theory of Practice*, Cambridge: Cambridge University Press.

Bourdieu, P. and Wacquant, L. J. D. (1992) *An Invitation to Reflexive Sociology*, Chicago: University of Chicago Press.

Bowers, C. A. (2001) *Educating for Eco-Justice and Community*, Georgia: The University of Georgia Press.

Briggs, J. (2005) 'The Use of Indigenous Knowledge in Development: Problems and Challenges,' *Progress in Development Studies* 5 (2): 99–114.

Byrne, J. (2000) 'From Policy to Practice: Creating Education for a Sustainable Future,' in K. A. Wheeler and A. P. Bijur (eds) *Education for a Sustainable Future: A Paradigm of Hope for the 21st Century*, New York: Kluwer Academic/Plenum Publishers, pp. 35–72

Chambers, R. (1979) 'Editorial. Rural Development: whose Knowledge Counts?' *IDS Bulletin* 10: 1–3.

—— (1983) *Rural Development: Putting the Last First*, Harlow: Longman.

Daniel, Y. (1996) 'Tourism Dance Performances: Authenticity and Creativity,' *Annals of Tourism Research* 23 (4): 780–97.

Davis, Susan (1997) *Spectacular Nature: Corporate Culture and the Seaworld Experience*, Berkeley: University of California Press.

Dews, G. J. David, Cordell, J. and Ponte, F. (1997) 'Report Prepared for Environment Australia and the Torres Strait Island Coordinating Council,' Unpublished paper.

Edensor, T. (1998) *Tourists at the Taj: Performance and Meaning at a Symbolic Site*, London: Routledge.

Ellen, R. and Harris, H. (2000) 'Introduction,' in R. Ellen, P. Parkes and A. Bicker (eds) *Indigenous Environmental Knowledge and its Transformations*, Amsterdam: Harwood Academic Publishers, pp. 1–33.

Escobar, A. (1995) *Encountering Development: the Making and Unmaking of the Third World*, Princeton, NJ: Princeton University Press.

Fien, J. (1993) *Education for the Environment: Critical Curriculum Theorising and Environmental Education*, Victoria: Deakin University Press.

Fien, J. and Maclean, R. (2000) 'Teacher Education for Sustainability: Two Teacher Education Projects from Asia and the Pacific,' in K. A. Wheeler and A. P. Bijur (eds) *Education for a Sustainable Future: A Paradigm of Hope for the 21st Century*, New York: Kluwer Academic/Plenum Publishers, pp. 91–111

Gray, W. and Sanders, W. G. (2006) *Views for the Top of the 'Quiet Revolution': Secretarial Perspectives on the New Arrangements in Indigenous Affairs*, Centre for Aboriginal Economic Policy Research (CAEPR), Discussion Paper no. 282.

Handler, R. and Saxton, W. (1988) 'Dissimulation: Reflexivity, Narration and the Quest for Authenticity in "Living History",' *Cultural Anthropology* 3: 242–60.

Harris, S. (1980) 'Culture and Learning: Tradition and Education in Northeast Arnhemland,' Abridgement of PhD dissertation. NT Department of Education, Darwin.

Janke, T. (1998) *Our Culture: Our Future: The Report on Australian Indigenous Cultural and Intellectual Property Rights*, Sydney: Michael Frankel & Co.

Karol, J. (n.d.) 'Bourdieu and Education for Sustainable Development: Analysis of an Interview.' URL accessed on 5 June 2008. Available at www.aare.edu.au/06pap/kar06523.pdf.

Karol, J. and Gale, T. (2005) 'Bourdieu's Social Theory and Sustainability: What is "Environmental Capital"?' in Peter L. Jeffrey (ed.) *Doing the Public Good: Positioning Education Research*, AARE 2004 International Education Research Conference papers, AARE, Melbourne. URL accessed at www.aare.edu.au/04pap/kar041081.pdf.

Kerwin, D. and Leon, M. (2002) 'A Comment on Indigenous Cultural Heritage Protection in Australia. Available at www.austlii.edu.au/au/journals/ILB/2002/24. html.

Langton, M., Epworth, D. and Sinnamon, V. (eds) (2000) 'Indigenous Social, Economic and Cultural Issues in Land, Water and Biodiversity Conservation: A Scoping Study for WWF Australia,' Volume One. Unpublished report for the Centre for Indigenous Natural and Cultural Resource Management, Darwin: Northern Territory University.

Langton, M., Mazel, O. and Palmer, L. (2006) 'The "Spirit" of the Thing: The Boundaries of Aboriginal Economic Relations at Australian Common Law,' *The Australian Journal of Anthropology*, September 17 (3): 307–21.

Lee, T. W. Martin and Wurm, J. (2006) *Garma Key Forum Report,* Darwin: Charles Darwin University.

MacCannell, D. (1973) 'Staged Authenticity: Arrangements of Social Space in Tourist Settings,' *American Journal of Sociology* 79: 589–603.

Magowan, F. (2001) 'Waves of Knowing: Polymorphism and Co-Substantive Essences in Yolngu Sea Cosmology,' *The Australian Journal of Indigenous Education* 29 (1): 22–35.

Magowan, F. (2007a) 'Honouring Stories: Performing, Recording and Archiving Yolngu Cultural Heritage,' in U. Kockel and M. Nic Craith (eds) *Cultural Heritages as Reflexive Traditions*, London: Palgrave Macmillan.

Magowan, F. (2007b) *Melodies of Mourning: Music and Emotion in Northern Australia*, Oxford: James Currey Publishers.

Neuenfeldt, K. (1994) 'The Essentialistic, the Exotic, the Equivocal and the Absurd: the Cultural Production and Use of the Didjeridu in World Music,' *Perfect Beat* 2 (1): 88–104.

Palmer, L. (2007) 'Interpreting "Nature": The Politics of Engaging with Kakadu as an Aboriginal Place,' *Cultural Geographies* 14 (2): 255–73.

Rose, D. (1999) 'Hard Times: An Australian Study,' in K. Neuman, N. Thomas and H. Ericksen (eds) *Quicksands*, Sydney: UNSW Press.

Sklar, D. (1994) 'Can Bodylore Be Brought to Its Senses?' *Journal of American Folklore* 107: 9–22.

Strang, V. (1997) *Uncommon Ground: Cultural Landscapes and Environmental Values*, Oxford; New York: Berg.

Tamisari, F. (2000) 'Meaning of the Steps is in Between. Dancing and the Curse of Compliments,' Theme issue, 'The Politics of Dance,' *The Australian Journal of Anthropology* 12 (3): 274–86.

Tamisari, F. (2005a) 'Writing Close to Dance: Reflections on an Experiment,' in E. Mackinlay, D. Collins and S. Owens (eds) *Aesthetics and Experience in Music Performance*, Cambridge: Cambridge Scholars Press.

Tamisari, F. (2005b) 'The Responsibility for Performance: The Interweaving of Politics and Aesthetics in Intercultural Contexts,' *Visual Anthropology Review* 21 (1–2): 47–68.

Taylor, J. (1997) 'Changing Numbers; Changing Needs? Indigenous Population Distribution 1991–1996,' Centre for Aboriginal Policy Research, Australian National University, Canberra.

Verran, H. (1998) 'Re-imagining Land Ownership in Australia,' *Postcolonial Studies* 2: 237–54.

Waitt, G. R. Figueroa and McGee, L. (2007) 'Fissures in the Rock: Rethinking Pride and Shame in the Moral Terrains of Uluru,' *Transactions of the British Institute of Geographers* 32 (2): 248–63.

Yothu Yindi Foundation (n.d.) 'The Healing Place.' URL accessed on 5 June 2008. Available at www.healingplace.com.au/yyf.html.

Chapter 11

'Cuca shops' and Christians

Heritage, morality and citizenship in Northern Namibia

Ian Fairweather

In August 1999 crowds gathered outside the palace of King Emanuel Kalauma Elifas of Ondonga to celebrate the official birthday of the King. Ondonga is the largest and most centralized of the 'Owambo'[1] kingdoms that occupy the Cuvelai floodplain in north-central Namibia. Unlike many of the Owambo kingdoms, in which kings were deposed by colonial interventions or occasionally by their own people,[2] Ondonga kept its monarchy throughout the colonial period and independence struggle. During this period, Ndonga kings have been alternately described as tyrants and celebrated as anti-colonial leaders.[3] King Elifas' brother Filemon, the previous ruler, had been deeply implicated in the machinery of indirect rule and was finally assassinated, allegedly by the South West Africa Peoples Organization (SWAPO).

In independent Namibia, governed by a democratically elected SWAPO party, King Elifas' status is that of 'traditional leader'. This role is not clearly defined, but, in the interests of banishing ethnic bias from politics, the constitution makes it impossible for 'traditional leaders' to hold political office. He still has rights to distribute land within the 'communal areas' and presides over a 'traditional court' administering Ndonga 'customary law' as originally codified by Finnish missionaries in the early twentieth century. In all respects, however, traditional leaders remain subject to the Namibian state which for most Oshiwambo-speaking people is indistinguishable from SWAPO.

SWAPO's relations with 'traditional' authorities remain ambivalent, but despite the hostilities of the liberation struggle, SWAPO leaders now frequently express their respect for 'traditional leaders' as custodians of Namibia's diverse 'cultural heritage'. Accordingly the King's birthday celebrations were attended not only by his subjects but by the then president Sam Nujoma. President Nujoma was a long-time SWAPO leader who still enjoyed immense popularity in Northern Namibia where the liberation war was fought. The president made no secret that his own ethnic background was Owambo, from the neighbouring kingdom of Ongandjera.

The celebrations went on for the whole day, centred on a stage erected in front of the palace. They consisted of speeches by local politicians, senior headmen and church leaders congratulating the King, thank you speeches from the King and his wife, a display of horsemanship by the King's hunters and a succession of performances by 'cultural groups' who performed 'traditional' dances and songs dressed in costumes ranging from those that approximate pre-colonial local dress styles, to those derived from European missionary dress. The president arrived at the palace by helicopter during the celebrations and, in front of a large crowd, mounted the stage and shook hands with the King, thus demonstrating the now friendly relations between SWAPO and the 'traditional' authorities.

This performance reveals a complex interplay of power relations between political and traditional elites neither of which functions independently of the other. Both seek to appropriate the power of 'heritage' to make visible their authority in the eyes of the audience who participate both as subjects of an Ndonga king and citizens of a modern democracy. The performance was carefully orchestrated to balance expressions of loyalty to the state and respect for the King, both of which were achieved by manipulating ideas about 'culture', 'heritage' and 'tradition'. The participants positioned themselves somewhere between the narrative of belonging to the nation as modern right-bearing citizens and that of membership of a distinctively local collective or 'tribe' defined by its 'traditional culture'. In doing so they constituted themselves as a 'heritage community' (Nic Craith 2007: 4) which is neither constrained nor encompassed by the notion of 'tribe'.

Charles Piot (1999) has described a comparable intervention of the state in the reproduction of Kabre tradition in post-colonial Togo. President Eyadema, himself Kabre, attends annual Kabre initiation ceremonies, ostensibly out of nostalgia for his roots. This transforms them into state spectacles and locates the Kabre within the representational space of the nation-state (Piot 1999: 102). Namibia's president Nujoma also understood the importance of spectacle to state power. His speeches emphasized the value of Namibian cultures as contributing to the 'national heritage' which has been suppressed by colonialism and apartheid. He frequently called upon Namibians to 'know their heritage' in order to be modern Namibian citizens as opposed to colonial subjects. This chapter will seek to shed light on the way that this kind of official rhetoric implicates certain understandings of the notion of 'cultural heritage' in a wider discourse about 'human rights' that has particular salience in post-apartheid Namibia.

It should be noted that the use of ethnic terminology is highly politicized in post-apartheid Namibia. The linguistically and culturally related people of the Cuvelai floodplain in north-central Namibia were referred to generically during the colonial and apartheid eras as 'Owambo'. For the purposes of this chapter, however, I am referring largely to Oshiwambo speakers who reside in the Kingdom of Ondonga and are therefore subjects of King Elifas. During my fieldwork I lived for 18 months in the village of Olukonda, on the site of the Nakambale Museum,[4] only 2 km from the residence of King

Elifas and 9 km from Oniipa, the headquarters of the Evangelical Lutheran Church in Namibia (ELCIN). The Lutheran Church is overwhelmingly predominant in Ondonga, but is less so in other 'Owambo' kingdoms.

Most of my informants, therefore, were residents of Olukonda and the surrounding villages and members of the church. I tried to become as closely involved with the community as I could and to speak to as many people as possible, but because of my own age, limited grasp of Oshindonga and perceived status I found myself gradually included in a group of elite, English-speaking young men, including one of King Elifas' younger sons. Furthermore, I was befriended by the family of the Pastor of Olukonda and by the staff of the museum and so many of my key informants were introduced to me by them.

Most residents of Olukonda are by no means wealthy, but by local standards they are not poor. My informants were mostly literate and some were highly educated. Several had studied abroad. Almost all identified themselves as members of ELCIN and many were active participants in the life of the local church. Although a number of my informants had been involved with SWAPO during the liberation struggle, and most supported the SWAPO government, few identified themselves as active members. Furthermore, many had kinship connections to King Elifas' family. My informants, therefore, are not representative of all Aandonga, but their perspective is widely shared, particularly among the post-independence generation.

Local heritage and global citizens

In much of Southern Africa, the ability to perform one's 'modernity' is closely identified with full moral personhood and categorically opposed to backwardness and 'tribalism', but this does not necessarily imply the rejection of indigenous culture. It has long been recognized that the attribution of prestige to European-style commodities like bottled beer and cultural practices like ballroom dances, does not necessarily constitute 'de-tribalization' or a loss of culture. Mitchell's study of the Kalela dance (Mitchell 1968), performed by ethnically homogeneous teams, dressed in neat European outfits, questioned the nature of 'tribalism' under urban circumstances, where 'tribal' or 'traditional' culture took on new forms and significances (Mitchell 1968: 32). More recently Werbner has described Africans' pursuit of style through Western consumer goods as a 'playful or aestheticized self-fashioning' (Werbner 2002: 2) that may reflect an adoption of 'the latest, most fashionable ways of being what one is not as well as the actual appropriation of modern subjectivism' (Werbner 2002: 2). The anthropological literature provides many examples of Africans' creative merging of the indigenous and the exogenous.

I want to suggest that Mitchell's observations about the importance of 'tribes' in the prestige systems that developed in urban environments of the

Copperbelt in the mid-twentieth century (Mitchell 1968: 32) may have something to tell us about the importance of 'heritage' to the politics of recognition in twenty-first century north-central Namibia. If the tribalism of the Kalela dance was a way of reproducing familiar rural identities in an urban context, might we be able to see contemporary heritage performances as attempts to reproduce a sense of local belonging in a nation that celebrates diversity and a homogenizing global system?

Anthropologists have often been concerned with the reproduction of local 'culture'. As Appadurai has reminded us, locality is a property of social life that must be produced and maintained (Appadurai 1996: 180). The production of locality need not imply boundedness or homogeneity and people often recognize the need to move with the times and be open to a wider world. Appiah has coined the term 'rooted cosmopolitanism' to describe persons who see themselves simultaneously attached to particular locales and yet able to appreciate the existence of different localities (Appiah 1998: 94).

Francis Nyamnjoh has suggested that post-colonial subjects negotiate vulnerability and subjugation through their relationships with others in contexts of 'conviviality' (Nyamnjoh 2002: 111). In north-central Namibia, the most obvious opportunities for this kind of conviviality are to be found in the small bars serving alcoholic drinks that line the tar roads. These bars are known as 'cuca shops' and whilst many are little more than shacks made from corrugated tin and selling traditionally brewed millet beer, the mark of a successful 'cuca shop' is a refrigerator, allowing the sale of cold, bottled beers. They serve as bastions of local sociality but also gateways to the wider world. They are family meeting places but they aspire to be international in their names, in the brightly painted exteriors and in the entertainment they offer. The more well-established often boast a pool table and a music system on which Angolan Qasa Qasa, South African Quito and Anglo-American rap music compete for popularity.

Cuca shops are family businesses, and they act as gathering places for the extended family and friends. They often stock various provisions from cigarettes to paraffin which are both sold and redistributed to the family members who come by. They are places for socializing, but also for conducting business deals and meetings arranging marriages, funerals and other family affairs. They also act as conduits through which knowledge of the wider world is passed, through the radio and in discussions among the clientele.

'Cuca shop culture' has its roots firmly in the experience of the liberation war when two major military bases in the towns of Ondangwa and Oshakati housed large numbers of South African and South West African troops, and PLAN combatants were active throughout the region. Cuca shops developed along the line of the new tar road that connected these bases to the rest of South West Africa, to cater for the troops. It was also inside the cuca shops that SWAPO's message of national independence was disseminated as combatants mixed with civilians, and plans to cross the border into exile were made and put into action. Open defiance of the regime was unwise, if not impossible in the shadow of the military bases, but it was expressed subtly in the brightly painted walls, often in SWAPO colours and imaginative names of the bars. During the struggle, therefore, 'cuca shops' exemplified the Oshiwambo speaker's ability to seemingly acquiesce in the face of power and violence whilst maintaining a playful but spirited resistance. Most 'cuca shops' now have new names representing the aspirations of a new generation of Oshiwambo speakers – 'BMW Safari centre' and 'USA No Money No Life bar' to name a couple, but many still incorporate a reference to national independence, or to the achievement of peace. Civil society as it is produced in the conviviality of the cuca shops is therefore deeply rooted in local experience, but it is also firmly embedded in the regional and global events that led to the birth of Namibia as a nation.

'Cuca shops' frequently serve as meeting places for local 'cultural groups' expressly concerned with the preservation and performance of 'traditional' music and dances. The production of 'heritage' in this context requires the expression of nostalgic memory in a global setting tied to issues of national identity and integration.

In her study of African popular culture Karin Barber has suggested that the habit of assigning African cultural productions into one of two categories roughly approximating to the 'traditional' and the 'modern' or 'Westernized', has become so pervasive that these categories are often used by the producers themselves (Barber 1997: 2). The binary nature of this paradigm has created a liminal space for African cultural performances that make use of available contemporary materials but cannot be defined as simply the products of 'culture contact' or 'corruption' by Western influences (Barber 1997: 2). Everyday performances of 'traditional culture' in north-central Namibia take place in a hybrid space that is not defined exclusively either by local experience or by a homogenizing globalization. This space is manifested in the unselfconscious hybridity of the 'cuca shop'.

Not only are nations comprised of multiple 'cultures' but multiple identities are accommodated by a single subject and people often seek interconnectedness beyond national identities (Werbner 1996: 15). In Namibia SWAPO asserts that a common citizenship identity is the source of unity for diverse cultures. Namibians themselves belong to churches, ethnic groups, football clubs and youth groups which, like the 'cuca shops', are rooted in the local whilst reaching out to the global. My informants' imagined communities are articulated alongside the SWAPO vision of a 'beautiful, contrasting Namibia together in unity'[5] but they are not encompassed by it, and to illustrate this I want to discuss another social institution through which both locality and globality are produced in north-central Namibia – the Evangelical Lutheran Church.

Unlike 'cuca shops', which are largely the domain of the young, male and relatively affluent, the Church is an all-pervasive institution. Handed over into local hands by the Finnish missionaries in the 1950s, the Finnish Lutheran Church, reconstituted as the Evangelical Lutheran Church in Namibia (ELCIN) mediates disputes, provides healthcare and education, dispenses charity and officiates from birth, through marriage and death. In each parish the church building serves as a gathering place for the whole community. As I have argued at length elsewhere (Fairweather 2004) the Finnish mission church was the first encounter that many Aandonga had with Europeans, bypassing both local traditional authorities and the colonial state.

The Church has always been associated with 'modernity', and with the international community. Allegiance to the Church in the past was expressed through the consumption of Western goods, particularly clothing. When the Finnish missionaries handed the church over to local hands the connections between Finland and North Namibia were maintained. Gradually missionaries were replaced by volunteers and Finns were closely involved with SWAPO and with the transition to independence which was finally presided over by Finnish diplomat Martti Ahtisaari.

ELCIN also played a decisive part in the liberation struggle beginning with an open letter to the administration in Pretoria from Namibia's first black bishop, Leonard Auala, in which he denounced the regime's failure to protect the human rights of Africans. The Church actively supported SWAPO's struggle without becoming synonymous with it. ELCIN still retains its legitimacy in the eyes of many Oshiwambo speakers, irrespective of SWAPO's success or failure as a government. Through its connections to its mother church in Finland the church has provided many opportunities for Aandonga to travel beyond Namibia that are not directly controlled by the SWAPO state.

The Church also sees its role as the protection and support of indigenous culture. It sponsors heritage events and cultural groups and maintains the Nakambale Museum. Finnish Lutheranism has therefore become a distinctive part of Ndonga identity, in which both the idioms of 'tradition' and 'modernity' are expressed.

If the Church has taken on the role of guardian of Owambo traditions, not least by establishing the Nakambale Museum, 'cuca shops' unashamedly celebrate modernity. Their brightly painted walls and fanciful names reach out to the wider world. What these institutions have in common, however, is that they both create imagined communities that extend beyond the ethnic and national collectivities through which civil society is expected to be produced in post-apartheid Namibia. They locate people as members of translocal communities but at the same time they construct these communities through distinctly local practices.

Heritage, rights and the politics of recognition

In his seminal essay on the politics of recognition, Taylor points out that fears about the recognition of minority groups tend to rest on the assumption that these groups are discrete. This appearance of discreteness can be made to foster intolerance, hatred and violence and act as a justification for the abuse of human rights in the name of national unity (Taylor 1994: 58). Twentieth-century nationalisms held members of the nation to share essential moral attributes and emotional attachments expressed in culture and heritage that constituted their national identity (Handler 1988: 6). In response, the aspirations of minority groups in Western democracies for the recognition of their human rights have increasingly come to include a demand for cultural recognition (Taylor 1994: 25). As Englund observes, postcolonial governments in Africa have had great difficulties in acknowledging and accommodating difference (Englund 2004: 9). They have sought to build nations from diverse populations with 'competing modes of belonging and identification' (Englund 2004: 2), often through authoritarian attempts to impose a 'national culture' which have been associated with sometimes extreme abuses of basic human rights.

The recent move to more liberal types of government has brought demands for the right to ethnic and regional representation, in ways that complicate older, nationalist discourses (Englund 2004: 2). In Namibia, the transition from occupation by South Africa to independent nation took place as recently as 1990 and the primary national liberation organization, SWAPO, remains in control of the state. Nationalist histories present SWAPO's struggle for independence as that of African people against the oppressive apartheid state and its systematic abuses of their human rights. Accusations that SWAPO committed its own abuses of human rights during the struggle have repeatedly been made, but they have met with only official silence and calls for SWAPO to be made accountable have received only limited popular support.[6]

Although sometimes accused of authoritarianism and bias toward the majority Oshiwambo-speaking ethnicity, SWAPO has largely avoided separatist demands. The accusation of ethnic bias is countered in official discourse with a call for 'unity in diversity'. Namibian citizenship is held up as the only legitimate grounds on which to demand rights and recognition whilst ethnic identity is commodified as 'heritage', the possession of which is the right of all Namibian citizens.

Pride in culture and history is presented by the state as essential for progress towards modernity, and the celebration of 'cultural heritage' is integral to the process of engendering nationalist passions. This politicization of 'cultural heritage' is, in part, a legacy of the politics of the apartheid era, during which the colonial power imposed itself through 'customary institutions' (Englund 2004: 19). Namibians' experience of the apartheid system, which denied people basic human rights on the basis of a discourse about discreteness rooted in the notion of a traditional, 'tribal culture' has made 'cultural heritage' an idiom through which feelings of fellowship obligation and passion are articulated.

As Ulf Hannerz has pointed out, 'natives' are often persons who not only belong to places but are confined in them by the exaggeration of differences and the characterization of places and people according to some single essential social cultural quality (Hannerz 1996: 92). This legacy complicates postcolonial processes of legitimating power and authority, charging the politics of recognition with a moral narrative in which Africans were denied access to 'modernity' through being identified as 'tribal', and also denied the full expression of their 'African-ness' by their subjugation to hegemonic European values.

Coming to independence late, in 1990, Namibians have witnessed the disintegration of many neighbouring states into ethnic conflict and civil war. The recent ethnic conflicts in Zimbabwe, Angola and Congo inform public discourse about ethnicity, nationality and identity in north-central Namibia and infuse SWAPO's message of 'unity in diversity' with moral force.

Werbner has drawn our attention to the way that the performance of nationalist nostalgia manifests tensions between local, regional and national interests. When the state seeks to appropriate the past in its production of 'national heritage', popular counter-movements emphasize rupture with it (Werbner 1998: 86). For Roland Robertson: 'One of the major features of modernity which has had a particularly powerful impact with respect to nostalgia is undoubtedly the homogenizing requirements of the modern nation state in the face of ethnic and cultural diversity' (Robertson 1990: 49).

In postcolonial Namibia, state-sponsored performances seek to root national identity in local traditions. 'Heritage' has become a matter of state policy and the state itself has become the agent of nostalgia for an idealized notion of 'tradition'. Knowledge of one's 'heritage' is often held up as essential for local, national and even global recognition. For my informants this requires the constitution of an Ndonga 'tradition', performed in heritage events and displayed to outsiders, but, perhaps for the reasons I have highlighted above, the nostalgia of my informants for a cultural rootedness expressed as local heritage does not translate into demands for political recognition on the basis of ethnicity.

Annie Coombes has described how, in South Africa, the ideal of 'community' attracts significant expenditure by the post-apartheid government into the public heritage sector and is seen to provide leverage in official circles. In this context, the discourse of heritage can become a means of authenticating a claim to 'community' (Coombes 2003: 2). The celebration of locality through the heritage industry can be both an arena in which nation building is achieved through the appropriation of local traditions into a national heritage and one that allows local communities to claim a share of the nation's resources and increase their own autonomy.

Jonathon Friedman's point that consumption of Western commodities can be regarded as a cultural strategy of self-definition (Friedman 1991), can also be applied to the consumption of 'heritage' as a commodity. For Friedman (1991: 312) consumption is a cultural strategy of self-definition or self-maintenance. The self-conscious marketing of the 'traditional' is part of a resurgence of local cultural identities that has accompanied the decline of modernist identities and fragmentation of the world system (Friedman 1991: 323). It is necessary, therefore, to see Namibians' consumption of 'heritage' alongside their consumption of bottled beer and 'hip hop' music as a locally specific demand for recognition.

As Jean and John Comaroff (1999: 17) have pointed out, the study of 'civil society' in Africa is often hampered by this Eurocentric tendency to see it as separate from the state. Furthermore, Nyamnjoh suggests that: '[d]emands for recognition of minorities in postcolonial Africa, for instance, do not necessarily defend an autonomous sphere of civic activism, but, on the contrary, represent an effort to become a part of, and thereby to transform, the state' (Nyamnjoh 2004: 3). The Aandonga do not see themselves in direct opposition to the state. The legacy of apartheid tends to transform any opposition between state and society into one between SWAPO as champion of Namibians' human rights and 'traditional authority', which raises the spectre of indirect rule. For this reason, emergent civil society in post-independence Namibia is neither subsumed by nor distinct from the SWAPO state. This ambivalent relationship is affirmed in delicately balanced performances like the one I described at the beginning of this chapter, in which respect for 'heritage' is a key idiom for making visible complex power relations.

Heritage as a moral good

The Council of Europe's 2005 *'Convention on the Value of Cultural Heritage for Society* defines 'heritage' as: 'a group of resources inherited from the past which people identify, independently of ownership, as a reflection and expression of their constantly evolving values, beliefs, knowledge and traditions' (Nic Craith 2007: 3). Máiréad Nic Craith (2007: 4) also draws attention to the Convention's definition of a 'heritage community' consisting of 'people who value specific aspects of cultural heritage which they wish, within the framework of public action, to sustain and transmit to future generations'. My informants' performances of Ondonga 'traditional culture' establish a 'heritage community' that extends beyond ethnic and national collectivities, even though their membership of these cosmopolitan communities is asserted through the production of the distinctively local.

Rene Lemarchand has shown how local responses in Africa to the state's project of nation building are refracted through the collective representations of distinct communities drawing on a more or less hybrid selection of cultural repertoires that can both legitimize and challenge the state (Lemarchand 1992: 179). The move towards preservation of 'cultural heritage' in north-central Namibia can be regarded as just such a response, aimed at the moral and cultural regeneration of the community by asserting both the importance of nationality and the significance of local ties.

Jean and John Comaroff (1993: xiv) have demonstrated that a concern with 'tradition' in Africa often expresses a complex, and often critical, commentary on Euro-American models of modernity, but not all Southern Africans are discontented with modernity. A generation of Aandonga who are now part of the new black elite are showing a nostalgic interest in their 'traditions'. They appeal to 'tradition' in Karin Barber's sense 'as an origin or influence which is co-opted to authenticate the modern by providing it with roots' (Barber 1997: 1). Both the churches and the 'cuca shops' are the sites of cultural performances that incorporate local traditions alongside global symbols and images, whether they are the affected styles of African American 'hip hop' or the internationally recognizable liturgy and trappings of Lutheran Christianity. In these performances, the boundaries between categories become blurred.

As Deborah James puts it 'the past is recreated to provide the grounds for an act of constitution of identity' (James 1999: 190). Drawing in this way upon tradition does not produce something static, but provides a sense of identity even as the performance adapts to suit contemporary circumstances (Ranger 1983: 259). It should not therefore be interpreted as simply nostalgia or conservatism, but as a project of social advancement (James 1999: 190). The appeal to the past reflects a desire to be rooted in a distinctive local identity whilst reaching out to global modernity. It is this very power to produce 'modernity' which is sought by my informants' appeals to tradition in public performances. The everyday performances that take place in the hybrid, liminal spaces of churches and 'cuca shops' therefore have potential to reveal the ways that globalization works through the performance of local identities.

A number of authors have pointed to the contentious nature of the terms 'heritage' and 'tradition' (Nic Craith 2007; Kockel 2007; Barber 1997). Ullrich Kockel (2007: 21) argues that 'heritage refers to cultural patterns, practices and objects that are either no longer handed down in everyday life (and therefore left to the curators) or handed down for a use significantly removed from their historical purpose and appropriate context'. For Kockel 'cultural practices and artefacts only become "heritage" once they are no longer in current active use' (Kockel 2007: 20). 'Tradition', for Kockel 'is created and recreated in a continuously evolving process. Culture becomes "heritage" only when it is no longer current, that is when it is no longer part of the process of tradition.'

Kockel's formulation of heritage assumes a rupture between a 'then' and a 'now'. Heritage is always, in some sense, a staged reconstruction of a vanished past. If this is so, can heritage ever have 'authenticity'? Or, in other words, can it establish the historically evolved legitimacy of an identity claim on which demands for rights and recognition can be based? My answer is yes, but one based on the assertion of both continuity and change. In performing their 'heritage' the performers both assert their claim to be the legitimate descendants of those whose traditions they perform, and at the same time lay claim to an identity not defined by those traditions.

This raises a question about how different the contexts in which 'tradition' is performed have to be before this appropriation becomes the production of 'heritage'. For instance, is young Namibians' appropriation of 'traditional' music and dance styles to assert their equality with wealthy travellers part of the continuous process of adaptation that constitutes 'tradition', or does it take them out of the process of tradition (Fairweather 2006)? Heritage performances like those I have described elsewhere at the Nakambale Museum (Fairweather 2003, 2005), or those of youth 'cultural groups' (Fairweather 2006) are clearly modified and appropriated as they are enacted, but the content of these performances is not handed down as part of a continuous process. 'Traditional' materials are rediscovered, reconstructed or invented for their purpose as heritage.

Whilst I agree broadly with Kockel's characterization of 'heritage' as resulting from a change in the process of transmission, the study of postcolonial societies such as that of Namibia complicates this picture and precludes any simple distinction between tradition and heritage on these grounds. The commodification of culture in a postcolonial environment where 'cultural tourism' is increasingly proffered as a source of income means that cultural patterns, practices and objects that are still in daily use and therefore 'traditional' can at the same time be taken out of context and used for new purposes, as Mitchell described in *The Kalela Dance* (Mitchell 1968).

On the other hand, the sense of rupture created by religious conversion, migration, liberation struggle, apartheid and 'globalization' has meant that for many there is no obvious continuity of 'tradition'; that which is apparently handed down in everyday life is often significantly removed from its historical purposes. This is apparent in contemporary use of the term 'Ohango', which in pre-colonial times described a girls' initiation ceremony, to refer to a modern church wedding. In a recent PhD thesis, Sayumi Yamakawa has provided a detailed comparison between the traditional Ohango ceremony and the contemporary marriage practices, often described as 'Doing Ohango in the church'. She observes that for most couples: 'The Church blessing is a vital part in Ohango, but the church ceremony alone is not considered enough. For Ohango to be "proper," the "traditional" parts before and after the church service have to be done' (Yamakawa 2008: 190). Clearly Ohango is regarded by Oshiwambo speakers as part of a living tradition with its roots in the past. However, their contemporary use of the term also implies a radical break with that past, as Yamakawa explains:

> Meanwhile, it is only in a specific situation that the term *Ohango* is used to refer to a female initiation ceremony. This meaning is only relevant when discussing the *Ohango* as it was practiced in the past, or as local people say, '[it was a] *long long time ago, before Christianity came to us*'.
>
> (Yamakawa 2008: 134–5)

These radically altered practices that constitute 'doing Ohango in the church' are clearly regarded by Aandonga as traditional, but at the same time, Aandonga would strongly reject the idea that contemporary wedding ceremonies are merely adaptations of the heathen girls' initiation ceremonies. The rupture between then and now brought about by conversion to Christianity is central to their appropriation of 'tradition' to ground contemporary identities. In short, the localizing of Christian wedding rituals into the format of Ohango is only possible because of a change in the process of transmission of tradition. Given the importance of this sense of rupture it is not productive to distinguish this adaptation of traditional material from the performance of 'traditional culture' in the context of 'heritage', such as the 'national cultural festival' (Fairweather 2007) or the Nakambale Museum (Fairweather 2003, 2005).

What is clear is that 'heritage', whether or not it can be clearly distinguished from 'tradition', is defined in the present. The valorization of a vanishing cultural heritage has the effect of making it an object of desire for those who feel uprooted and disconnected from their imagined rural home, and communities who are able to construct themselves as the custodians of heritage are in a position to take the moral high ground. The notion of an 'Owambo cultural heritage', therefore, has powerful, moral resonances, especially for those who spend most of their lives away, either in towns, or abroad.

Conclusion

In Northern Namibia it is considered important for people to 'know their past' in order to share in a national identity founded on the principle of 'unity in diversity'. The idiom of salvage and preservation in which this imperative is articulated gives the impression that the 'cultural heritage' being preserved is a static homogeneous entity, but, I have argued that the Aandonga's nostalgic construction of a vanishing heritage constitutes a re-assertion of their rights as modern cosmopolitan citizens.

The celebration of King Elifas' birthday with which I began this chapter brings together church, state and traditional authority (or 'tribe'), without merging them. They remain distinct forms of community to which the residents of Ondonga feel they belong to different degrees in different circumstances. SWAPO's call for 'unity in diversity' requires the state to recognize citizens' right to cultural distinctiveness whilst neutralizing the threat of ethnic separatism. This is managed by conflating ethnic identity with 'cultural heritage'. The latter can be publicly recognized in state-orchestrated performances without conceding to collective claims for rights or privileges implicit in the assertions of the former.

In this chapter, however, I have demonstrated the inadequacy of ascribing to the postcolonial state hegemonic control of the narrative of citizenship expressed through the idiom of a 'national heritage'. The attempt to include the cultural diversity of postcolonial subjects whilst at the same time subsuming ethnic and religious identifications into a unified national identity attaches symbolic importance to the cultural capital possessed by 'traditional authorities' and rural villagers, opening up a space for the negotiation of postcolonial subjectivities. The birthday celebration was a large-scale performance in which the idiom of 'cultural heritage' allowed allegiances to be negotiated without open conflict. The King requires both the church's blessing and the state's recognition to rule effectively, but both church and state also must court the cooperation of the King in their attempts to appropriate the idiom of local heritage in producing local legitimacy.

The heritage performances that take place in Ondonga must be understood in their own terms as a framework in which appropriate relations between individuals and various local and extra-local collectivities can be understood. The church and the 'cuca shops' are both arenas where a sense of local community is generated and sustained. Throughout the independence struggle these institutions provided the means for the Aandonga to develop a robust civil society in difficult circumstances that was neither an extension of the apartheid state nor manifest in open resistance to it. Whilst independence has brought a welcome peace and a questionable degree of prosperity at the hands of a new state perceived as legitimate, it is these preexisting structures that continue to underpin the development of civil society in rural North Namibia. Although the SWAPO state seeks, like a creeping vine, to graft itself onto these institutions, the constructions of 'heritage' produced through them allow a distinctive local history and experience to be remembered and accommodated into the structures of everyday life whilst the present moment is distinguished from the past by means of an appeal to the global, the modern and the civilized that reaches beyond the nation-state and aspires to membership of an international community.

Notes

1 This ethnic terminology is often regarded as offensive in post-apartheid Namibia and the term Oshiwambo-speaking people is regularly used to refer to the people speaking one of a number of related 'Owambo' languages as an ethnic collective. Most people in Ondonga speak a language known as Oshindonga. In this language, the name of the kingdom – Ondonga, its language Oshindonga, and its people Aandonga are derived from the root 'Ndonga'. I have therefore attempted

to retain local usage by referring to the subjects of this chapter as the Aandonga, meaning people of Ondonga, throughout.
2 King Mandume of UuKwanyama was deposed and killed by South African forces in 1917. King Ipumbu of Uukwambi was deposed and exiled by South African forces in 1932. The last king of Ombalantu is said to have been deposed by his own people and replaced by a council of headmen just prior to colonial intervention in the region.
3 King Nehale is remembered for his cattle raid on the German fort at Namutoni and at least one Ndonga king was arrested by South African forces for refusal to comply with the orders of the Native Commissioner.
4 The Nakambale Museum is located in the premises of the first Christian Mission Station in North Namibia. I have discussed at length elsewhere (Fairweather 2003, 2005) the regular performances of local heritage that take place for tourists there.
5 From Namibia's national anthem.
6 For a fuller account of the SWAPO state's manipulation of the history of the liberation struggle see Melber (2003), and for an account of SWAPO's refusal to address the issue of human rights abuses see Saul and Leys (2003).

Bibliography

Appadurai, Arjun (1996) *Modernity at Large – Cultural Dimensions of Globalization*, Minneapolis: University of Minnesota Press.
Appiah, K. A. (1998) 'Cosmopolitan Patriots,' in P. Cheah and B. Robbins (eds) *Cosmopolitics: Thinking and Feeling Beyond the Nation*, Minneapolis: University of Minnesota Press.
Barber, K. (1997) 'Views of the Field,' in K. Barber (ed.) *Readings in African Popular Culture*, The International African Institute in association with Indiana University Press and James Currey.
Comaroff, J. L. and Comaroff, J. (1993) 'Introduction,' in J. L Comaroff and J. Comaroff (eds) *Modernity and its Malcontents: Ritual and Power in Postcolonial Africa*, Chicago and London: University of Chicago Press.
Comaroff, J. L. and Comaroff, J. (1999) 'Introduction,' in J. L Comaroff and J. Comaroff (eds) *Civil Society and the Political Imagination in Africa*, Chicago and London: University of Chicago Press.
Coombes, A. (2003) *History after Apartheid – Visual Culture and Public Memory in a Democratic South Africa*, Durham and London: Duke University Press.
Englund, H. (2004) 'Introduction: Recognizing Identities, Imagining Alternatives,' in H. Englund and Francis B. Nyamnjoh (eds) *Rights and The Politics of Recognition in Africa*, London: Zed Books.
Englund, H. and Leach, J. (2000) 'Ethnography and the Metanarratives of Modernity,' *Current Anthropology* 41 (2): 225–48.
Fairweather, I. (2003) 'Showing Off – Nostalgia and Heritage in North-Central Namibia,' in *Journal of Southern African Studies* 29 (1): 279–95.
—— (2004) 'Missionaries and Colonialism in a Postcolonial Museum, or How a Finnish Peasant can become an African Folk Hero,' *Social Analysis* 48 (1): 16–32.
—— (2005) 'The Performance of Heritage in a Reconstructed Post-apartheid Museum in Namibia,' in M. Bouquet and N. Porto (eds) *Science, Magic and Religion: The Museum as a Ritual Site*, Oxford: Berghahn.

—— (2006) 'Heritage, Identity and Youth in Postcolonial Namibia,' *Journal of Southern African Studies* 32 (4): 719–36.

—— (2007) 'We All Speak with One Voice: Heritage and the Production of Locality in Namibia,' in Ullrich Kockel and Máiréad Nic Craith (eds) *Cultural Heritages as Reflexive Traditions*, London: Palgrave.

Friedman, J. (1991) 'Consuming Desires: Strategies of Selfhood and Appropriation,' *Cultural Anthropology* 6 (2): 154–63.

Handler, R. (1988) *Nationalism and the Politics of Culture in Quebec*, Wisconsin: The University of Wisconsin Press.

Hannerz, U. (1996) *Transnational Connections*, London: Routledge.

James, D. (1999) *Songs of the Women Migrants. Performance and Identity in South Africa*, London: Edinburgh University Press.

Kockel, U. (2007) 'Reflexive Traditions and Heritage Production,' in Ullrich, Kockel and Máiréad Nic Craith (eds) *Cultural Heritages as Reflexive Traditions*, Basingstoke and New York: Palgrave.

Lemarchand, R. (1992) 'Uncivil States and Civil Societies: How Illusion Became Reality,' *Journal of Modern African Studies* 30 (2): 177–91.

Melber, H. (2003) *Re-Examining Liberation in Namibia: Political Culture since Independence*, Uppsala, Sweden: Nordic Africa Institute.

Mitchell, J. C. (1968) *The Kalela Dance,* Rhodes Livingstone Paper no. 27, Manchester: Manchester University Press.

Nic Craith, M. (2007) 'Cultural Heritages: Process, Power, Commodification,' in Ullrich Kockel and Máiréad Nic Craith (eds) *Cultural Heritages as Reflexive Traditions*, Basingstoke and New York: Palgrave.

Nyamnjoh, F. B. (2002) 'A Child is One Person's Only in the Womb: Domestication, Agency and Subjectivity in the Cameroonian Grassfields,' in R. P. Werbner (ed.) *Postcolonial Subjectivities in Africa*, London: Zed Books, pp. 111–38.

Nyamnjoh, F. (2004) 'Reconciling "the Rhetoric of rights" with Competing Notions of Personhood and Agency in Botswana,' in H. Englund and Francis B. Nyamnjoh (eds) *Rights and the Politics of Recognition in Africa*, London: Zed Books.

Piot, C. (1999) *Remotely Global, Village Modernity in West Africa*, Chicago and London: University of Chicago Press.

Ranger, T. (1983) 'The Invention of Tradition in Colonial Africa,' in Eric Hobsbawm and Terence Ranger (eds) *The Invention of Tradition*, Cambridge: Cambridge University Press.

Robertson, Roland (1990) 'After Nostalgia and the Phases of Globalization,' in B. S. Turner (ed.) *Theories of Modernity and Postmodernity*, London: Sage.

Saul, J. and Leys, C. (2003) 'Lubango and After: "Forgotten History" as Politics in Contemporary Namibia,' *Journal of Southern African Studies* 29 (2): 333–53.

Taylor, C. (1994) 'The Politics of Recognition,' in A. Gutmann (ed.) *Multiculturalism: Examining the Politics of Recognition*, Princeton, NJ: Princeton University Press.

Werbner, Pnina (2002) *Imagined Diasporas Among Manchester Muslims*, Oxford: James Currey.

Werbner, R. P. (1996) 'Multiple Identities, Plural Arenas,' in R. Werbner and Terence Ranger (eds) *Postcolonial Identities in Africa*, London: Zed Books.

Werbner, R. P. (1998) 'Smoke from the Barrel of a Gun: Postwars of the Dead, Memory and Reinscription in Zimbabwe,' in R. P. Werbner (ed.) *Memory and the Postcolony: African Anthropology and the Critique of Power*, London: Zed Books.

Werbner, R. P. (2002) 'Introduction,' in R. P.Werbner (ed.) *Postcolonial Subjectivities in Africa*, London: Zed Books.

Yamakawa, S. (2008) 'Youth in Transition: The Status of Youth, Marriage and Intergenerational Practices in Northern Namibia,' Unpublished PhD thesis, University of Manchester.

Part III

Rights in conflict

Chapter 12

Protecting the Tay Nguyen gongs

Conflicting rights in Vietnam's central plateau

William Logan

With the emergence of the concept of 'intangible cultural heritage' in the last decade, a new set of human rights issues confronts heritage professionals. These relate to 'cultural rights'; that is, group and individual rights to maintain those heritage elements that underpin cultural identity and to enjoy self-determination in cultural terms. There is a need to tread warily in dealing with intangible cultural heritage since a totally different set of ethical issues arises when seeking to protect 'practices, representations, expressions, knowledge, skills' – as the 2003 UNESCO *Convention for the Safeguarding of Intangible Heritage* defines intangible heritage – for these heritage elements are embodied in people. It is not ethically possible to 'own' people in the way that we do the tangible heritage of physical places and artefacts, nor to buy and sell, destroy, rebuild or preserve them (Logan 2007a, 2008, 2009 in press). Although the Convention came into force fairly quickly with the requisite 30 states signed up by January 2006, a number of countries which have a strong record in other forms of cultural heritage conservation have misgivings about it and have so far refused to ratify it.

The Convention refers to the notion of human rights as a way of shaping and, indeed, limiting the proposed intangible list. Frequently, however, cultural rights as one form of human rights and the one most directly linked to intangible cultural heritage, comes into direct conflict with other human rights, such as women's rights, or the rights of children to be children rather than young labourers or soldiers. Conceptions of what is essential to cultural identity vary, of course, across time and from one part of the world to another. But, in some instances, opposing claims to cultural rights may be put forward by different groups locked in conflict in the same time and place.

These complexities are discussed in this chapter through a case study of the hill-tribes of the Tay Nguyen or Central Highlands region of the Socialist Republic of Vietnam. Here claims to the community's right to protect traditional culture, including local religious practices, clash with the right to religious freedom, especially at the individual level. Complicating the situation is the underlying resource competition in this part of Vietnam that has boiled over recently into violent clashes with the authorities in 2001 and 2005. State-initiated population migrations into the central uplands have impacted upon Tay Nguyen land tenure rights and created major land use changes. The intervention of Christian sects and anti-communist overseas Vietnamese (*Viet kieu*), notably in the United States, adds to the brew. Unsurprisingly, the Vietnamese state reasserted its control over the Tay Nguyen area and people. Yet, at the same time the state also chose to embark upon a campaign to celebrate and protect one of the most distinctive features of the Tay Nguyen's intangible heritage, its gong-playing culture.

Given this complex and highly politicized context, what does the decision to inscribe the gong-playing culture mean? The chapter seeks to explicate this decision and, in so doing, raises questions about cultural heritage theory and practice that relate not only to Vietnam but to other parts of the world where there are clashes of rights claims.

The Tay Nguyen gongs

In November 2005 the Socialist Republic of Vietnam celebrated the addition of its 'Tay gong-playing skills' to the then 90-strong list of intangible heritage items proclaimed by UNESCO as 'Masterpieces of the Oral and Intangible Heritage of Humanity'. This focused the world's attention on the plateaus of the mid-Tay Nguyen region which claims to have more gongs than any other area inside or outside Vietnam – about 6,000 sets in 20 minority groups in the four provinces of Dak Lak, Kon Tum, Lam Dong and Gia Lai (Pleiku district). Gong-playing has played a central role in the traditional life of the Tay Nguyen peoples. According to UNESCO (2006: Section 2.1), the gongs are 'permanent historical witness of the development of the people's daily lives' and 'the unique symbol of the highlanders' cultural traditions'. The gongs are featured in most rituals, such as ceremonies to welcome the New Year, celebrate the rice harvest or the construction of a new communal house, bid farewell to soldiers going to war and celebrate their victories. They mark the life cycle, being used in the *thoi tai* (blowing the ears) ceremony to usher the new-born child into life, in weddings and in the *bo ma* (leaving the grave) ceremony to bring the dead to the sacred world. The gongs are valued as a medium of communication between people and their deities. According to the Central Highlanders' conception, behind each gong resides a deity and the older the gongs, the more powerful the deities are said to be. Additionally, the gongs have an economic value and represent a symbol of wealth and power. A gong set was once as valuable as 30 buffaloes but has inflated to 85 or more (Alperson *et al.* 2007).

This cultural and economic significance notwithstanding, these days the young Tay Nguyen people are seen to be losing interest in gong-playing and the gong culture generally, while the men with gong-tuning and playing skills are ageing and declining in number (UNESCO 2006: Sections

2.1–2.2). Taking advice from Dr Tran Van Khe, an ethnomusicologist at the Paris Sorbonne noted for focusing world attention on traditional music, the UNESCO Hanoi Office commenced an Action Plan in 2006 to stabilize the gong-playing culture. With funding from the government of Norway, the project seeks to develop an inventory of practitioners and nomination of

Figure 12.1 Inter-generational transmission of traditional gong-playing skills (Courtesy: UNESCO Hanoi Office).

Figure 12.2 Young men learning traditional skills in a village gong club (Courtesy: UNESCO Hanoi Office).

a select group to the Vietnamese Government for recognition as 'National Practitioners', to re-energize the village gong clubs so that the skills will be better valued and transmitted to young people, to establish training courses and to promote gong-playing nationally and internationally through performances and publications.

Minority rights

The Vietnamese Government selected the gong-playing culture for submission to the Masterpieces list because it was seen as having the strongest case of all the items on the country's own intangible list established under the 2001 *Law on Cultural Heritage*. Already the cycle of Nguyen Dynasty court music and dance had been inscribed in 2003 as Vietnam's first Masterpiece, a paradoxical action by one of the world's remaining communist regimes, as Long (2003) has explained. Others on the tentative list include lullabies from Central Vietnam, Quan Ho antiphonal singing from 49 villages in Bac Ninh Province near Hanoi, Ca Tru singing and instrumental chamber music, the dances of the Thai minority, and various kinds of puppetry including the internationally known water puppetry developed in Vietnam's rice fields (ACCU 1998: 106–7).

Vietnam has 54 officially recognized ethnic groups that provide a rich cultural diversity and intangible cultural heritage. Two groups make up the bulk of the lowlanders – the Kinh who comprise 87 per cent of the total Vietnamese population of 85.3 million (July 2007), and the Hoa (ethnic Chinese of the Han linguistic family), who form 1.5 per cent of the total. The other minorities mostly live in the mountainous areas and have highly complex cultural characteristics. For instance, languages from several ethno-linguistic families are spoken in villages located in the same valley or even in the same village. In the Tay Nguyen region, where the population totals over 2 million, the ethnic mix is very varied, with, for instance, the Ba-Na belonging to the Mon-Khmer language group living alongside the Gia-Rai and Ede who are classified as part of the Austronesian language group.

Despite their significant cultural differences, in common Kinh parlance and in much official policy in Vietnam, the hill-tribes tend to be lumped together. The Kinh have traditionally looked down on them, placing little value on cultural diversity and wanting to assimilate them into the lifestyle of the Kinh majority. They have largely been ignored in histories of Vietnam written by the Kinh Viet or the French who colonized Vietnam in the nineteenth and first half of the twentieth centuries. They played no part in imperial Vietnam and, apart from the Catholic missionaries who ventured into the plateaus and mountains, they were largely ignored by the colonial French who concentrated in lowland towns and ports. Only where French-owned plantations were set up in the mountains or when the colonial government decided to establish a new summer capital at Da Lat on the southern edge of the Tay Nguyen region did the French come into close contact with them.

Nearly all the hill-tribes lacked traditional writing skills and their oral histories were inaccessible and hence disregarded. Vietnamese ethnologists, according to Rambo (2005: 39–40), have been handicapped by reliance on a Soviet theoretical commitment to 'a rigidly unilineal model of cultural evolution', with the consequence that the various ethnic groups were placed on a 'ladder of evolutionary progress'. Western ethnographers and anthropologists, at least in colonial times, tended to view all the hill-tribes through Orientalist eyes, which, it can be argued, further reinforced the Kinh sense of superiority. The early French referred to them as 'sauvages' – a translation of the Vietnamese term 'moi' once used for the hill-tribes people. As late as 1998 a Vietnamese official outlining her country's approach to safeguarding intangible cultural heritage at a regional seminar in Tokyo was still able to describe 53 of Vietnam's 54 ethnic group cultures as being merely folklore, with only the Kinh culture being based on written transmission and scholarship (ACCU 1998: 105).

Patricia Pelley (1998) describes the efforts made by the Vietnamese government from the 1950s to deal with the ethnic identity question as national independence was achieved. One of these was the introduction of legislative and administrative programmes to 'sedentarize the nomads' and to draw the younger generation into the mainstream through education policies and employment creation. Another effort, striking to the heart of ethnic minority identity issues, was to draw up an official list of recognized ethnic groups – the 54 groups we have been discussing compared with the 90 or so ethnic groups recognized by some non-government analyses. As with the appointment of Buddhist religious leaders, the granting of official recognition was a way of bringing the groups under control, of setting in place social structures in which a leadership layer felt an obligation to accede to Hanoi's dictates.

Many of the ethnic minority traditions had been interrupted during the long period of independence wars so that the same Vietnamese official speaking in Tokyo could note that even the over 40s generation had forgotten their intangible cultural heritage (ACCU 1998: 107). Gong-playing was losing its function as a dialogue with the deities and was increasingly restricted to traditional ceremonies where it was performed merely as entertainment. In 1977 the national cultural authorities had determined that such ceremonies were superstition and they were stopped (ACCU 1998: 109). A revival began in the 1990s when cultural policies eased and the Ministry of Culture and Information, together with the Association of Vietnamese Folklorists, began to organize annual festivals and competitions at ethnic district, provincial and regional levels.

It is clear that there has been a softening of the assimilationist approach in recent times. The speech by Deputy Prime Minister Nguyen Thien Nhan at a Hanoi education conference in January 2008 typifies this shift (*Viet Nam News* 2008). Reviewing ethnic minority boarding schools' performance in the decade 1997–2007 and outlining the course of development to 2010, Nhan maintained, on the one hand, that the ethnic minority children were not getting enough general education and Vietnamese language instruction in the boarding schools created for them. On the other hand, he insisted that other educational activities should be organized according to the traditions of each ethnic group, such as encouraging students to wear their national dress. The pupils would study their ethnic cultures and languages but also learn about the other cultures in their areas.

This policy softening towards ethnic minorities brings the Vietnamese Government more closely into line with the various international statements on minority rights, such as the United Nations' 1966 *International Covenant on Civil and Political Rights* (ICCPR) and 1992 *Declaration on the Rights of Persons Belonging to National or Ethnic, Religious and Linguistic Minorities*, and UNESCO's 2001 *Declaration on Cultural Diversity*. Nevertheless, to the Vietnamese majority and the Government of Vietnam today, how to incorporate the cultures of the minority hill-tribes peoples into the Vietnamese self-image continues to be a complex and sensitive issue. This is not merely a question of cultural heritage protection; it involves a fundamental ethical, political and administrative question: how can Vietnam bridge the economic and cultural divide between the country's dominant lowlanders and the ethnic minorities, most of whom live in impoverished circumstances in the mountainous north and centre of Vietnam? Of course this is not a dilemma just for Vietnam but is replicated in all countries where dominant ethnic or racial groups have an advanced standard of living and ethnic or racial minorities live in poverty and ill-health.

There is also the ongoing argument in Vietnam about the nature of democracy and the form that best suits the particular needs of the country. The Kinh majority governs, but through a political structure still dominated by a single party – the Communist Party of Vietnam – although many commentators see the country being transformed by 'creeping pluralism' (Porter 1993; Logan 2000: ch. 8; Koh 2006). In a democracy, majority rule is appropriate; however, it is usually argued that democracies must also respect the rights of minority groups, including at least some aspects of their cultural identity and underlying heritage.

Cultural rights

Indeed the maintenance of one's culture is seen in the UN arena these days to be part of one's unalienable human rights. Since at least 1966, when UNESCO's General Conference adopted the *Declaration on the Principles of International Cultural Cooperation*, it has become the standard view of the international agencies that, as Article 1 states, 'Each culture has a dignity and value which must be respected and preserved' and 'every people has the right and duty to develop its culture'. Such statements of principle set aside the myriad complexities that arise when governments or NGOs seek to apply them. All around the world political tensions emerge, for instance, when cultural diversity is seen to be undermining the social cohesion of the peoples united within a political state or when claims to cultural rights conflict with other human rights (Logan 2007b).

With regard to Vietnam specifically, there is little written about cultural rights – or, indeed, human rights generally. The book edited by Oscar Salemink (2001) outlined Vietnam's rich cultural diversity. Originating in a 1994 UNESCO International Experts Meeting on the 'Preservation and Revitalisation of the Intangible Cultural Heritage of the Ethnic Minorities in Vietnam', it is an important early attempt to propose measures to preserve cultural diversity in a developing country. This helped the push for the 2001 *Law on Cultural Heritage*, a law that is advanced by global standards in incorporating intangible heritage alongside the tangible. Its implementation is less 'advanced', however, in the sense that it relies almost entirely on top-down governmental and bureaucratic decisions about what is to be regarded as significant Vietnamese heritage. Neither Salemink's book nor the law refers specifically to the notion of cultural rights or to the difficulties of conflicting rights claims.

A handful of other publications treat human rights generally in Vietnam. The Harvard Law School research associate Ta Van Tai (1988) traced the pre-modern Vietnamese record of what we now call human rights, arguing that this record matched many of today's international human rights standards. Vo Van Ai (2000) focused on the contradictions between the post-independence official Vietnamese discourse about human rights and the internal repression of dissent, but is now outdated. From the point of view of this chapter, John Gillespie's 2006 work is most useful, giving a brief outline of the place of cultural rights in Vietnamese history before focusing on the post-colonial situation. Like Keyes (2008), he sees the official approach in Vietnam being essentially inclusive, although assimilationist. He notes that Vietnam's 1959 Constitution gave ethnic minorities a degree of autonomy as a reward for their support in the anti-colonial struggle. After reunification of North and South in 1975, however, while the new 1980 Constitution supported policies of equality and rights to culture and language, it gave priority to the maintenance of unity among all ethnic groups – the majority Kinh and the minorities. This subordination of cultural rights to national unity was reaffirmed in the 1992 Constitution.

A fourth publication on human rights in Vietnam, by Gammeltoft and Hernø (2000: 475), reinforces the point that the state – through the Ministry of Culture (previously Ministry of Culture and Information) – has had enormous power to decide which strand or representation of a cultural and ethnically diverse society is given legitimacy. The way the ethnic groups are identified is dubious, and many have, as Michaud and Turner (2006) point out, a transnational identity, either existing in locations subsequently bisected when colonial boundaries were imposed or ignoring these and moving backwards and forwards across boundary lines on a daily or seasonal basis. Gammeltoft and Hernø see the MOC's power waning in recent years as a result of increased internationalization. They argue that in contrast to the officially sanctioned set of Vietnamese values (social duties, collective obligations, hierarchically ordered social relations) which dominates the public discourse, it is now possible to see notions of rights in the Western sense (individual freedom, autonomy, more equal social relations) emerging as a 'hidden transcript'. It is true that since the Sixth Party Congress in 1986 when the *doi moi* (economic renovation) principles were adopted, Vietnam has rejoined the global financial and trading systems and become a major target for international tourism. It is also apparent that international tourism has been a powerful factor in encouraging the Vietnamese authorities to appreciate the hill-tribe people better – if largely as a resource to be exploited by the tourism industry.

Contact with the outside world has brought pop music, Western dress and modern hairstyles to the Tay Nguyen young generation. This further undermines the distinctive local culture and gives rise to concerns about the cultural impact of globalization. From a human rights perspective, the young Tay Nguyen people as individuals should have the right to choose their own lifestyle. But what of the group identity and heritage? A major difficulty in many of the human rights instruments is that they are concerned more with individual than group, community or societal rights and, indeed, have often been criticized as enshrining an individualistic Western priority that is not culturally appropriate in many other parts of the world. Group rights have become better accommodated, however, since the landmark assertion in Article 27 of the 1966 ICCPR that:

> In those States in which ethnic, religious or linguistic minorities exist persons belonging to such minorities shall not be denied the right, in community with other members of their group, to enjoy their own culture, to profess their own religion, or to use their own language.

In any case, it is questionable how free any of us are as individuals or groups, in the West or the non-West, to choose freely in the face of the massive taste-formation processes engineered by global companies in the music, fashion and media industries. This is precisely the kind of concern about the perceived negative impacts of globalization that led to UNESCO's adoption in 2005 of the *Convention on the Protection and Promotion of the Diversity of Cultural Expressions*.

Economic rights

The question arises how best to protect the cultural rights of ethnic minority groups. Is the commodification of their cultures through cultural tourism a problem that requires a policy response, or is it, on the contrary, part of the solution? The 1986 *doi moi* economic reforms have clearly improved life for the minorities in Vietnam. Many tribes traditionally suffered from malaria, iodine deficiency, tuberculosis and scabies, and their children were kept at home to work the land. The hill-tribe people remained largely illiterate in a country whose national literacy rate is claimed to have reached around 90 per cent under the communist regime by the 1980s. Since then the tyranny of remoteness has been reduced, giving better access to health care and education.

Clearly many members of ethnic groups see the paid employment in jobs often controlled by the Kinh as the way to move out of the poverty that surrounds most of the minorities. Under such circumstances, it is not ethically easy to argue for the maintenance of traditional ways of life. Indeed, some Asian countries have argued vehemently that to prevent development would be acting against their people's basic human right to live free from poverty. This view was codified in *The Bangkok Declaration*, signed at an Asian regional meeting of the UN World Conference on Human Rights in 1993, which asserted that 'all countries, large and small, have the right to determine their political systems, control and freely utilize their resources, and freely pursue their economic, social and cultural development' (Article 6). While recognizing that human rights are universal in nature, the Declaration insists that they 'must be considered in the context of a dynamic and evolving process of international norm-setting, bearing in mind the significance of national and regional particularities and various historical, cultural and religious backgrounds' (Article 8). In short, the articulation of these views in the 1990s – often referred to as the 'Asian values debate' – took the exceptionalist position that conditions in Asia were different and that the right to protect cultural traditions had to be set aside until such time as standards of living had improved through economic development.

A question for heritage professionals, therefore, is how to respond to situations where local communities prefer to achieve higher standards of living by rejecting tradition and modernizing their cultures. Is it an appropriate response to try to shore up the traditional behaviours and skills that make up their intangible cultural heritage? In the Tay Nguyen case, does the programme to protect the gong-playing culture fly in the face of the rights of Tay Nguyen people to modernize and achieve better living standards? Or will it have the effect of turning a traditional set of skills into an economic resource that will help achieve these social goals?

In fact, since the opening up of Vietnam to the global economy and international tourism the market has taken on a primary role in shaping the country's 'new cultural heritage' (Logan 2009). Alongside the feudal Sino-Viet heritage that gives the Kinh their sense of pedigree and the twentieth-century legacy of the independence struggle under Ho Chi Minh and the socialists, the French cultural layer is now firmly included, thanks largely to French media and tourist interests as well as the efforts of the French government and investors to restore France–Vietnam links. It was slower for the ethnic minorities in the mountains to have their cultures recognized as an integral part of the national culture due to the national campaign to force the minorities to assimilate with the mainstream. But already tourism is having a significant impact on remote hill-tribe people in places such as Sapa in the north, an impact that needs to be carefully monitored to ensure that tourism does not destroy aspects of the hill-tribe culture that the people themselves see as critical identity supports.

Political rights

Vietnam is one of the world's few remaining communist countries and political rights, especially to form opposition parties, are severely restricted. Even now, according to Chen (2006: 54), Vietnam severely limits civil and political rights in order to maintain the one-party rule that is seen as essential to hold the country together and to prosper. Chen notes that religious organizations and activities are tightly regulated by law and that the media are state owned, editors are subject to control and politically sensitive issues are not able to be discussed. Nevertheless, some environmental and heritage issues, such as the Golden Hanoi Hotel issue (Logan 2002, 2006), have generated public controversy and show that state power can be brought to a standstill by culture on occasions. Commentators such as Gillespie (2006) and Chen (2006) also believe the situation is improving. Chen argues (p. 509) that the future of human rights in Asia turns on shifting attitudes in China, Vietnam, Singapore and Malaysia and is 'cautiously optimistic'. Gillespie (pp. 452–7) sees in Vietnam today the state permitting an increasingly diverse range of associations to flourish, even if political associations remain tightly controlled; the state is using more and more rights-based arguments to balance the public good against individual civil, political and economic rights. Having adopted a mixed-market economy, it is indeed hard to see how further political liberalization in Vietnam will not occur, the 'creeping pluralism' mentioned previously.

In one sense the ethnic minorities are well served in terms of political rights: they are given preferential access under the electoral laws to approximately 15 per cent of the seats in the National Assembly and 10 per cent in the Vietnamese Communist Party's central committee. This limited affirmative action began in the 1990s and the first ethnic minority representative became a member of the Communist Party's Politburo and chairman of the National Assembly in 1992. This was more than tokenism according to many observers (*The Economist* 1992). However, the ethnic groups rarely vote as a bloc, according to Gillespie (2006: 476), and are more likely to represent regional party or national views than any cohesive ethnic perspective.

In other ways their political activities seem more restricted or at least carefully monitored. This follows from a long history of political instability in the upland plateaus and highlands of Vietnam and resistance by the hill-tribes to mainstream Kinh Vietnamese governments, whether of the capitalist South or communist North. In the early 1960s the Central Highlanders fought President Ngo Dinh Diem's transplantation of northern Catholics onto their lands. In the 1970s and 1980s many fought with the French and Americans against the communists. They formed a small insurgency movement called FULRO (*Front Uni pour la Libération des Races Opprimés* or Unified Front for the Struggle of Oppressed Races). As a result they found themselves distrusted by the communist governments that were established in the North from 1955 and in unified Vietnam after 1975. The failed attempt by the Hanoi government to outlaw the hill-tribes' traditional customs and language in the 1970s has been mentioned. Of course, official suspicion of the hill-tribes' motivations partly reflected a general anxiety about state independence, territorial integrity and social cohesion, all of which needs to be understood in the context of a nation that fought for generations against Chinese and Western colonial dominance.

Land use rights

In Tay Nguyen country, however, human rights issues remain highly sensitive, ostensibly as a result of a number of land rights-based clashes between the hill-tribes and the authorities in the last ten years. Elsewhere in this volume Jérémie Gilbert sees land competition as the common and greatest source of tension between dominant and minority groups wherever indigenous peoples exist because the heritage that is the basis of their identity and existence as distinctive groups is deeply embedded in land and therefore linked to the protection of traditional territories. In the central plateaus, land competition was certainly high among the key historical, demographic and political factors that had created a climate of intense frustration and seemed to dash, yet again, the ethnic minorities' longstanding hopes of gaining independence. They saw a steady stream of Kinh Viet immigrants into what used to be almost their exclusive home, a result both of government-sponsored resettlement schemes aimed at easing population pressure in lowland Vietnam and spontaneous migration since 1975 (Evans 1992).

The 1992 Constitution stipulates that the country belongs to all the people (Article 17) and the state manages the land (Article 18). State law supporting lowland immigration and agricultural investment in the highlands overrides customary law and 'strike[s] at the heart of minority cultural practices and communal relationships grounded in a swidden [shifting slash-and-burn] agricultural economy' (Gillespie 2006: 476). The hill-tribes often lack official titles to the large tracts of customary forest land that they occupied, but a national land-titling programme made problems worse when land use rights were issued to them because this converted land into an alienable commodity and, according to Gillespie, exposed the hill-tribes to unscrupulous lowland settlers and corrupt local officials and eventual dispossession in some localities. High illiteracy rates led to the perception that Hanoi discriminated against them in education, health and other social service provisions. In 1999–2000 plummeting coffee prices made worse the already high poverty levels, setting the scene for a political crisis.

In February 2001, several thousand members of Tay Nguyen minorities held a series of demonstrations calling for independence, return of ancestral lands and religious freedom – in defiance of the state constitution and law. An official reaction was to be expected and, indeed, the Vietnamese authorities responded with a show of force, deploying police and soldiers to disperse the protesters. Authorities arrested hundreds of highlanders, sometimes, according to the US-based Human Rights Watch (HRW 2002), using torture to elicit confessions and public statements of remorse. Travel was restricted in and out of the region and the 1,000 or so highlanders who fled across the national border were forcibly repatriated by Cambodia and punished by the Vietnamese authorities. The political conflict focused attention on the land rights conflicts in the Central Highlands and has produced at least one scholarly analysis (see McElwee 2008). These disturbances broke out again in April 2004. The central plateaus were closely monitored and at times closed off to foreign diplomats, journalists and tourists (Asian Centre for Human Rights 2004).

Religious rights

The HRW points to generalized human rights violations, including the use of excessive punishment, violation of the right to freedom of assembly, and violation of the right to freedom of religion. The last-named is seen in the destruction and/or closure of churches and official pressure on Christians to abandon religion under threat of legal action or imprisonment. But this picture is complicated by the presence of foreign evangelical Protestant sects – an intervention that fans Hanoi suspicions of deliberate US-backed involvement. According to HRW (2006: 2), the Vietnamese government has persistently blamed the turmoil on agitation and manipulation of the local population by 'hostile foreign forces', meaning Montagnard groups in the US demanding religious freedom, land rights and a separate state, and using religion as a cover for separatist political activities. The Hanoi government's perception that this amounts to a threat to national unity is fuelled by the link between some independence advocates and former members of the now pro-US FULRO. Although FULRO's armed struggle effectively died out in 1992, many members at that time converted to Christianity (HRW 2002: 9) and some moved to the US where they formed a Montagnard Foundation Inc. Led by a Gia Rai-American, Kok Ksor, this organization has been among those accused by the Vietnamese Communist Party of organizing the February 2001 demonstrations.

Neither the HRW nor Amnesty International totally rejects Hanoi's interpretation. Indeed, HRW openly acknowledges that the recent upsurge in adherence to Protestant evangelical Christianity was at least one of the causes of conflict. There were American Protestant missionaries working in the area and there was clear evidence of Internet messages from Tay Nguyen minority groups based in the US in the days leading up to the outbreak of violence. Whether this amounted to a deliberate bid to unsettle the Hanoi government's hold on the area has yet to be clearly demonstrated. In any event, a crack-down on some foreign missionary activities followed, notably on the Dega Protestant sect (*Tin Lanh Dega* in Ede language, literally 'Sons of the Mountains Good Word Church'). Dega Christianity is linked with Ksor's effort to build support for an independent 'Dega' homeland in 2000 (HRW 2002: 9), making it no surprise that the sect is officially banned. HRW estimated in 2002 that more than 250,000 (25 per cent) of the Tay Nguyen hill-tribe population were Christian, with the 'Dega Christians' being a significant sub-set. Another sect, the New Life Fellowship Vietnam, which had been started in the mid-1980s by an American couple, had its worship services stopped by the police in August 2005.

But as well as cracking down on some foreign missionary activities, several other missionaries have been recognized. This follows Hanoi's standard practice of dealing with religious groups. As with all organizations, the government bans independent religious associations and only recognizes those that have been approved by the Vietnamese Communist Party's Fatherland Front. However, by international comparison the Vietnamese state's attitude to religion has been relatively benign. Buddhist, Daoist and Confucian temples and pagodas and Christian churches were not closed down even during the height of ideological purity in the 1960s and 1970s, although the powerful Buddhists lost control over much property. The government insisted that it would recognize only one Buddhist organization and that it had the right to veto leadership appointments. There had been four government-sanctioned religions in Vietnam up until the Tay Nguyen crisis: the Vietnam Buddhist Church, Cao Dai, Hoa Hao and the Catholic Church. In April 2001 the Evangelical Church of Vietnam (ECVN) was added to the list. Established in 1911 and known in Vietnamese as Tinh Lanh ('Good News'), its branches had developed a strong Vietnamese leadership structure and more than 100,000 adherents. During 2005 a further 29 of the 1,200 ethnic minority churches closed in 2001 were registered by the government and re-opened, while local officials turned a blind eye to religious gatherings in numerous unregistered church houses (HRW 2006: 3–4).

In its June 2006 report on the Vietnamese national situation, HRW took the view that Vietnamese officials, recent reforms notwithstanding, were

> blurring the lines, not making the distinctions required by international law, and continuing to crack down on what should be protected political and religious expressions and behaviour. This is a violation of the basic human rights that Vietnam is obligated to uphold as a signatory to the International Covenant on Civil and Political Rights. (p. 2)

Amnesty International (2004) agreed, insisting that:

> Whilst there is no doubt that overseas Montagnard groups have been linked to the public protests both in 2001 and April 2004, Amnesty International believes that to blame 'outsiders' for the unrest avoids addressing fundamental and underlying problems including land rights' pressures from internal migration and differences of religion and culture.

From the Vietnamese government's point of view, as Gillespie points out, 'State tolerance of religious activity is predicated ... on religions contributing to state socio-economic objectives. Religions must generate patriotic sentiments and uphold the "Great Unity" ' (pp. 459–60). Thus the authorities maintain that their treatment of religions has always been consistent with provisions in the *International Convention on Religious Freedom* that permits states to prohibit religious activities that infringe 'political security and social order'.

It is easy for political prejudices to come into play with regard to the right of sovereign nations with popularly elected governments to rule without external interference. But how does one judge this scenario in terms of cultural rights? Should the foreign missionaries be stopped because they are undermining the traditional culture of the ethnic minority group? Or does that infringe the minority group's and the individual's right to choose whatever religion they want? HRW claims that recent reforms liberalizing religious activity in the Tay Nguyen region are in response to US designation of Vietnam in 2004 as 'Country of Particular Concern' for religious freedom violations. The US does not officially acknowledge involvement in the missionary activities in Vietnam, in the same way that it is not seen to back the Fa Lun Gong in China. But adopting Nye's concept of 'soft power' (2004), it can be argued that the US seeks to exert influence by setting the discourse, using human rights arguments to undercut the Vietnamese regime's status in the eyes of the world. Such tactics fit the American state's continuing attack on socialist states and its apparent inability to accept its loss in the Vietnam War. One conclusion that might be drawn is that this is primarily about power in the global setting, and only secondarily about human rights – and even further down the track about cultural diversity and cultural heritage.

Rights to self-determination

This chapter has sought to highlight the various conflicting rights claims made by or involving the Tay Nguyen people. In this context, what does Vietnam's inscription of the gong-playing culture onto the UNESCO intangible heritage list signify? The Vietnamese government's action seems paradoxical but most likely reflects a carefully thought-out pragmatic position. Bolstering traditional elements of Tay Nguyen minority culture seems at first glance to run against the government's worry that the hill-tribes' desire to differentiate themselves from the majority population threatens national unity. However, it may show a realization that the recent political unrest is linked to the lack of economic and educational opportunities and that certain cultural practices, such as gong-playing, can be cultivated as economic resources to draw revenue into the Tay Nguyen region through increased cultural tourism. If this is the case, then the tourism industry is again clearly at the forefront of the re-valorization of Vietnam's minority cultures as it has been among the ethnic minority groups around Sapa in the north.

Other tourism projects, including the development of ecomuseums in Daklak Province, are being promoted by the central and provincial governments. But by promoting the gongs through UNESCO, the government can be seen to be working at the highest international level to support the local traditions and, at the same time, helping to raise living standards. This may have the effect of placating local separatist voices and of quietly drawing the Tay Nguyen minority into the mainstream through increasing their economic links to the national and international tourism industries. This does not appear to mean that the general assimilationist approach has been abandoned, but merely that there has been some further softening in that approach. Of course, the recognition by the world community of the high level of significance of the Tay Nguyen gong-playing also impacts upon the attitudes of mainstream Vietnamese. It is therefore likely that nominating the gong-playing culture to UNESCO is seen as a way of using cultural heritage as a focus of national Vietnamese pride and nation-state formation more generally.

But perhaps this is attributing a more strategic approach on the part of the central government than has really existed. Nominating the gongs may simply have been the result of the normal activities of the responsible government department, the Ministry of Culture (now reconfigured as the Ministry of Culture, Sport and Tourism), and the Vietnamese National Commission for UNESCO. It was their responsibility to propose heritage items to UNESCO and, as mentioned, the gong-playing culture was seen to have the strongest case. Perhaps the national government in Hanoi, the provincial authorities and the gong-players themselves had little involvement in the decision-making process. While further investigation is required to clarify this point, such a conclusion would be in line with Porter's view (1993) that Vietnam is governed by a system of bureaucratic socialism in which the bureaucrats made and implemented decisions on behalf of the one-party state and the general public had little role to play or influence.

In any event, the gong-playing culture was successfully nominated and the UNESCO Action Plan is under way. An inaugural gong culture festival was held in November 2007 in Buon Me Thuot city. Aimed at 'honouring the gong culture and improving the community's awareness of the need to preserve this valuable culture', it attracted 25 gong performance groups, including one from Laos and another from the Republic of Korea (My An 2008: 37). Meanwhile, the Viet Nam Folk Art Association, a group of dedicated folklore experts, ethnomusicologists and culture bureaucrats under the leadership of Professor To Ngoc Thanh, has been working on a 'Vision 2010' programme to build up a network of gong-players and supporters (*Viet Nam News* 2005). Membership now stands at almost 1,000 but, since they are mostly between 60 and 70 years old, the sustainability of the group is in question. What will be the worth of Tay Nguyen's gong-playing if the living context is lost? Performances may be sound- or video-recorded, the instruments collected in museums, and the skills handed down to an elite group of players trained in specially funded schools. A poor alternative is for gong-playing to become a show for tourists, exotic but ultimately empty.

Conflicting rights claims make the task of the heritage professional exceedingly difficult. How do we respond as professionals to instances where various claims to cultural practices based on human rights are in conflict with each other? How do we deal in practice with situations where cultural heritage is used by powerful actors, both domestic and external, to obtain political goals that are essentially unrelated to heritage conservation? Our personal world view inevitably comes into play in setting the parameters for how we intervene as professionals. But, if we have the freedom of choosing how to act, so too should the individuals whose heritage we are considering. Not only is the ability to maintain one's culture a form of human rights, but more fundamental is the right to determine one's own life circumstances. In Tay Nguyen country we have clearly seen how people, as groups and individuals, want secure food and water supplies and improved housing and hygiene. Abandoning, modifying or commodifying traditional culture may be the price to be paid for winning improved standards of living. Let them decide for themselves.

Bibliography

Alperson, P., Nguyen Chi Ben and Ngoc Thanh (2007) 'The Sounding of the World: Aesthetic Reflections on Traditional Gong Music of Vietnam,' *Journal of Aesthetics and Art Criticism* 65 (1): 11–20.

Amnesty International (2004) *Socialist Republic of Viet Nam: Renewed Concern for the Montagnard Minority*. Available at http://web.amnesty.org/library/print/ENGASA4 1005 2004; accessed 20 February 2009.

Asian Centre for Human Rights (2004) 'Behind the Razor's Wire: Montagnards of Vietnam,' *ACHR Review*, 7 July [weekly on-line commentary and analysis]; accessed 10 November 2007.

Asia-Pacific Cultural Centre for UNESCO (ACCU) (1998) *Preservation and Promotion of the Intangible Cultural Heritage. 1998 Regional Seminar for Cultural Personnel in Asia and the Pacific, Tokyo, 24 February–2 March 1998*. Tokyo: ACCU. Available at www.accu.or.jp/ich/en/pdf/1998_Tokyo.pdf; accessed 21 February 2009.

Chen, A. H. Y. (2006) 'Conclusion: Comparative Reflections on Human Rights in Asia,' in R. Peerenboom, C. J. Petersen and A. H. Y. Chen (eds) *Human Rights in Asia: A Comparative Legal Study of Twelve Asian Jurisdictions, France and the USA*, London: Routledge.

Dournes, J. (1980) *Minorities of Central Vietnam: Autochthonous Indochinese Peoples*, London: Minorities Rights Group (Report No. 18).

(The) Economist (US) (1992) 'Minor aspects: Vietnam,' 325 (7779) 3 October: 34.

Evans, G. (1992) 'Internal Colonialism in the Central Highlands of Vietnam,' *Sojourn* 7 (2): 274–304.

Gammeltoft, T. and Hernø, R. (2000) 'Human Rights in Vietnam,' in M. Jacobsen and O. Bruun (eds) *Human Rights and Asian Values: Contesting National Identities and Cultural Representations in Asia*, Noralic Institute of Asian Studies 'Democracy in Asia' Series, No. 6, Richmond, Surrey: Curzon Press, pp. 159–77.

Gillespie, J. (2006) 'Evolving Concepts of Human Rights in Vietnam,' in R. Peerenboom, C. J. Petersen and A. H. Y. Chen (eds) *Human Rights in Asia: A Comparative Legal Study of Twelve Asian Jurisdictions, France and the USA*, London: Routledge.

Human Rights Watch (2002) *Repression of Montagnards: Conflicts over Land and Religion in Vietnam's Central Highlands*, New York: HRW.

Human Rights Watch (2006) *No Sanctuary: Ongoing Threats to Indigenous Montagnards in Vietnam's Central Highlands* 18 (4): 2–4.

Keyes, C. (2008) 'Ethnicity and the Nation-states of Thailand and Vietnam,' in P. Leepreecha, D. McCaskill and K. Buandaeng (eds) *Challenging the Limits: Indigenous Peoples of the Mekong Region*, Chiang Mai: Mekong Press.

Koh, D. W. H. (2006) *Wards of Hanoi*, Singapore: Institute of Southeast Asian Studies.

Logan, W. S. (2000) *Hanoi: Biography of a City*, Sydney: UNSW Press; Seattle: University of Washington Press; Singapore: Select.

Logan, W. S. (2002) 'Golden Hanoi, Heritage and the Emergence of Civil Society in Vietnam,' in W. S. Logan (ed.) *The Disappearing Asian City: Protecting Asia's Urban Heritage in a Globalizing World*, Hong Kong: OUP.

Logan, W. S. (2006) 'The Cultural Role of Capital Cities: Hanoi and Hue, Vietnam,' in K. C. Ho and H.-H. M. Hsiao (eds) *Capital Cities in Asia-Pacific: Primacy and Diversity*, Taipei, Taiwan: Center for Asia Pacific Area Studies, Academia Sinica.

Logan, W. S. (2007a) 'Closing Pandora's Box: Human Rights Conundrums in Cultural Heritage Protection,' in H. Silverman and D. F. Ruggles (eds) *Cultural Heritage and Human Rights*, New York: Springer.

Logan, W. S. (2007b) 'Reshaping the "Sunburned Country": Heritage and Cultural Politics in Contemporary Australia,' in R. Jones and B. Shaw (eds) *Loving a Sunburned Country? Geographies of Australian Heritages*, Aldershot: Ashgate.

Logan, W. S. (2008) 'Cultural Heritage and Human Rights,' in B. J. Graham and P. Howard (eds) *Ashgate Research Companion to Heritage and Identity*, Aldershot: Ashgate.

Logan, W. S. (2009) 'Hanoi, Vietnam: Representing Power in and of the Nation,' *City* 13 (1): 87–94.

Logan, W. S. (2009 in press) 'Playing the Devil's Advocate: Protecting Intangible Cultural Heritage and the Infringement of Human Rights,' *Historic Environment*.

Long, C. (2003) 'Feudalism in the Service of the Revolution: Reclaiming Heritage in Hue,' *Critical Asian Studies* 35 (4): 535–58.

McElwee, P. D. (2008) 'Ethnic Minorities in Vietnam: are Globalization, Regionalism and Nationalism Hurting or Helping Them?' in P. Leepreecha, D. McCaskill and K. Buandaeng (eds) (2008) *Challenging the Limits: Indigenous Peoples of the Mekong Region*, Chiang Mai: Mekong Press.

Michaud, J. and Turner, S. (2006) 'Imaginative, Adapted, and Transnational Economic Strategies for Marginal Actors in a Centralised State: The Hmong and Yao (Dao),' in Lao Cai Province, Northern Vietnam, paper presented to the *Vietnam Update 2006: Dilemmas in Difference: New Approaches to Ethnic Minorities in Vietnam* conference, Australian National University, 23–4 November.

My An (2008) 'Gonging in Central Highlands,' *Vietnam Economic News* 3: 37.

Nye, J. (2004) *Soft Power: The Means to Success in World Politics*, New York: Public Affairs.

Pelley, P. (1998) ' "Barbarians" and "Younger Brothers": the Remaking of Race in Postcolonial Vietnam,' *Journal of Southeast Asian Studies* 29 (2): 374–91.

Porter, G. (1993) *Vietnam: The Politics of Bureaucratic Socialism*, Ithaca, NY: Cornell University Press.

Rambo, A. T. (2005) *Searching for Vietnam: Selected Writings on Vietnamese Culture and Society*, Kyoto: Kyoto University Press.

Salemink, O. (ed.) (2001) *Viet Nam's Cultural Diversity: Approaches to Preservation*, Paris: UNESCO Publishing.

Tai, T. V. (1988) *The Vietnamese Tradition of Human Rights*, Berkeley: Institute of East Asian Studies, University of California, Berkeley.

UNESCO (2006) *Action Plan for Safeguarding the Space of Gong Culture in Dak Nong Province, Viet Nam*, Project Document, Hanoi: UNESCO Hanoi Office.

UN World Conference on Human Rights (1993) *The Bangkok Declaration.*

Viet Nam News (2005) 'Here today, gong tomorrow,' 15 May. Available at http://vietnamnews.vnagency.com.vn/showarticle.php?num=01INN150505 accessed 26/2/2009.

Viet Nam News (2008) 'Education key to ethnic development,' 23 January: 1, 3.

Vo Van Ai (2000) 'Human Rights and Asian Values in Vietnam,' in M. Jacobsen and O. Bruun (eds) *Human Rights and Asian Values: Contesting National Identities & Cultural Representation in Asia*, Richmond: Curzon (Nordic Institute of Asian Studies 'Democracy in Asia' Series, No. 6).

Chapter 13

The rights movement and cultural revitalization

The case of the Ainu in Japan

Yuuki Hasegawa

The Ainu are one of the indigenous peoples in Japan. From the mid-nineteenth century, their culture was forbidden and ignored through the actions of the assimilation policy and their land and natural resources were taken away by the Japanese government. The 1980s marked the rise of the Ainu rights movement, in the face of severe marginalization.

This chapter outlines the process of the rights movement and cultural revitalization of Ainu culture from the experiences of colonization. It consists of four parts. The first part deals with the process of dispossession from the late nineteenth century for the purpose of providing an historical background. The second part is on the process of organizing a rights movement for obtaining status as indigenous peoples, particularly after the 1960s, and the social situation of the Ainu. In the third part, I will explain the kind of cultural revitalization that has been realized by the Ainu accompanying increasing rights movements, such as the registration of Ainu culture as national cultural property. In the fourth part, I will discuss current cultural activities following the adoption of the Ainu Culture Promotion Act in 1997.

Colonization and assimilation policy

Internal colonization from the late nineteenth century

The Ainu traditionally lived in the territories now known as the north of Honshu, Hokkaido, the south of Sakhalin and Kurile islands. Following the commencement of modernization and construction of the modern nation state in 1867, the Japanese government unilaterally annexed Ainu traditional territory, renaming it 'Hokkaido' in 1869. Integration of traditional Ainu territory with the rest of Japan was carried out systematically by the Colonization Commission (later Hokkaido government from 1886) and the national government. Ainu individuals were officially registered under the Census Registration Law (1871) as 'former aborigines' and were treated as second-class citizens (Emori 2007; Siddle 1996).

From the 1870s through to the 1900s, a number of forced settlements were conducted in the traditional territories. The 1875 Treaty of St Petersburg which established the borders between Russia and Japan, drew a line right through Ainu traditional territories. Because of this treaty, Kuril Ainu and Sakhalin Ainu were forced to move to Hokkaido. In Hokkaido itself, many Ainu communities were forced to move out of newly established urban areas and areas unilaterally declared farmland of the Emperor (Miyajima 1996).

During this time Japanese immigration accelerated. The population of Hokkaido was only 58,487 people at the time the Colonization Commission was established, but by 1935 it had reached 3 million (Emori 2007). Traditional land was taken away by regulations which encouraged Japanese immigrants to come to Hokkaido to practise agriculture, and forced the Ainu onto the least viable land for farming. However, many Ainu could not adopt Japanese agriculture and suffered starvation through the prohibition of traditional hunting and fishing.

Through this massive migration process, the Ainu suffered dispossession of their territory, lost their means of survival, were struck down by new diseases and were forced into poverty. In 1873, the population of the Ainu was 16,272, 14.63 per cent of the total population, but by 1936, the population of the Ainu of 16,591 was a mere 0.54 per cent of the total population (Emori 2007). Sixty-seven years since the establishment of the Colonization Commission, the Ainu had become a socially, economically and politically disadvantaged minority in their own territory.

Systematic assimilation policy

The assimilation policy directed at the Ainu was implemented by the government in order to 'civilize' the Ainu from their 'barbarian' culture. In the 1870s, the Colonization Commission created a number of regulations to forbid the practising of traditional culture and customs by the Ainu (Emori 2007). It included a prohibition on the speaking of their language and the conducting of traditional hunting. The tradition of tattooing a woman's face and hands as proof of adulthood was also prohibited as a 'vulgar' custom.

In 1899, the Hokkaido Former Aborigines Protection Act was enacted with the purpose of remedying the problem of Ainu living in poverty. The main provisions of this act were to: 1) provide a maximum five hectares of land per household with conditions; and 2) establish an elementary school in Ainu communities. The provision of land accelerated the shift of Ainu towards agriculture, but the majority of land granted was barely suitable for farming as the best fertile and flat land had already been taken by Japanese immigrants. Furthermore, the Act had the condition that if the Ainu could not cultivate the land granted within 15 years, it would then be taken back. Although by 1916, half of the Ainu were engaged in farming, their average cultivation area and production amount was only one-fourth that of Japanese immigrants (Emori 2007).[1]

The Hokkaido Former Aborigines Protection Act also provided for the establishment of 24 'Former Aborigine Schools' across Hokkaido from 1901 to 1922 (Ogawa 1997). 'Former Aborigine Schools' played an important role in the government's assimilation policy. The curriculum was based on Japan's Policy of Imperialism which was an assimilation and aggrandizement policy demanding loyalty to the Japanese Emperor and was also conducted in Ryukyu (Okinawa Islands), Taiwan and Korea following its use on the Ainu. The curriculum was different from that of an ordinary Japanese school (Ogawa 1997). Ainu language and customs were forbidden to be used, and Ainu children were taught to respect the Emperor. The attendance rate of the school increased from 44.6 per cent in 1901 to 98.5 per cent in 1916 (Emori 2007). 'Former Aborigine Schools' were also used to educate adults by forcing their attendance at school ceremonies and ceremonies for the Emperor, reinforcing Japanese culture.

The Hokkaido Former Aborigines Protection Act is an act for protecting the Ainu in name only. As a result of its implementation, severe assimilation policies were carried out and fear of marginalization led the Ainu of this generation to regard their Ainu identity negatively, with many abandoning the custom of transmitting their Ainu culture to future generations.

Growth of interest toward the Ainu as 'the dying race'

Cultural and biological distinctions of the Ainu were pointed out with curiosity by researchers and the general public in a humiliating way, while at the same time the Ainu were being compelled to become Japanese by the government. With regard to academic fields during this period, Ainu Studies formed and grew under colonization, developing the disciplines of anthropology, archaeology and linguistics in order to research and preserve the racial origins of the Ainu and 'dying' languages (Siddle 1996).

The Anthropological Association was established in 1884 through the influence of Western academia in Tokyo. As the theory of Darwinism took hold with academics at the end of the nineteenth century, Japanese anthropologists became increasingly interested in the Ainu as an ancient people who were thought to be on the verge of extinction. Professor Yoshikiyo Koganei at the Imperial University (then Tokyo University), a member of the Anthropological Association, was a scholar who played a crucial role in Ainu Studies through research of Ainu skulls. He collected 164 skulls from Ainu graves without obtaining any permission from Ainu people and measured the bodies of living Ainu people by pretending to be a doctor on his trips around Hokkaido in the 1880s. His essay on skeletons and body shape of Ainu using data collected in this manner was highly admired internationally (Ueki 2008). The theft of skulls, skeletons and artefacts from Ainu graves and their subsequent spoiling were carried out in the name of research until after the Second World War.

Anthropologists played a part in the creation of a stereotype image of Ainu through expositions which were a form of media to demonstrate national power to society in general. From 1872 to 1922, groups of living Ainu were put on display at national and international expositions in Tokyo and Osaka as well as overseas in St Louis and London. For instance, Professor Shogoro Tsuboi, a founder of the Anthropologist Association, organized the 'human being pavilion (Jinruikan)' at the Fifth Domestic Industrial Promotion Exposition at Osaka in 1903 (Hasegawa 2005). Living Ainu were shown together with Ryukyu people, Taiwan indigenous groups and so on as a part of a 'races of the world' exhibit. Displays of Ainu were used to show Japan to the Japanese public and Western society as a developed and imperialized country.

Ainu Studies have had a significant influence in forming the status of the current Ainu collection in domestic museums. Most Ainu collections lack basic information such as the place and date they were obtained or the owner's name. In that time, constitutional anthropology was a major field focused on Ainu communities. Cultural anthropological field work had not been carried out during the period in which Ainu culture was disappearing. Kotani (2004) points out that the late establishment of a national anthropological museum is one of the primary causes for the inadequacy of the Ainu collection. In the end, the majority of ethnographical Ainu artefacts which now make up Ainu collections in museums and cultural institutions were collected directly through antique dealers and third parties.

Struggle for recognition

Rights movement after the Second World War

Despite the policies of colonization and assimilation, many Ainu struggled to retain their identity and improve their living standards. In 1946, after the end of the Second World War, the Ainu Association of Hokkaido (hereafter AAH) was established with the purpose of improving living standards in Ainu communities (Siddle 1996). At this time, there was still strong discrimination against Ainu, even though the end of the Second World War brought democracy to Japanese society.

Just after its establishment, the AAH played an active role in attempting to stop land originally granted to Ainu by the Hokkaido Former Aborigines Protection Act being redistributed as part of the farmland reform. This reform was promoted by the government for returning land owned by rich landlords to the poor farmers who were leasing it, but Ainu unjustly became subject to these reforms as well. AAH lobbied the Hokkaido government and related government departments to exclude granted land from the farm-land reform. Unfortunately they failed, with the government redistributing 34 per cent of granted land (Emori 2007). By the 1960s, many Ainu were compelled to move to the city to find work because of the farmland reforms. This was a period of high economic growth in Japan and many Ainu left their communities and came to live in cities such as Sapporo and Tokyo.

From the late 1960s, the Ainu rights movement started to gain some momentum. Around the centenary of the anniversary of Hokkaido in 1968, there was a movement towards increasing the awareness of the historical perception of colonization among the Ainu and support groups.

The campaign to enact a proposal for a New Law for the Ainu People and to abolish the Hokkaido Former Aborigines Protection Act commenced in 1980, and was driven mostly by the AAH (Siddle 1996). The proposal was composed of a Preamble and Grounds for the Proposal with six provisions. The purpose of the proposal was to recognize the Ainu as people with a distinct culture and to secure rights as an indigenous people. The proposal sought the recovery of rights through the eradication of racial discrimination, ethnic education and economical independence. It clearly stated that 'Ainu problems' were the product of the historical processes during the building of the modern nation state. The provisions included basic human rights, right to political participation, the promotion of education and culture and support for industry to provide economical independence.

The Hokkaido Governor's private advisory panel had discussed the proposal since 1984 and recommended that the Government enact the New Ainu Law with almost all of the same content as the original proposal, with the exception of the right to political participation such as securing a parliamentary seat for an Ainu representative. In 1988, AAH, together with the Hokkaido governor and the Hokkaido parliament, requested the Japanese government to enact the proposal of the New Ainu Law (Siddle 1996). The discussion at a government level was conducted by a private advisory panel of the chief cabinet secretary from 1995 and led to the enactment of the Ainu Culture Promotion Act as well as the abolishment of the Hokkaido Former Aborigines Protection Act in 1997. This Act will be discussed in further detail later.

During the process of enacting the proposal, the concept of indigenous rights was central to the Ainu rights movement. Generally, indigenous rights are inherent rights, including political, economical and cultural rights, more specifically land rights and the right to self-determination. This concept is defined differently depending on the demands and situation of each indigenous peoples around the world (Xanthaki 2007). The Ainu rights movement underwent a shift in order to demand collective rights as indigenous peoples, not as an ethnic minority, in order to demand recognition of past colonization and assimilation policies and to achieve the adoption of an integrated policy for the Ainu people, not a welfare policy.

While the proposal was being discussed by the Hokkaido government, discriminatory statements were publicly made by the Prime Minister. In 1986, the former Prime Minister Yasuhiro Nakasone, stated that Japan was a racially homogeneous nation. This statement by the Prime Minister influenced the Ainu to begin appealing against their situation to the international community as well (Emori 2007). Since 1987, Ainu representatives have attended UN meetings related to indigenous peoples including the former *Working Group on Indigenous Populations* and the *Permanent Forum on Indigenous Issues*.

Giichi Nomura, the former executive director of AAH, was invited to give a speech at the United Nations General Assembly during the inauguration of the World Year of Indigenous Peoples in 1992. He called upon the Japanese government and other member states to build a 'new partnership' with indigenous peoples (Nomura 1994). It was an historical speech for Ainu who had struggled to have their demands for indigenous rights heard since commencing political activities in the 1960s.

Through the 1990s, efforts from various Ainu enabled the creation of an Ainu organization in the Tokyo metropolitan area. The Ainu Association of Rera established Rera cise, an Ainu food restaurant, in 1993, after receiving strong support from related support groups (Reranokai 1997). The Ainu now living in the Tokyo area have long requested the Tokyo government to provide communal space to be used for transmitting culture and to use as a base for rights movements. In the absence of such a venue, Rera cise plays an important role as a place for transmitting culture and conducting meetings for organizing movements as well as providing a place for Ainu individuals to work.

Although the court decision on the Nibutani Dam and the Ainu Culture Promotion Act[2] were both issued in 1997, as stated by Professor Hideaki Uemura (1997: 27), a long-time activist for indigenous peoples' rights, 'the two documents represent complete opposites from the respective areas of justice and administration'. The Nibutani Dam court decision was made at the Sapporo District Court over the dam construction on the Saru River in Nibutani having the densest population of Ainu. The decision stated that construction of the dam by the government was illegal because the government did not conduct enough research on the impact on Ainu culture. The decision recognized the Ainu as indigenous peoples and also that the Ainu have cultural rights under Article 27 of the *International Covenant on Civil and Political Rights*. It was a landmark decision towards achieving full recognition.

The latter document, the Ainu Culture Promotion Act, was enacted as a result of the campaign to enact the proposal for a New Law for the Ainu People. However, the Act only includes the cultural part of the proposal. The purpose of the Act was for the promotion of Ainu culture in order 'to contribute to the development of diverse cultures in our country'. Through the process of enactment, the recognition of indigenous rights was omitted, even though it was the foundation of the proposal. Furthermore, the indigeneity of the Ainu was not recognized in the Act itself, only in a supplementary resolution of the Act.

The Ainu movement after the Second World War achieved a number of outcomes such as the formation of a powerful Ainu organization and the promotion of movements at national and international levels aimed at recovering economic, social and political status within the society.

Current social and economical situation of the Ainu

The situation of the Ainu is unclear at a national level because the Japanese government has never taken any nation-wide surveys or measures. There are no indicators which refer to ethnicity or indigeneity in the national census.

Since 1974, the Hokkaido government has promoted measures to improve the living conditions, housing and education of Ainu through the Hokkaido Utari Welfare Measures. The Hokkaido government conducted a survey of the living conditions of Ainu for the first time in 1972 and the Hokkaido Utari Welfare measures were developed based on the results of this survey, having been promoted since with support from the national government. The fifth-term measures (2002–2008)[3] are now being implemented. The basic purpose of the measures is to 1) stabilize living conditions, 2) improve education, 3) stabilize employment and 4) promote industry.

According to the Survey on the Hokkaido Utari Living Conditions[4] conducted in 2006 by the Hokkaido government, the population of Ainu is 23,782. That is 0.4 per cent of the total population of Hokkaido. About 60 per cent of the Ainu living in Hokkaido live in the sub prefectures of Hidaka and Iburi. The latest figures on the population of Ainu outside Hokkaido are only available from an actual conditions survey conducted in the Tokyo Metropolitan Area in 1988/9, which estimated the Ainu population at 2,700.

According to the surveys conducted by the Hokkaido government and the Tokyo government the general social and economical status of Ainu is lower than that for ordinary Japanese. The latest survey on the Hokkaido Utari Living Conditions shows the average socio-economic situation of Ainu is worse than for ordinary Japanese with regard to employment, welfare assistance and education. The number of Ainu receiving welfare assistance is 1.6 times higher than the average for Hokkaido. The university entrance rate is 17.4 per cent which is half the general average for Hokkaido. Regarding discrimination 16.9 per cent of respondents indicated they had experienced discrimination, that they could remember, while 13.8 per cent indicated that they had not experienced discrimination themselves but knew someone who had (Ainu Affairs group 2006).

The Tokyo government conducted a survey on living conditions for Ainu in Tokyo in 1974 and again in 1988/9 with the help of Ainu associations in

Tokyo. These two surveys show that Ainu in Tokyo in the 1970s and late 1980s faced financial difficulties as a result of low academic qualifications and had limited opportunity to find work outside of blue collar jobs. They also showed a desire to transmit and learn Ainu traditional culture and requested their own place to learn, such as a community centre, and to be given opportunities to learn (Tokyo Government 1975, 1989).

Comprehensive measures are required to solve the social difficulties encountered in Ainu communities not only in Hokkaido, but throughout Japan. A nation-wide survey represents the best means for facilitating the development of such measures by gaining an understanding of the actual situation.

Cultural revitalization

Cultural management by Ainu

Despite the policies of assimilation and colonization, at the end of the Second World War, Ainu culture was still well preserved in some areas. During the 1980s, the Ainu commenced various activities to revitalize traditional culture. The cultural revitalization movement developed in parallel with the rise of the rights movement.

Traditional ceremonies

The revitalization of traditional ceremonies has been carried out in Ainu communities since the 1960s. In Ainu culture ceremonies are carried out by households and communities to thank the Gods of nature (*kamuy*). One of these ceremonies is known as *asir cep nomi* which is held each autumn as a welcome ceremony for salmon, an important source of food for Ainu. *Asir cep nomi* was revitalized in Sapporo in 1982 with the purpose of recovering fishing rights for salmon and transmitting culture to the next generation. Although it was originally first revitalized in Sapporo, *Asir cep nomi* is now conducted all over Hokkaido. In the same way, the bear-sending ceremony, *iyomante*, was also revitalized to preserve and transmit traditional customs and knowledge from Ainu elders to the next generation.

Furthermore, a memorial service for ancestors, *icarpa*, is now carried out in many communities. The *shakushain* memorial service in Shizunai, and *nokamap icarpa* in Nemuro are conducted once a year. Both are memorial services for Ainu who were killed in battles with Japanese during the Edo era. In Tokyo, the *sinrit mosir koicarpa* service has now been regularly held since 2003. This is a commemoration for four young Ainu who passed away as a result of being forced to attend a boarding school in Tokyo in the 1870s and for those Ainu who died alone after coming to live in the Tokyo area. The creation of a memorial service is significant not only for the act of

Figure 13.1 Traditional dancing plays a vital part in the transmission of Ainu culture (Tokyo icarpa) (Courtesy: Makiko Ui).

Figure 13.2 The Fire God is the most important god in Ainu life. Here an Ainu prays to the Fire God during a Kamuynomi, a traditional ceremony (Courtesy: Makiko Ui).

Figure 13.3 Wood carving has a long tradition amongst Ainu (Courtesy: Makiko Ui).

revitalizing traditional Ainu culture, but as recognition of history told from the perspective of the Ainu.

The revitalization of traditional ceremonies and the creation of memorial services have had a large impact on cultural activities and identity building for Ainu. Traditional foods, dance, language and handicrafts are all essential to holding ceremonies. Masahiro Nomoto, who is an Ainu curator from the Ainu Museum, described his experience of attending *iyomante* as a life-changing experience, where he first realized that cultural activities such as dancing, carving and fishing were all interconnected and integral to the conducting of a ceremony. After he had experienced *iyomante*, he found the confidence to identify as an Ainu (Nomoto 2000: 199–200).

Furthermore, ceremonies create a place for Ainu from all over Japan to meet. In Tokyo, *icarpa* is an opportunity for Ainu living in Tokyo as well as attending from Hokkaido to get together and share the experience of a traditional ceremony. The revitalization of ceremonies presents Ainu with greater cultural and social opportunities.

Museums

Several institutions were created as a part of the trend towards recovering the rights and culture of the Ainu.

In 1972, the Nibutani Ainu Cultural Information Centre was opened in Nibutani with the support of AAH. Its establishment was led by Shigeru Kayano who had built his own private Ainu collection containing 2,000 artefacts from around the region, taking him close to 20 years to create. Kayano devoted his later years to the revitalization of Ainu culture through not only collecting and researching cultural objects but also by making efforts to preserve the language through the publishing of an Ainu language dictionary. It was anger at Japanese scholars digging up graves to collect bones and taking away the few remaining traditional artefacts from Ainu households which inspired Kayano to take decisive action (Kayano 1994).

The collection of the Nibutani Ainu Cultural Information Centre was transferred to the newly established government-funded Nibutani Ainu Culture Museum in 1992 and the Information Centre was renamed the Shigeru Kayano Nibutani Ainu Information Centre. These two museums in Nibutani are key institutions in facilitating cultural transmission amongst the Nibutani community and provide an opportunity for non-Ainu visitors to learn Ainu culture and history.

The Ainu Museum was opened as an independent foundation by the Ainu themselves in Shiraoi in 1984. Shiraoi has been a tourist destination since the early twentieth century for attracting Japanese tourists wanting to see a traditional Ainu village, and the establishment of the museum was made possible through the profits of tourism. The purpose of the Ainu Museum is the transmission, preservation and exhibition of Ainu culture and history and its establishment has provided the Ainu with an opportunity to introduce their history and culture to the general public. Its activities have expanded to include cultural exchanges with overseas museums such as in Finland and Russia (Akino 1999).

Language

As the rights movement progressed, the Ainu themselves started to realize the importance of language in regaining their identity and culture due to the core role played by language. However, after 140 years of colonization and assimilation policy, the Ainu language is no longer used in daily life and there are few native speakers left. According to the Survey on the Hokkaido Utari Living Conditions in 2006, only 4.6 per cent of Ainu answered 'Can have a conversation' or 'Can speak a little' for the question on Ainu language ability. Compared to past surveys, the Ainu speakers are now mostly the older generation aged in their 60s (Ainu Affairs Group 2006: 43). Because of discrimination against Ainu, speakers tend not to use Ainu language in public, even to their children.

The Ainu language has been treated as a 'dying' language among Japanese scholars since the 1920s. In the 1980s, AAH started to organize Ainu language classes in various regions in Hokkaido. There are now 14 classes with more Ainu language study groups located in the Tokyo area as well. In the 1990s, Ainu dictionaries on several dialects were published. Also in 1994, AAH published *akor itak* (our language) as the first text book in which Ainu collaborated with Japanese scholars on how to teach the language.

Professor Hiroshi Nakagawa (1999: 372), an Ainu language specialist and a contributor to language revitalization, points out that gradual changes in language learning and preservation have accompanied the rise of the rights movement. He takes Toshi Ueda, one of the Ainu elders from Biratori, as an example in explaining the uncertainty of the number of actual Ainu capable of speaking the language. Ueda only started to speak in Ainu and share the oral literature which she learnt from her sister after her sister's death in the 1980s. From the time she started to talk in Ainu, until her death in 2005, her contribution to the preservation and revitalization of the language was enormous. The number of young Ainu learning Ainu language is gradually increasing. However, it is apparent that strong efforts are required to revive the Ainu language, not only by the Ainu themselves but also national and regional governments.

A culture which was once almost lost has gradually been recovered in various regions through the initiative of local Ainu over the last 30 years. These areas of cultural revitalization, traditional ceremonies, the establishment of museums and language activities together play a core role in cultural activities and have been realized in parallel with the increased influence of the rights movement. The few remaining elders with traditional know-ledge have made enormous contributions to the efforts to revitalize Ainu culture by passing on their knowledge to future generations.

Registration as national cultural property

After the Second World War, a new national cultural property protection system was created. This system was based on the Cultural Property Protection Act which was enacted in 1950. In this national system, cultural property is categorized into tangible and intangible, tangible folk and intangible folk, monuments, cultural landscapes and groups of traditional buildings.

Traditional dancing

In 1984, Ainu traditional dancing was registered as an important intangible folk cultural property under the national cultural property protection system. The significance of traditional dancing is the transmission of charac-teristics of religion and daily life and provides an insight into the origins of dancing itself (Agency for Cultural Affairs 2008). Traditional dancing con-tains expressions on working life and imitations of animals and is used as a significant component of religious rituals as well. There are currently 17 tra-ditional dancing groups in Hokkaido registered under the Hokkaido Ainu Traditional Dancing Coalition Protection Association.

The registration of traditional dancing was realized through the lobbying of AAH in its efforts to preserve the whole of Ainu culture during the 1970s. At first, AAH established the Ainu Intangible Culture Transmission Preservation Association under the authorization of the Hokkaido Education Council, the body in charge of cultural property protection, in 1976. This led to the support of Ainu culture by the Hokkaido government which then influenced the national government (Higashimura 2001). The registration of traditional dancing as a national property had a very positive effect on the Ainu. It gave Ainu traditional dancing a more respected status and provided opportunities to perform this dancing at major venues such as the National Theatre. There is no doubt that Ainu no longer hesitate to perform dancing in public.

Nibutani collection

In 2002, 1,121 artefacts from the Ainu collections at Nibutani Ainu Culture Museum and Shigeru Kayano Nibutani Ainu Cultural Information Centre were registered as important tangible folk cultural property. The collection was named the 'Collection of living materials used by Ainu in Nibutani and surrounding regions of Hokkaido' (hereafter Nibutani collection). This was the third registration of an Ainu collection following the 'Ainu dugout' in

1957 and the collection of 750 Ainu living materials from Hakodate in 1959.

A feature of the Nibutani collection is the accompanying information on the creator, its usage and the origin of the piece as well as its raw materials. The Nibutani collection covers all aspects of Ainu lifestyle and shows traditional culture from the perspective of the objects used in daily life. It is divided into different areas of Ainu lifestyle, which are clothes, food, household objects, fishing, farming and making of tools, transportation, social life, religion, traditional knowledge, performing arts and a person's life including childhood, marriage and death. One-fourth of the collection is comprised of religious objects including ceremonial tools, sacred shaven wooden sticks, known as *inaw*, and altars (Yoshihara 2004).

The Nibutani collection was mainly created from objects in the Nibutani region by Shigeru Kayano. It is unique among Ainu collections in museums because it is based on one specific region. Hideki Yoshihara (2004: 10), curator at Nibutani Ainu Culture Museum, stresses that the registration of the Nibutani collection strengthens not only ethnic identity but also regional identity. Furthermore, it reaffirms that Ainu traditional culture is highly valued and should be preserved and transferred among Ainu.

The registration and protection of several aspects of Ainu culture as national cultural property has enabled Ainu communities to regain a sense of pride for their culture and strengthened their identity as Ainu. The process of registration accompanied the rise of the rights movement.

Culture as a whole

Limitations of the Ainu Culture Promotion Act

The Ainu Culture Promotion Act was enacted in 1997 with the objective of promoting and cultivating Ainu culture. The enactment of this law led to the establishment of the Ainu Culture Foundation.[5] The main aim of the Foundation is the promotion of Ainu culture, language and research on Ainu and the dissemination of information on Ainu culture. The Foundation seeks to achieve these aims by funding a range of cultural projects.

To promote language, the Foundation implements projects such as training for language teachers, advanced language classes, language radio programmes and speech contests. Also the Foundation provides classes to learn and restore traditional handicrafts such as wood carving and embroidery. Since the law was enacted, such projects have given new opportunities for Ainu to learn and transfer Ainu language and Ainu culture.

However, the Ainu Culture Promotion Act and its implementation by the Foundation have had two fundamental problems from the beginning. The first is that even though the law is for the protection of Ainu culture, it does not recognize the basic cultural rights for Ainu. It also lacks any provisions stating that responsibility for Ainu culture should be transferred to the Ainu themselves. This means that Ainu have no self-determination over their own culture under this law. It is a law to promote Ainu culture, for which the Ainu bear no responsibility.

For instance, the Act does not include the right to use and learn Ainu language as a formal language in Japan. The law provides certain language programmes at a limited community level, but not for the whole Ainu community or at a national level. The Ainu language is not taught in the formal education system.

The second problem is that Ainu culture in this law has a limited definition, as stated in the second article of the Act.[6] The definition given in this law does not include secret and historical sites, natural resources or traditional knowledge. Yet culture and language have a strong connection with heritage sites and require a proper cultural environment in order to prosper.

In addition, this Act does not ensure the use of land and natural resources in traditional ceremonies. As an example, *asir cep nomi*, the welcome ceremony for salmon mentioned above, has been revitalized in many regions; however, rights to fish for salmon are yet to be recovered. Only two regions; Sapporo and Chitose, apply for and are granted permission by the Hokkaido government to catch a limited number of salmon using the traditional fishing style for this ceremony once each year, and yet salmon fishing is inseparable from the intentions of this ceremony. The use of permanent land and natural resources for holding ceremonies and gathering of materials for making tools is indispensable for the passing down of traditional culture.

Ten years after enactment of the Ainu Culture Promotion Act

For centuries intangible and tangible cultural heritage was handed down amongst Ainu families and communities across many different regions. Culture is not something to be learned in a classroom. It is passed down to the next generation in their natural surroundings, as part of their daily life.

At the time of writing ten years had passed since the Ainu Culture Promotion Act was enacted. The work of the Foundation has been recognized as promoting Ainu culture, but only to a certain extent. The Act has limitations for enabling Ainu to fully enjoy their culture even though the Ainu have gained opportunities to learn their culture.

In its current form, the Act provides opportunities only for those Ainu who are able to sacrifice time from their work and other duties to engage in cultural activities. This Act does not have any benefit for those Ainu who are unable to engage in cultural activities. The survey in 2006 shows 48 per cent of Ainu in Hokkaido have not engaged in any cultural activities. The survey also shows that Ainu have requested the government to emphasize support for educating children (78 per cent) and for living and employment

(50 per cent) more than support for Ainu culture (32 per cent) (Ainu Affairs group 2006). It is clear that cultural activity is not a priority among those Ainu who still suffer economical and social difficulties as a result of past colonization and assimilation policy.

Furthermore, there are demands to create career opportunities for Ainu engaging in Ainu culture. There are few opportunities to use the knowledge and skills related to Ainu culture in a career such as a language teacher or curator. Once the Ainu recover their culture, it is necessary to provide opportunities for using it in their work as well as their daily life.

For this reason, it is essential to realize economical and social security for Ainu, to enhance recognition of Ainu culture and the status of Ainu as indigenous peoples, and to widen the appeal of Ainu within society. It is obvious that the Ainu Culture Promotion Act is not the only tool that can be used for promoting the cultural and social situation of the Ainu. The Ainu need to continue to demand that the Government take comprehensive measures to promote not only culture, but also to improve the social and economical situation of the Ainu at a national level.

The adoption of the United Nations *Declaration on the Rights of Indigenous Peoples* by the UN General Assembly in 2007 accelerated the recognition of Ainu as indigenous peoples by the Japanese government. On 6 June 2008, the Diet passed a resolution calling for the recognition of the Ainu people as indigenous peoples. On the same day, the Chief Cabinet Secretary made a statement recognizing that Ainu people are indigenous to the northern part of Japan, especially Hokkaido, and as an indigenous people, possess a unique language, religion and culture.

In accordance with the statement made by the Chief Cabinet Secretary, a panel of experts was established. The panel of experts was set up to discuss the economical and social status of Ainu and to visit Ainu communities in Hokkaido and Tokyo to form a proposal toward the establishment of comprehensive measures concerning Ainu. After visiting Ainu communities the experts expressed their concern on the serious situation of cultural transmission as well as the poor quality of living standards among Ainu communities. Ainu communities demand not only the establishment of social welfare measures but also the addressing of economical and cultural issues such as repatriation of skulls and management of national forests (*Hokkaido Shinbun* 16 October 2008). Ainu organizations urge the expert panel to use the United Nations *Declaration on the Rights of Indigenous Peoples* as a fundamental standard in its deliberations, rather than mere reference material. This trend is a positive step toward future Ainu policy.

Since the late nineteenth century, the Ainu have experienced enormous cultural change as well as social and economical change. Their culture was almost lost after only two generations of colonization and assimilation. The rights movement organization since the 1980s has improved the status of Ainu in Japanese society and contributed to the revitalization of Ainu culture. This process of revitalization means more than just the transmission of culture, but refers also to the creation of communal places and a strengthening of the Ainu identity. Despite this progress, the Ainu still face social and economical difficulties in society. In addition to the recognition of cultural rights, the full revitalization of culture requires the securing of the daily life needs for all Ainu.

Notes

1 In the 1870s, Japanese immigrants received up to 500 hectares (Uemura 2008: 56).
2 Official name is 'Act for the Promotion of Ainu Culture, the Spread of Knowledge relevant to Ainu Traditions, and an Education Campaign (1997 Law No. 52)'.
3 Renamed the 'Promotional policy concerning the improvement in living standards of the Ainu'.
4 The survey has been conducted six times (1972, 1979, 1986, 1993, 1999 and 2006) with the purpose of reviewing the measures.
5 Official name is 'The Foundation for Research and Promotion of Ainu Culture'.
6 Article 2 (definition) 'The Ainu culture' in this law means the Ainu language and culture properties such as music, dance, crafts and other cultural properties which have been inherited by Ainu people, and other cultural properties are developed from these.

References

(The) Agency for Cultural Affairs (2008) *Cultural Heritage Online*, Tokyo: Agency for Cultural Affairs. Available at http://bunka.nii.ac.jp/Index.do;jsessionid=A6F1C4 A42AE9A7CA4F6A43220EC89211 (accessed 8 June 2008).
Ainu Affairs group (ed.) (2006) *Heisei 18 nen Hokkaido Ainu seikatsu jittai chosa houkokusho*, Sapporo: Ainu Affairs group, Administrative Division, Department of Environment and Lifestyle, Hokkaido Government.
Akino, S. (1999) 'The Ainu Museum Foundation,' in William W. Fitzhugh and Chisato O. Dubreuil (eds) *Ainu: Spirit of a Northern People*, 183–6, Arctic Studies Centre: National Museum of Natural History Smithsonian Institution in association with University of Washington Press.
Emori, S. (2007) *Ainu minzoku no rekishi*, Tokyo: Sofukan.
Hasegawa, Y. (2005) 'Ainu minzoku to shokuminchi tenji 1903 nen kara 1913 nen no hakurankai kara,' in Engeki 'Jinruikan' joen wo jitsugen sasetai kai (ed.) *Jinruikan huinsareta tobira*, 70–97, Osaka: Yugengaisha attowa-kusu.
Higashimura, T. (2001) '[Bunkazai] toshiteno [Ainu koshikibuyou],' in *The Liberation of Humankind: A Sociological Review*, 15:98–118, The Japanese Association of Sociology for Human Liberation.
Hokkaido Shinbun (2008) 'Ainu yushikishakon donaisisatsukanryo,' 16 October.
Kayano, S. (1994) *Our Land Was a Forest: An Ainu Memoir*, Boulder: Westview Press
Kotani, Y. (2004) 'Kaigai Ainu bunkazai chosa: Mokuteki to keika, shushu no rekishi, chosa kenkyu no seika,' in Y. Kotani (ed.) *Kaigai no Ainu bunkazai: Genjo to rekishi*, 6–22, Nagoya: Nanzan Anthropological Institute.

Miyajima, T. (1996) *Ainu minzoku to Nihon no rekishi*, Tokyo: Sanitsushobo.

Nakagawa, H. (1999) 'Ainu Language: Present And Future,' in William W. Fitzhugh and Chisato O. Dubreuil (eds) *Ainu: Spirit of a Northern People*, 371–3, Arctic Studies Centre: National Museum of Natural History Smithsonian Institution in association with University of Washington Press.

Nomoto, M. (2000) 'Ainu minzoku hakubutsukan ni okeru katsudo,' in Foundation for Research and Promotion of Ainu Culture (ed.) *Heisei 11 nen Fukyu keihatsu semina houkokusho*, 198–205, Sapporo: Foundation for Research and Promotion of Ainu Culture.

Nomura, G. (1994) 'Giichi Nomura,' in E. Alexander (ed.) *Voice of Indigenous Peoples Native People Address the United Nations*, 68–71, New Mexico: Clear Light Publication.

Ogawa, M. (1997) *Kindai Ainu kyoikuseidoshi kenkyu*, Hokkaido: Hokkaido daigaku tosho kankokai.

Reranokai (1997) *Rera cise heno michi- koshite Tokyo ni Ainu ryoriten ga dekita*, Tokyo: Gendaikikakushitsu.

Siddle, R. (1996) *Race, Resistance and the Ainu of Japan*, Oxon: Routledge.

Tokyo Government Planning and Coordination Department Investigative Section. (ed.) (1975) *Tokyo zaiju utari jittai chosa houkokusho*, Tokyo: Tokyo Government Planning and Coordination Department Investigative Section.

Tokyo Government Planning Council Investigative Section (ed.) (1989) *Tokyo zaiju utari jittai chosa houkokusho*, Tokyo: Tokyo Government Planning Council Investigative Section.

Ueki, T. (2008) *Gakumon no bouryoku – Ainu bochi ha naze abakaretaka*, Yokohama: Shunpusha.

Uemura, H. (1997) 'Nibutani damu hanketsu to Ainu bunka shinkoho,' *SEKAI*, 636: 27–30, Tokyo: Iwanami Shoten.

Uemura, H. (2008) *Shitte imasuka? Ainu minzoku ichimon itto*, Tokyo: Buraku Liberation Publishing House.

Yoshihara, H. (2004) 'Ainu no seikatsu korekushon ha dou ikasarete irunoka,' *Bunkazai* 493: 9–11, Tokyo: Agency for Cultural Affairs

Xanthaki, A. (2007) *Indigenous Rights and United Nations Standards: Self-determination, Culture and Land*, Cambridge: Cambridge University Press.

Chapter 14

Cultural heritage and human rights in divided Cyprus

Susan Balderstone

Thirty-four years after the Greece-inspired coup and subsequent Turkish invasion of Cyprus in 1974, Famagusta's former Law Courts, burnt out during the fighting, are a stark reminder of events which bear ongoing consequences for the island today. About a kilometre further along the main road in which they stand, on the other side of a security fence, are several kilometres of the bombed out beachside precinct, comprising ruins of highrise apartments and hotels. Left to rot, they are held by the occupying power, Turkey, as a possible bargaining tool in any political solution to the Cyprus problem. Within the Venetian walls of the old city stand the medieval ruins of another, earlier invasion, when the Ottoman Turks finally overthrew the then outpost of the Venetian Republic in 1571. These have long received star billing as tourist attractions; only now is the same rating beginning to apply to the ruins of the last century.

A pragmatic approach to heritage management in both the Turkish-occupied north and the Cyprus government-controlled south has been funded from the United States Aid Agency (USAID) and more recently from the European Union (EU) through the United Nations Development Programme (UNDP). This has resulted in a focus on heritage conservation as a path to economic development through tourism, with many damaged buildings being conserved for new uses. However, a large number of churches and monasteries in the north have yet to be repaired, and there has been no willingness on the part of the Turkish authority in the north to deal with them. These places, regarded by Greek Cypriots as part of their cultural heritage, have become a human rights issue, with the decision by the Church of Cyprus to take the matter to the European Court of Human Rights (Stylianou 2008).

Background

Cyprus, located in the Eastern Mediterranean close to Syria, Turkey and Egypt is geographically described as part of the Levant, a strategic meeting place of East and West. As such, it has a long, well-documented history of war, conflict and occupation by competing powers (Hill 1952; Hunt 1990; Panteli 2005; Drousiotis 2006). At the beginning of our common era, Cyprus was part of the Roman Empire. As in the rest of the eastern Roman world, previously subject to the Hellenistic successors of Alexander the Great, Greek was the lingua franca of the island. Cyprus was famous for its cult of the Greek goddess Aphrodite, and was reputedly her birthplace. Christianization of the island began with the visit of St Barnabas and St Paul in 45 CE. By the fourth century, the bishops of Cyprus were strong and influential, achieving autocephalous status within the early Orthodox Church in the fifth century. Many large basilicas were built all over the island from the fourth to sixth centuries. The wealth of the church attracted Arab raids in the seventh and eighth centuries and these together with numerous earthquakes destroyed many of the buildings of the previous centuries. In the ninth century, Byzantine governorship was re-established and some prosperity recovered during the following two centuries (Coldstream 1981: 18). Through all this the Orthodox Church survived and reasserted its presence. To this period date the earliest painted churches that are now included on the World Heritage List.

The Crusaders arrived in the late twelfth century and subsequently established a Latin kingdom on the island under the Lusignans. Three centuries later, the Venetians took over, lasting 82 years until the arrival of the Ottoman Turks in 1571. In the early nineteenth century, the Greek struggle for independence from Turkey, 1818–1821, had repercussions in Cyprus. The emergence in Greece of 'The Great Idea' envisaging the restoration of the Christian Orthodox Byzantine Empire and the liberation of all Greeks under Ottoman control was the foundation of later attempts in Cyprus to achieve *enosis* or union with Greece.

Britain took over administration of the island in 1878 as part of the settlement of hostilities between Russia and Turkey and made Cyprus a Crown Colony in 1925. The British period ended with Independence and the creation of the Republic of Cyprus in 1960. Britain retained sovereignty over its military bases, and the rights of the two major ethnic communities, Greek and Turkish, were to be guaranteed by Britain, Greece and Turkey. The first president of the Cyprus Republic was Archbishop Makarios, prelate of the Cyprus Orthodox Church. But ongoing troubles between the Greek and Turkish Cypriot communities finally led to the Military Junta then in control of Greece attempting a coup to remove Makarios in 1974. In response, Turkey invaded and occupied the northern third of the island. The ceasefire line or Green Line still divides the island and the old walled capital, Nicosia, is divided in half from east to west (Figure 14.1). Cyprus' other historic walled city, Famagusta, is included in the Turkish occupied area.

Around 180,000 Greek Cypriot refugees from the north were resettled in the south, initially in specially created villages. About 71,000 Turkish Cypriots from the south moved to the north and were mostly accommodated in

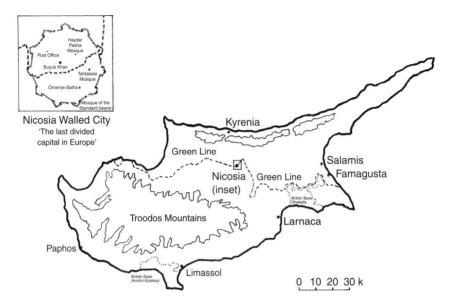

Figure 14.1 Map of divided Cyprus (Susan Balderstone).

vacated Greek Cypriot property. As well, in an echo of Ottoman practice, Turkey resettled 60,000 Turks from the mainland in the north (Drousiotis 2006: 263). With this separation of the ethnic communities, the country was effectively partitioned. UN forces patrol the Green Line, and the Turkish military continue to occupy the northern third of the island. In 1983 the Turkish administration in the north formalized itself as the Turkish Republic of Northern Cyprus (TRNC), but as an occupying power is not recognized as such by any State except Turkey. The most recent attempt to solve the Cyprus division, the Annan Plan, was accepted by Turkish Cypriots but rejected by Greek Cypriots in the referendum of 2004.

However, since 2003, when accession of the Republic of Cyprus to the EU was imminent, there has been an agreement between both sides to open crossing points to allow Cypriots from either side to visit their former homes and participate in each others' economies. Some trade is allowed across the Green Line, and there is cooperation between municipalities in relation to power and sewerage. It is widely acknowledged that the Cyprus government in the south achieved a super-human task in providing homes, employment and infrastructure with a stable and increasingly prosperous economy in the wake of 1974. The opening of the Green Line crossing points was aimed at enabling the relatively isolated and impoverished north to participate in this prosperity and eventually achieve social and economic parity with the south. The access has caused major emotional responses for many, with Greek Cypriots finding their former properties occupied by Turkish Cypriots and vice versa or in some cases that they have been sold on to foreign owners. There are some well-publicized law suits in progress involving these in the European Court of Human Rights (Lisle 2007: 107).

One of the major factors in the prosperity of the south has been tourism. Cyprus' most favoured destination before 1974 was the white, sandy beach stretching to the east along the coast from Famagusta. Largely developed by Greek Cypriots with the then fashionable high-rise hotels, this area known as Varosha, part of the area occupied by Turkey, was fenced off in the aftermath of partition and held as a possible bargaining factor in negotiations for a settlement. Deprived of this area, Greek Cypriots were confined to the south, where the sand is mostly grey or the beaches stony, but nevertheless developed hotels and resorts around man-made coves and small fishing shelters. Initially concrete high-rise along the lines of Varosha, and somewhat chaotic and unplanned in the aftermath of 1974, development became more rational, low-rise and more in tune with the landscape as planning laws began to be applied.

Issues of identity and human rights

The Christianization of the populace that took place gradually from the first century CE has been considered by some to be the real key to Cyprus' identity. Lawrence Durrell observed that Cyprus was Byzantine rather than Hellenic (Durrell 1978: 121), and in the view of historian Franz Georg Maier (1968: 55):

> Cyprus belonged to the Byzantine empire for almost nine centuries – longer than any other foreign power. No other epoch was so decisive in the fate of the island as the years of Eastern–Roman–Byzantine domination; every aspect of its culture, landscape and national character was moulded for all time in the centuries within the Graeco-Christian world.

Certainly the Orthodox Church survived through the centuries and plays a major role in the life and culture of Greek Cypriots, who continue to celebrate religious festivals and saints' days throughout the year. The Greek Cypriot identity is expressed physically in its churches and monasteries, and culturally through the Greek language and the Orthodox Church. Three centuries of Ottoman rule brought the abolition of feudalism and an influx of Turkish settlers, mostly soldiers (Dakin 1981: 21), and it has been noted that in the Ottoman period domestic building traditions and farming practices were common to both Greek and Turkish Cypriots (Schriwer 2002: 211–14; Given 2000: 214–21). The British brought even more commonality in these with the imposition of new laws and regulations.

An insight as to what this means for Cypriot heritage management can be gained by visiting heritage places on both sides that have been conserved since 1974. It is clear that a high degree of professionalism in heritage management and conservation as demonstrated at Ottoman and British period sites exists on both sides. Antiquities and Planning Laws appear to have been implemented with no more than the same degree of deviation due to development pressures as can be found anywhere. In the Turkish-occupied north, however, there has been little serious concern for the key heritage places closest to the Greek Cypriot heart – the churches and monasteries. Many lie open and unsecured, their interiors looted and vandalized. *The Cyprus Weekly* (Stylianou and Molyva 2006: 6) reported a declaration adopted by the EU Parliament in July 2006 condemning the pillaging of Christian churches and monasteries in the occupied north and calling for their protection and restoration 'to their original Greek Orthodox status'. The report stated that more than 200 churches, chapels and monasteries in the occupied north have been desecrated, converted into mosques, or used as military depots, hospitals, stables and nightclubs, and have had their religious artefacts, including more than 15,000 icons, illegally removed to unknown locations. The web site of the Ministry of Foreign Affairs of the Republic of Cyprus gives detailed figures for desecrations and losses.

The submission of the declaration to the EU parliament followed publication of a profusely illustrated book in Greek, *A View of the Land – From the Soul* by Greek Cypriots Anna Marangou and Michaelis Georghiades, sponsored by the Cultural Foundation of the Kykko Monastery. The book highlighted the issue of the importance of religion to the Greek Cypriot identity (Efthyvoulos 2006: 28–9). The authors had travelled all over the north, visiting the places they knew before 1974 and photographing the abandoned and now ruined churches and monasteries. They described their emotional feelings and reactions on entering the north for the first time after the crossings were opened. They were fearful that the opening of the crossings would not last but were greatly relieved when they were welcomed by Turkish Cypriots. They felt the stirring up of deep, emotional wounds as they realized what they had lost. Beautiful, haunting photographs portrayed derelict churches and monasteries in graphic detail.

Other Greek Cypriot visitors to the north have been distressed to find their village churches open and desecrated, robbed of icons and used for hay storage or animal shelters. They see the neglect and desecration of the history and monuments of their Church as a deliberate strike against their Greek identity, a further reason for rejecting reunification. However, the neglect also applies to Christian sites other than Greek Orthodox, such as the Armenian monastery of Sourp Magar (Leonidou 2007: 6).

Turkish Cypriots have been subject to the secular influence of Turkey following the separation of state and religion with the rise of Ataturk after the First World War. The emergence of Islamicists in Turkey seeking the restoration of the Caliphate seems to have had little impact on them. They have found their abandoned villages and mosques in the south with security fences no longer maintained and their buildings used by local farmers. The Mosque of the Standard-bearer located on the Constanza bastion in the government-controlled half of walled Nicosia, commemorating the soldier who led the Ottoman assault on the Venetian city has been frequently vandalized despite being restored in 2003 and fenced off by the municipal authority. But there has not been the same anguished outcry from the Turkish Cypriots over their mosques as there has been from the Greek Cypriots over their churches.

In fact, Turkish Cypriots seem mostly concerned about the loss of their Cypriot cultural identity under continued occupation by the Turkish Army. The tradition for Turkish Cypriots is one of secularism, not mosque attendance, although the authority seems to be trying to change this with the building of large new mosques in the areas to which they have relocated Anatolian settlers from the mainland. (This phenomenon should perhaps be seen in the light of the large, new, Greek Orthodox churches proliferating in the government-controlled south – some reaching capacities not seen in Cyprus since the fourth century.)

Turkish Cypriots regret their lack of resources to record family histories, traditional handcrafts, costumes, folk songs and dances. This is partly due to fear of their Turkish Cypriot identity being submerged in that of the Turkish mainland as represented by Turkish immigrants since 1974 and the Turkish military occupation forces. The Turkish Cypriot community has been increasingly depleted since Cyprus became part of the EU, easing the departure of Cypriot passport holders, including Turkish Cypriots born in Cyprus before the occupation who can obtain Cypriot passports. The ratio of Turks to Turkish Cypriots in the occupied north has been estimated to be now about 2:1 (Ministry of Foreign Affairs, Hellenic Republic of Greece 2008). The emphasis on 'folk' heritage is also a consequence of secularization having diverted the focus of Turkish Cypriot family and community life away from religion. A relevant factor is that the Ethnographic Museum of Cyprus, which was first established in the old Archbishopric in south Nicosia in 1950 as the Cyprus Folk Art Museum (Egoumenidou c.1998: 99) was not accessible to people in the north after 1974 until the Green Line crossings were opened in 2003. It contains collections of nineteenth- and early twentieth-century Cypriot 'folk art' including costumes, wood carved objects, embroidery and woven cloth. There has been no equivalent repository in the north for family collections.

It is possible that the neglect and misuse of Christian places is as much to do with Turkish secularism as with anti-Greek or anti-Christian sentiment. The lack of regard for the spiritual values of such places is similar to the way in which religious places under communist regimes such as China have been used for factories and warehouses (Alexander et al. 1994), and it appears to apply to mosques as well as churches. In the Turkish-occupied northern half of the walled city of Nicosia, the former fourteenth-century Gothic St

Catherine church which was converted to the Haydar Pasha Mosque by the Ottomans became redundant as a mosque last century. It was conserved and converted to an art gallery by the Turkish authority's Department of Antiquities and Museums after 1975 by its own team of 15–16 specialized tradesmen. Panels of softboard have been fixed around the walls to the height of a string course below the window sills to enable the hanging of artworks, and picture lighting suspended from a rod spanning the single hall/nave. The *mihrab* (wall niche facing Mecca) and *mimbar* (pulpit) from the mosque period have been retained as physical pointers to past Islamic use, but all other evidence has gone. The Latin Catholic origins of the church are not interpreted, although evident in its Gothic architecture.

The Orthodox Church hierarchy has become increasingly frustrated by the lack of response from the north to its calls for better care of the churches. In April 2007 Cypriot Archbishop Chrysostomos II stated his intention to unilaterally clean and restore Christian sites in the north. In reply, the Director of the Turkish Cypriot Department of Religious Affairs, Ahmet Yonluer said that the preservation of places of worship in Cyprus should embrace all the religious sites on the island, regardless of their location, origin or faith (*Cyprus Observer* 2007). He proposed that they should restore one church in the north at the same time as one mosque in the south. But as Chrysostomos pointed out, many of the mosques in the government-controlled south have already been restored. In the face of no further progress on the matter, the Church of Cyprus subsequently announced that it had decided to take Turkey to the European Court of Human Rights over its continuing refusal to allow access to the Christian Orthodox places of worship belonging to it in the occupied areas (Stylianou 2008).

The Greek Cypriots have been careful to publicize their conservation of mosques and other Islamic religious sites. At a ceremony celebrating the restoration of the Ali Dede Mausoleum in Limassol just days before the EU parliament adopted the declaration described above, the Department of Antiquities officer was quoted as saying that the policy of the Antiquities Department is to 'restore every mosque or Muslim monument in the free part of the island' (Leonidou 2006). Also, according to the lavishly illustrated publication produced by the Association of Cypriot Archaeologists – *Muslim Places of Worship in Cyprus* (Association of Cypriot Archaeologists 2005), more mosques operate today in the government-controlled areas of the island than in the past. These actions signal support by the Cyprus government for the proposal made by the Parliamentary Assembly of the Council of Europe (PACE) Committee on Culture, Science and Education; Sub-Committee on the Cultural Heritage, for the establishment of an international foundation for the protection of the cultural heritage of the whole of Cyprus (PIO 2004).

However, there has been no matching response from the north. It was noted by Cyprus Attorney General Petros Clerides in addressing a seminar of the European Consortium for Church and State Research on the right of thought, conscience and religion (Article 9 of the *European Convention on Human Rights*) hosted in Cyprus in January 2008, that Turkey continues to violate human rights in the areas occupied by its troops since 1974. In particular, he referred to 'the violation of freedom of religion associated to ethnic origins of Greek Cypriots living in occupied Cyprus' (*Hellenic News of America* 2008). While there are several international conventions regarding the protection of cultural property (Cyprus Embassy to the EU 2008), this is apparently the only human right as recognized by the European Court of Human Rights that can be invoked in regard to cultural heritage, apart from the right of access to property.

Heritage protection and tourism

The current Antiquities Law as applied in the government-controlled south of Cyprus goes back to that enacted by the British in 1935, which was primarily intended to control archaeological excavations and protect ancient monuments of the Graeco-Roman, Byzantine, Medieval and Venetian periods. It is administered by the Department of Antiquities set up in the same year. But the more significant law in relation to urban and rural heritage is the Town and Country Planning Law of 1972, which enables protection of buildings, groups of buildings or areas of special historical, architectural, social and other interest or character through designation in Local Plans. An increasing awareness of the importance of buildings of the more recent period, together with government funding in the south, has resulted in the protection of traditional 'folk' architecture and mansions deriving from the Ottoman period, as well as some of the European-style buildings of the British period (Egoumenidou *c.*1998: 102–19). Tourism has been encouraged to the hinterland villages and mountains in the south through government grants for agritourism involving the repair and adaptation of traditional houses as holiday cottages and small inns, as well as for the conservation of historic churches, water mills, wine presses, olive presses and other features of interest.

In the north, the Turkish administration was not in a position to develop tourism due to its illegality and consequent lack of recognition as a state. Flights carrying tourists from Britain or other parts of Europe to north Cyprus must land in Turkey en route, and these tourists cannot then legally enter the south. Up until 2003 the north was considered something of a backwater, despite the fact that most of the major monuments of Cyprus' colourful past are located north of the Green Line. Then with Cyprus' accession to the EU imminent, and Turkey's hope to follow soon, investors moved in. Since the opening of the Green Line crossings, holiday units and resorts have appeared around Kyrenia and Famagusta. A new four-lane highway connects Nicosia to Kyrenia, and Nicosia to Famagusta.

More and more tourists are being brought into the north via Larnaca airport in the south, without spending time or money in the south. A report in the *Cyprus Mail* (Christou 2007: 8) noted that tourism to the south had declined, while arrivals to the north rose by 30 per cent in the first four months of 2007.

Recognition of the potential of tourism-generated economic activity to achieve parity between the two communities was demonstrated early on by the instigation of a Master Plan for the divided walled city of the capital, Nicosia. This was identified as necessary to the revitalization of the greater city on each side and it was hoped would contribute to an eventual settlement. Initiated in 1979 by the then Mayors of the respective halves of the divided city, Lellos Demetriades (representing the Greek Cypriot community) and Mustafa Akinci (representing the Turkish Cypriot community), it focused on bringing the two sides together for a common purpose. Studies of infrastructure and services needs were carried out together with analysis and assessment of the historic and culturally significant places and precincts. Rehabilitation projects were identified for certain areas, which included consideration of urban design and traffic issues, together with the conservation and reuse of particular monuments as well as housing precincts.

Implementation of the Master Plan began in 1989 with funding for bi-communal projects initially via the United Nations High Commission for Refugees (UNHCR) and later from USAID and UNDP through the UN Office of Project Services. A guide book to the almost 100 projects carried out to date provides an impressive record. It relates to a walking tour map covering both sides of the divided city, with the sites clearly identified. Since Cyprus' accession to the EU in 2004, funding from the EU has been made available to both sides through the Partnership for the Future Programme via UNDP, not only for bi-communal projects within Nicosia but also in Famagusta and in rural and mountain areas in the south.

Cultural heritage conservation and presentation

Apart from the difficult situation created by the stand-off between the Church of Cyprus and the Turkish administration in the north, there are other issues relating to cultural heritage, connected to the way in which heritage places are presented. The key challenge for heritage professionals on both sides is recognition of not only all periods of an individual site or area, but also the social and spiritual values attached to places by different communities in the face of ongoing failure to achieve an overall settlement. The high degree of professionalism in heritage management and conservation on both sides since 1974 has been documented by Anthony Hyland for the north (Hyland 1999: 66–72) and for the south by Euphrosyne Egoumenidou

(Egoumenidou *c*.1998: 98–133). After 1974, responsibility for the care of churches in the north fell to Evkaf, the Kibris Vakiflar Foundation set up under the Ottomans to manage religious property. Those considered to be of major historic and architectural value are managed by the TRNC Department of Antiquities and Museums.

Five churches in the north have been conserved by the Turkish authority's Department of Antiquities and Museums and converted into museums. While a conscientious and professional approach has been applied to these projects, there is a lack of empathy for the spiritual value the places hold for Greek Cypriots. For instance, at the place sacred to the memory of the Apostle Barnabas, regarded as the founder of the Church of Cyprus, the eighteenth-century monastery church built over the fifth-century church that originally commemorated the site of his tomb has been carefully conserved as an icon museum, with archaeological finds displayed in the former monks' rooms around the courtyard. As a tourist site it is well done. But for Greek Cypriot pilgrims there is no sense of the venerability of the place. The fifth-century church was financed by the emperor Zeno, who was convinced by the discovery nearby in 478 CE of relics believed to be those of St Barnabas to award the Church of Cyprus autocephalous status as an Apostolic foundation. The archaeological remains of the eastern section of Zeno's fifth-century basilica project lie beyond the apse of the existing church and contain the tomb intended for the relics of St Barnabas. But this is neither interpreted nor accessible to pilgrims or other visitors, and is overgrown with destructive vegetation.

Nearby at Salamis, the archaeological remains of the basilica of St Epiphanios lie abandoned and overgrown, barely discernible amongst the giant fennel and other vegetation.[1] Epiphanios, Bishop of Salamis from 367 CE until his death in 403 CE, was a dominating figure in the history of the early church in the East. The patriarchal seat was established at Salamis (Constantia) after an earthquake devastated Paphos in 365 CE, and Epiphanios' tomb was located in his great church. Epiphanios was a key participant in the great theological debate of the fourth century (Englezakis 1995: 39). He was recognized as a father of orthodoxy who refused to compromise his essential understanding of Christianity by bending to any influences from Graeco-Roman antiquity and his writings are valued for the information they provide on the religious history of the fourth century (Saltet 1999). The later Campanopetra basilica nearby accommodated the continued influx of pilgrims who came to Salamis long after Epiphanios' death to venerate him as a Saint. It is also overwhelmed with weeds and thistles, to the extent that the marble and *opus sectile* paving is being lifted and stonework dislodged.

The two church sites are perhaps symbolically the most important church sites in Cyprus after St Barnabas. Hardy (2008) makes the point that under UNESCO's 1954 Hague Convention, the Turkish authority could support

Figure 14.2 Neglected remains of the fifth-century church of St Barnabas near Salamis: *Opus sectile* floor being destroyed by vegetation (Susan Balderstone).

Figure 14.3 Neglected remains of the fifth-century church of St Barnabas near Salamis: Apse overgrown with vegetation (Susan Balderstone).

the legitimate Department of Antiquities of Cyprus in 'safeguarding and preserving its cultural property', but claims that this does not happen because the Cyprus government refuses to work in the occupied areas. On the other hand, Fotini Papadopoulou, wife of the then President of the Republic of Cyprus, stated in a lecture given at a cultural event in Paris that: 'important heritage sites have suffered serious destruction because (of) the occupying regime not preserving them and not allowing the Cyprus government to renovate them, in association with the international organizations like UNESCO' (*Cyprus Weekly* 2006).

Within the walled city of Nicosia many of the heritage places common to both communities dating from the Ottoman and British periods have been conserved as part of the Nicosia Master Plan. Grand Ottoman period mansions of very similar form and layout have been conserved on both sides of the Green Line. In the north is the former home of Dervish Pasha, publisher of the first Turkish newspaper in Cyprus. In the south is the former home of Hadjigeorgakis Kornesios, Greek dragoman or interpreter to the Porte. This project won a Europa Nostra award in 1988. There has been some sensitivity amongst Turkish professionals in the north that the Dervish Pasha mansion, which was the first to be tackled by the Turkish authority and is displayed as an ethnographic museum using life-size costumed figures, is not up to date in terms of current trends in museum display. However, the display clearly expresses Turkish Cypriot concern for the loss of their Cypriot traditions and customs. More recent projects in north Nicosia, such as the Eaved House and the Great Inn (Buyuk Khan), reflect current conservation philosophies with regard to retaining the evidence of all periods. The Eaved House also presents some of the family and social history of past owners. The Buyuk Khan accommodates musical and dance performances in the central courtyard while housing antique shops, a café, and art and craft workshops in the surrounding rooms. The period of British use as a prison is demonstrated by retention of two prison cells.

In south Nicosia, projects involving Ottoman period places include the Omeriye Baths, which received a Europa Nostra award in 2006 and is still used as public baths, the Axiothea Mansion, now the University of Cyprus Cultural Centre, and the Tahtakale Mosque (Figure 14.4), conserved as 'representative of religious Islamic architecture' (UNDP 2006: 69). Buildings of the British period have also been conserved on both sides, to equivalent standards, including the former Nicosia Power Station (now the Municipal Modern Art Centre) in the south, and the former Post Office in the north. Areas of traditional housing have been rehabilitated on both sides.

Figure 14.4 Tahtakale Mosque, south Nicosia, restored under the Nicosia Master Plan (Susan Balderstone).

Conclusion

A planning and environment consultant in Nicosia concluded that: '[o]ne of the biggest achievements of the Nicosia Master Plan was the development of excellent communication and joint decision meetings by the planners of the two communities' (Caramondani 2006). Apparently, there has been no similar opportunity for the professionals in the two Departments of Antiquities to work together, exchange ideas and build mutual respect. There is a lack of consideration in Turkish Cypriot conservation projects for Greek Cypriot sensibilities regarding their Christian heritage. On the other side, the Greek Cypriots strive to assert their superiority in heritage conservation through winning awards and have already achieved ten or more Europa Nostra awards (*Europa Nostra* 2004). This perceived superiority engenders Greek Cypriot disdain for the way in which historic places in the north are presented with costumed figures demonstrating a past way of life. Such disdain displays a distinct lack of awareness of Turkish Cypriot sensibilities in relation to their social and intangible heritage.

With more than 43,000 Turkish troops stationed permanently in the north (Ministry of Foreign Affairs, Hellenic Republic of Greece 2008), there is ongoing fear and distrust of the administration in the north by Greek Cypriots. This situation is not necessarily comfortable for Turkish Cypriots either. Ownership complications relating to property which incorporates listed buildings or antiquities can apply to both sides. Something like a UN-sponsored Cyprus Heritage Strategy, which would require bi-communal cooperation between the heritage authorities, religious organizations and municipalities of both sides, would seem to be the next step in building on the success of the Nicosia Master Plan.

Pressure for something to be done has come from frustrated foreign institutions wanting to work in north Cyprus. In June 2007 two foreign professors at the East Mediterranean University in Famagusta – an institution not recognized by the Cyprus government because of the illegality of the Turkish occupation – managed to have the walled city of Famagusta added to the World Monuments Fund's Watch List of endangered sites threatened by conflict (Bahceli 2007: 9; *Cyprus Weekly* 2007). There was suspicion on the Greek side that they in fact wanted to set up a team to manage restoration funds from the WMF employing other foreign experts and archaeologists in the occupied areas, taking away any opportunity for Greek Cypriot involvement. Nevertheless, the initiative could result in a process for Famagusta that is similar to the Nicosia Master Plan. In December 2007, the Greek Cypriot refugee mayor of Famagusta and the town's Turkish Cypriot representative participated in a separate initiative sponsored by the UN Peacekeeping Force in Cyprus (UNFICYP) and the EU. Talks took place between the Greek and Turkish Cypriot communities aimed at bi-communal cooperation on the conservation of the old walled city of

Famagusta. The talks also involved the vice-president of *Europa Nostra*, and were reported as paving the way for a bi-communal approach to the protection of Cypriot cultural heritage in general (Stylianou 2007).

Shortly after the election of a new President of Cyprus, Christofias in February 2008, the Ledra Street Green Line crossing was opened in the centre of old Nicosia, increasing the relevance of the Nicosia Master Plan to the life of the city. Then, following a meeting in Paris attended by the vice-president of *Europa Nostra*, Costas Carras and the Greek and Turkish Cypriot mayors of Famagusta, Greek Cypriot mayor Alexis Galanos connected the human rights of refugees to return to their homes in Varosha with the future of the old town's cultural heritage: '[w]hat's important for us is that cultural heritage and human rights go hand-in-hand. The residents of the ghost town must return. Our efforts are within the framework of the tragedy suffered by our people' (*Cyprus Mail* 2008). This invocation of human rights in relation to cultural heritage was designed to garner European support. 'We need to win the Europeans over to our cause' said Galanos. The agitation over church property and human rights by Archbishop Chrisostomos II to the European Court of Human Rights is also aimed at getting the support of Europe. It seems clear that lack of adherence to the UN conventions on cultural property by the Turkish authority has had the result of causing activists such as Galanos and Chrisostomos to turn to the European avenue of human rights.

It may be that more progress in relation to the cultural heritage of the whole island will result from cultural heritage projects included in confidence-building measures announced in June 2008 following a meeting of the leaders of the Greek Cypriot and Turkish Cypriot communities (Foreign and Commonwealth Office 2008). The opportunity will be there perhaps in these projects for each community to recognize the cultural sensibilities of the other, and to demonstrate this understanding in the way the cultural heritage of Cyprus is conserved and presented.

Note

1 As at May 2009, action has been taken to remedy the situation. Vegetation has been removed and new signage provided.

References

Alexander, Nathan and Rushman, Gordon (eds) (1994) *Tianjin Urban Conservation Strategy*, Melbourne: Australian Institute of Urban Studies.

Association of Cypriot Archaeologists (2005) *Muslim Places of Worship in Cyprus*, Nicosia.

Bahceli, Simon (2007) 'Alarm Bells Ring for Old Famagusta,' *Sunday Mail*, Nicosia, 10 June.

Caramondani, Anna (2006) 'NICOSIA – The Last Divided City in Europe.' Available at www.undp-unops-nmp.org.

Christou, Jean (2007) 'Tourism in the North Soaring: Arrivals until April up 30 per cent,' *Cyprus Mail*, Nicosia, 5 May.

Coldstream, Nicholas (1981) 'Introduction to the Monuments and Early History of Cyprus,' in Ian Robertson (ed.) *Cyprus*, London and Tonbridge: Ernest Benn Limited.

Cyprus Embassy to the EU (2008) 'Destruction of Cultural Heritage.' Available at www.cyprusembassy.net/home/index.php?module=page&cid=15 (accessed 7 October 2008).

Cyprus Mail (2008) 'Optimism after Heritage Talks,' *Cyprus Mail*, Nicosia, 9 April.

Cyprus Observer (2007) 'Yonluer Protests Greek Cypriot Orthodox Church's Unilateral Approach to Religious Sites,' *Cyprus Observer*, Nicosia (north), 27 April–3 May: 6.

Cyprus Weekly (2006) 'First Lady Gives History Lecture in Paris,' *Cyprus Weekly*, Nicosia, 30 June–6 July.

Cyprus Weekly (2007) 'Famagusta Listing "Adverse Development",' *Cyprus Weekly*, Nicosia, 15–21 June: 16.

Dakin, Douglas (1981) 'Introduction to the Later History of Cyprus,' in Ian Robertson (ed.) *Cyprus*, London and Tonbridge: Ernest Benn Limited.

Drousiotis, Makarios (2006) *Cyprus 1974: Greek Coup and Turkish Invasion*, Mannheim und Mohnesee: Bibliopolis.

Durrell, Lawrence (1978) *Bitter Lemons of Cyprus*, London: Faber and Faber (first published 1957).

Efthyvoulos, Alex (2006) 'A View of the Land – From the Soul: A Labour of Love on the Occupied North,' *Cyprus Weekly*, Nicosia, 28 April–4 May.

Egoumenidou, Euphrosyne (*c*.1998) 'Cypriot Monuments of the Recent Past and their Integration in the Modern Environment,' in Dr E. Karpodini-Dimitriadi, *Ethnography of European Traditional Cultures: Society Cultural Tradition, Built Environment*, European Seminar II–Proceedings: Centre for Vocational Training, Institute of Cultural Studies of Europe and the Mediterranean: 98–134.

Englezakis, Benedict (1995) 'Epiphanius of Salamis, the Father of the Cypriot Autocephaly,' in Silouan and Misael Ioannou (eds) *Studies on the History of the Church of Cyprus, 4th–20th Centuries*, translated by Norman Russell, London: Variorum/ Ashgate Publishing Ltd.

Europa Nostra (2004) 'European Cultural Heritage Review 2004: Our Hope for a Peaceful Future is Based on our Common Cultural Heritage,' Interview with Mr Pefkios Georgiades, Minister of Culture and Education, The Republic of Cyprus, *Europa Nostra* 1: 23.

Foreign and Commonwealth Office UK (2008). Available at www.fco.gov.uk/ en/about-the-fco/country-profiles/europe/cyprus/?profile=all# (accessed 7 October 2008).

Given, Michael (2000) 'Agriculture, Settlement and Landscape in Ottoman Cyprus,' *Levant* 32: 209–30.

Hardy, S. A. (2008) 'Cultural Heritage Ethics in a Divided Cyprus,' Paper presented at the 6th World Archaeological Congress, Dublin, Republic of Ireland, 29 June–4 July. Available at http://human-rights-archaeology.blogspot.com/2008/07/ cultural-heritage-ethics-in-divided.html (accessed 5 October 2008).

Hellenic News of America (2008) 'Turkey Inserts Religious Elements to Cyprus Problem.' Available at www.hellenicnews.com (accessed 18 January).

Hill, Sir George (1952) *A History of Cyprus Volume IV: The Ottoman Province – The British Colony 1571–1948*, Sir Harry Luke (ed.). Cambridge University Press.

Hunt, Sir David (1990) *Footprints in Cyprus: an Illustrated History*, London: Trigraph Limited (first published 1982).

Hyland, A. D. C. (1999) 'Ethnic Dimensions to World Heritage: Conservation of the Architectural Heritage of the Turkish Republic of Northern Cyprus,' *Journal of Achitectural Conservation*, March, 1: 59–71.

Leonidou, Leo (2006) 'Mausoleum Restored,' *Cyprus Mail*, Nicosia, 5 July.

Leonidou, Leo (2007) 'Armenian Pilgrimage to Monastery in North: Emotional Return to Ruined Holy Site,' *Cyprus Mail*, Nicosia, 8 May.

Lisle, Debbie (2007) 'Encounters with Partition: Tourism and Reconciliation in Cyprus,' in Louise Purbrick, Jim Aulich and Graham Dawson (eds) *Contested Spaces*, Basingstoke: Palgrave Macmillan.

Maier, Franz Georg (1968) *Cyprus from the Earliest Time to the Present Day*, translated from the German by Peter Gorge, London: Elek Books Ltd.

Ministry of Foreign Affairs of the Republic of Cyprus (2008). Available at www.mfa.gov.cy/mfa/mfa2006.nsf/cyprus07_en/cyprus07_en?OpenDocument (accessed 5 October 2008).

Ministry of Foreign Affairs of the Hellenic Republic of Greece (2008) 'Cyprus – Parameters of the Problem.' Available at www.mfa.gr/www.mfa.gr/en-US/Policy/Geographic+Regions/South-Eastern+Europe/Cyprus/The+Parameters+of+the+Problem+and+the+Solution/ (accessed 7 October 2008).

Panteli, Dr Stavros (2005) *The History of Modern Cyprus*, Hertfordshire, England: Topline Publishing.

PIO (Cyprus Press and Information Office) (2004) 'Measures for Turkish Cypriots after the Partial Lifting of Restrictions on Movement along Ceasefire Line,' Press Release 30 April 2004, in Association of Cypriot Archaeologists 2005, *Muslim Places of Worship in Cyprus*, Nicosia: 101.

Saltet, Louis (1999) 'Epiphanius of Salamis,' *Catholic Encyclopaedia*, Vol. XIII: Online edition.

Schriwer, Charlotte (2002) 'Cultural and Ethnic Identity in the Ottoman Period Architecture of Cyprus,' Jordan and Lebanon *Levant* 34: 197–218.

Stylianou, Philippos (2007) *Cyprus Weekly*, Nicosia, 14–20 December.

Stylianou, Philippos (2008) 'Church Taking Turkey to European Rights Court,' *Cyprus Weekly*, Nicosia, 11–17 January (interview on 8 January).

Stylianou, Philippos and Demetra Molyva (2006) 'EU Parliament Calls on Turkey to Protect and Restore Pillaged Churches in Occupied North,' *Cyprus Weekly*, Nicosia, 7–13 July: 6.

UNDP, UNOPS (2006) *Walled Nicosia: a Guide to its Historical and Cultural Sites*, Nicosia Master Plan.

Chapter 15

Leaving the buildings behind

Conflict, sovereignty and the values of heritage in Kashmir

Tim Winter and Shalini Panjabi

Given recent events in Iraq, Afghanistan and the Balkans, the role cultural heritage plays in post-war reconstruction continues to be seen as an important and complex issue that warrants critical attention. There is a growing recognition that heritage policies need to address a multitude of agendas, and extend their goals beyond the restitution of objects or the reconstruction of buildings and other structures. However, if cultural heritage is to be integrated within wider goals of post-conflict economic reconstruction and societal recovery, stronger ties need to be made with today's humanitarian or developmental aid frameworks. This chapter explores the possibility of such links within the context of Srinagar, the capital city of Indian-administered Kashmir. In particular it focuses on the issue of housing as a focal point for understanding the interweaving cultural and economic rights of Srinagar's citizens.

With the conflict in the region enduring for more than 15 years, the city – regarded as one of the most important pre-modern urban landscapes in South Asia – has suffered extensive physical damage. Nonetheless, Srinagar remains the cultural and political heart of a wider collective identity rooted in the Kashmir Valley. As such, it presents a rich example of a city that would strongly benefit from an approach that recognizes the intimate dialogue between the built environment and the socio-cultural and economic needs of the population. However, as we shall see, if the heritage of a city like Srinagar is to be discussed in more holistic, less fabric-based terms, addressing wider goals of cultural sovereignty, multi-culturalism or security poses unfamiliar questions and challenges.

Humanitarian heritage

Global media coverage of the destruction of the Mostar Bridge in 1993 powerfully reminded the world about the impact war and conflict can have on sites of historical, religious or architectural value. Indeed, not since the Second World War and the widespread destruction of Europe's cities has so much attention been paid to the destruction of the built environment and the enterprise of its reconstruction. For Barakat (2005b), this 'reawakening' occurred because the Balkans conflict became 'a personalized war' for the Western media as it took place in a region where Europeans and North Americans took their holidays. Paralleling, and interfacing with, this renewed media interest has been a steadily evolving heritage discourse – both in academia and policy – that has sought to grapple with the difficult relationships between heritage and episodes of war, genocide and armed conflict. The 1954 *Hague Convention on the Protection of Cultural Property in the Event of Armed Conflict* remains the definitive mechanism and point of reference for safeguarding heritage sites threatened with destruction. Its widespread ratification, of course, has not prevented buildings, sacred objects or artworks being damaged or destroyed. The Dome of the Rock in Jerusalem or Babri Masjid in Ayodhya are two notable examples of the many places that have become the focal point of inflamed hostilities or tensions in recent decades. In reflecting upon the challenges such places pose, Bevan (2006) and Chamberlain (2005) illustrate why creating effective strategies for protecting cultural heritage sites during times of conflict remains a difficult and sometimes illusive problem.

The threats of destruction or desecration are not the only challenges war poses to the heritage community. Equally problematic is the 'commemoration' of past atrocities and other difficult histories. Prolonging the memory of oppression, injustices or the loss of lives has long been the responsibility of the memorial or the preserved symbolic structure. Indeed, while the popularity of this genre perhaps reached its zenith in the aftermath of the First World War, parks, walls of honour, statues, museums or iconic ruins endure as universally adopted devices for capturing – or indeed in some cases invoking – a national or personal memory. Invariably these spaces or structures are set aside from the everyday; demarcated as sites of reflection, contemplation and peaceful tranquillity (Beazley 2007; Kirshenblatt-Gimblett 1998). Enduring debates surround the effectiveness of material culture as *lieux de mémoire*. Forty and Küchler (2001), for example, point towards the role forgetting plays in the process of commemoration. Robert Bevan's (2006) book *The Destruction of Memory* also provides us with a historical panorama of such themes. As Bevan reminds us, the loss of memories caused by the destruction of architecture can in fact sometimes be an essential step towards reconciliation and the reduction of hostilities.

In these studies we begin to see one of the two themes that dominate academic analyses addressing the relationship between heritage and episodes of war and conflict. Reflections on memory form part of an ongoing conversation about the value of destruction and restoration at the symbolic level, and the impact of such efforts on group identities. Operating at a more technical 'fabric'-based level, other heritage studies have discussed the legal dimensions of heritage protection and the merits of different conservation 'philosophies'. Given the sustained attention given to the symbolic level, it is not surprising to find that academics, along with planners, consultants and architects have all concentrated on sites pertinent to 'collective identities', to use Stanley-Price's (2007) term. The restoration of mosques, temples, statues or bridges is often seen as a powerful metaphor for a wider socio-cultural restoration. Moreover, projects undertaken in Bosnia, Sri Lanka and Cambodia have shown why a sensitivity towards the various symbolic values communities impart on sites is absolutely vital if reconstruction is to be used as a positive tool for reconciliation (Wijesuriya 2007; Winter 2007).

Whilst not denying the validity of such efforts, Ascherson (2007), however, suggests that the attention given to sites of 'collective identity' is somewhat misplaced. He argues there is very little evidence to show that collective identities are actually dissolved or undermined through the destruction or deliberate attacking of symbolically important sites. He states 'assaults on group identity through cultural destruction, in short, very seldom work' (Ascherson 2007: 22). Writing in *After the Conflict*, Barakat (2005b) builds upon this idea, arguing that greater attention needs to be given to the reconstruction of everyday structures, ones that combine functional and cultural importance. For Barakat efforts to protect or restore domestic residencies can be a highly effective tool for creating a sense of personal security and local 'ownership' over a post-conflict reconstruction process; both of which, he suggests, are critical factors for successful intervention programmes. Refugees from Afghanistan and Palestine who keep keys for decades are also cited as an example of the important role played by the home as a marker of memory and cultural continuity.

Similarly, within his analysis of the restoration of the built environment in post-conflict societies, Zetter claims domestic housing is of paramount importance for re-establishing a sense of socio-cultural security (Zetter 2005: 156). In shifting the attention away from structures that symbolically capture or project a collective identity towards structures like domestic housing, both Barakat and Zetter place great emphasis on understanding the connections between the built environment and their surrounding social, institutional and political contexts. This is deemed crucial if interventions targeting the physical infrastructure are to operate at multiple levels and achieve multiple ends. Indeed, Zetter's focus on housing is underpinned by a concern for addressing the economic and social security rights of citizens. In harmony they suggest, however, that this is rarely achieved due to the emphasis given to technocratic approaches. As Zetter states:

> By focusing on lower order deliverables and measurable outputs – e.g. contract completions, costs per housing unit, buildings restored – physical reconstruction projects have frequently failed to address or measure progress towards the 'higher order' objectives which they serve such as reintegration, social and civil society development, economic needs and strategies for peace.
>
> (Zetter 2005: 160)

In order to achieve these 'higher order' goals he identifies four essential parameters that need to be followed: 'building a strategic framework; linking
relief and rehabilitation to recovery and development; rebuilding institutional capacity; enabling and empowering people as key resources in these
processes' (Zetter 2005: 160). Clearly, in making such assertions, these
authors call for a better integration between reconstruction programmes
focusing on the built environment, including heritage structures, and the
wider agendas of post-conflict humanitarian aid.

This chapter considers some of the implications of adopting such an
approach for the urban landscape of Srinagar, Kashmir. Of course, given that
'the Kashmir question' remains an emotive and violent one, it would be mis-
leading to approach Srinagar today as a post-conflict space undergoing
regeneration and restoration. Equally, however, treating the city as a frozen
space ensnared by violence and tension would miss the everyday shifts
between decay and regeneration, abandonment and reoccupation, and hostility and reconciliation. Our analysis is also given impetus through the voices
of Srinagar's residents, who desire to look to the future rather than merely
waiting for the conflict to subside; sentiments that Barakat neatly abstracts
and sees as universal:

> Post-war reconstruction begins in the hearts and minds of those who
> suffer the horrors of war and want to change societies so that there is no
> return to mass violence. For them planning for reconstruction often
> begins during conflict and is an essential part of negotiating their way
> towards peace.
>
> (Barakat 2005a: 1)

For Barakat then, cultural heritage needs to form part of a vision for development and societal reconstruction that is planned for in advance. The vernacular heritage of Srinagar's old city presents a number of valuable
opportunities here. As one of South Asia's most intact pre-modern urban
landscapes, its extensive housing stock represents a heritage resource that can
help strengthen a sense of security and participation among the city's residents. Indeed, if we follow the arguments of Barakat and Zetter, any intervention towards conserving the historic architecture will be most effective if
it forms part of a humanitarian effort that is geared towards peace and
stability. This means, by implication, that an outside intervention would not
claim neutrality in the conflict, but instead orient itself towards human
rights concerns. In such a context heritage becomes part of an agenda promoting economic and physical security, financial independence and a right
to a choice of housing. According to Zetter, prioritizing the issue of housing
to achieve such goals is warranted because it 'constitutes social capital and
an important and cultural commodity which reflects the rights of people to
live where they choose' (2005: 156). Clearly then, if we are to take the con-

servation of Srinagar's heritage in such directions a number of logistical and philosophical issues need to be addressed. The remaining sections of this chapter sketch out some of these challenges.

Srinagar – 'perhaps the most threatened yet valuable site in India'

The World Monuments Fund (WMF) has declared the old city of Srinagar as 'perhaps the most threatened yet valuable site in India', placing it on its 2008 List of Most Endangered Sites.[1] As the capital city of Indian-administered Kashmir, and the political, economic hub of the Kashmir Valley, Srinagar has a rich and extensive vernacular heritage. Situated in a mountainous valley, and oriented around the Jhelum River and many lakes, most notably the Dal Lake, the city has a unique material culture comprised of houseboats, wooden bridges, mosques, bazaars and hundreds of wooden houses. It is also home to some of the finest and most elaborate Mughal gardens in the region (Khan 2007).

Records indicate that Srinagar has existed as a settlement from at least the third century BC. Not surprisingly, the built environment today reflects a long, complex history of shifting religious, cultural and political influences. Around the time the city was established, Buddhism was being introduced to the Kashmir Valley by emperor Ashoka. By the end of the fourteenth century Hindu and Buddhist rule came to an end across the Kashmir Valley as the region came under the control of various Muslim rulers, including the Mughal emperor Akbar. It later came under the influence of the Sikhs and then the Hindus, after the treaty of 1846 between the British and the Dogra rulers of neighbouring Jammu (Zutshi 2003). The Dogra rulers discriminated in various ways against the Muslim populace, and the anger against this rule intensified when the Dogra ruler Hari Singh acceded, under pressure, to India in 1947 – when the country gained independence and was partitioned. With India reneging even on the limited promises of autonomy, and with support from Pakistan, the movement turned violent in 1989. For the next 16 years, the valley was caught in a web of intensive and horrific violence. The situation has been returning to 'normalcy' in recent years, though the political situation remains largely unchanged.

Srinagar, as a physical space, remains unique in various ways. Set at a high altitude in a mountainous valley, a lot of the architecture of the city is oriented towards either the Jhelum River or one of the lakes. There are wooden bridges and bathing areas (*ghats*) along the river, apart from the numerous old and beautifully crafted houseboats that, while they are a favourite of the tourists, are also home to many residents of the city. The long, joint rows of timber and masonry structures, with their sloping roofs and carved windows and doors, create a cityscape that is quite different from any other. At the crossroads of various civilizations, Srinagar has a rich cultural past that is reflected in its many mosques, shrines, temples, grand houses, gardens and bazaars. As Langenbach states:

> Srinagar, and other cities and villages in Kashmir are distinguished today for more than their monumental buildings and archaeological sites – they are unique in the world for their vernacular residential architecture. It is an architecture generated out of a distinctive use of materials and way of building, but in the modern world it is being rapidly displaced by reinforced concrete and other modern materials and systems.
>
> (Langenback 2007: 9)

Located in an area prone to earthquakes, the traditional, vernacular architecture of Srinagar is also noted for its resilience to seismic activity. In describing this earthquake-resistant vernacular construction, Langenbach identifies two distinct styles: *taq* and *dhajji dewari*. Although not specifically a Kashmiri term, *taq* refers to a type of building that employs a system of ladder-like horizontal timbers bedded into masonry-bearing walls. These timbers ensure the brick, mud or stone of the walls are held in place and tied into the wooden floors. Whereas the Persian term, *dhajji dewari*, literally meaning 'patch quilt wall', refers to a style of panelled construction comprised of tightly packed wood and masonry (Langenbach 2007). Characterized by hundreds of structures built from these two construction styles, the 'old city' remains a remarkable example of a large, relatively intact, historic urban landscape; one that endures as a dynamic 'living' city characterized by residences and shops in use today that have been passed on through generations.

It should also be noted that, in other respects, the 'old city' remains similar to other old urban settlements in South Asia. It is a crowded space characterized by narrow, winding lanes and buildings abutting each other, with a mix of residential, commercial and religious structures. The city consists of many *mohallas* (quarters or neighbourhoods), demarcated variously by trades and communities. Some *mohallas* are identified as Shia Muslim or Hindu, and the streets and bazaars are often distinguished by the predominance of one trade like silverware or spices or utensils (Khan 2007).

The ongoing conflict has had a paradoxical impact on the architecture of the old city, with some areas being destroyed while others have actually been preserved by the war. The political and economic isolation of the region since the early 1990s has meant Srinagar has not witnessed the modernization and 'concretization' that has become commonplace in other Indian cities. However, this isolation, along with the ongoing conflict and resultant economic 'poverty' has also meant the old city lies in a bad state of disrepair with hundreds of buildings literally crumbling away (Figures 15.1 and 15.2). The civic infrastructure too has been neglected through this period, and the river and the lakes need to be urgently revived. The reclamation of waterways has also occurred at a more rapid pace, and with roads being built

Figure 15.1 Residential structures along Jhelum River, Srinagar (Tim Winter).

Figure 15.2 Abandoned houses, central Srinagar (Tim Winter).

over canals, it becomes a challenge to interpret the overall layout of the city today. Quite simply, as one of the most important historic cities in South Asia, an urban landscape of immense cultural and architectural significance, Srinagar urgently requires far greater attention than it has received to date.

At this point it is worth noting the prevailing factors that have contributed to the neglect of Srinagar as a heritage site, as they will undoubtedly continue to inhibit the development of any heritage discourse in the coming years. Since 1990 the city has been the site of sustained violent conflict. The conflict has still not been resolved, and the Kashmir Valley remains tense with regular incidences of violence. Naturally the preservation of the past is considered a relatively low priority for both residents and local bureaucrats who are understandably more concerned with the everyday challenges of living in a conflict zone. Moreover, as a pivotal political and symbolic hub of the Kashmir Valley, Srinagar acts as an epicentre of the disputed territory of Jammu and Kashmir. This means that the material culture of the old city is a place that constantly reminds residents of past hostilities and enmities, bereavements and regrets. And as we shall see shortly, the governance and stewardship of the built environment have contributed to the contours of the conflict.

Currently administered as part of India, Srinagar falls under the remit of the country's national heritage programme. However, in recent decades the principal focus of the heritage movement in India has been directed towards the monuments and religious structures of 'classical' eras. While organizations like the India National Trust for Art and Cultural Heritage (INTACH) have endeavoured to widen the scope and time frames of the heritage discourse in the country, vernacular, wooden architecture less than two centuries old remain low on the list of conservation priorities. In the case of Srinagar, this means that whilst the World Monuments Fund has identified what they refer to as the 'Srinagar heritage zone', no such legal or policy frameworks exist on the ground. In 2005 INTACH completed a cultural resource-mapping report, and although this has provided a comprehensive documentation of the heritage of the city and its environs, little progress has been made towards developing some sort of legislative or protective framework.[2]

The political situation in Kashmir also creates major obstacles for interventions by the international heritage community. As an important step towards any future policy UNESCO produced a lengthy report in 2007 entitled *Guidelines for Preserving the Earthquake-Resistant Traditional Construction of Kashmir* (see Langenbach 2007). However, any move towards adding Srinagar to the World Heritage List or List of Endangered Sites would require its nomination by the State Party, i.e. India. For Kashmiris seeking autonomy for the region, or its accession to Pakistan, any collaboration between Delhi and a United Nations organization such as UNESCO would be politically charged. Indeed, any such interventions are likely to be seen as attempts to further integrate Srinagar within an Indian national heritage, and as such be regarded as a threat to the cultural and political sovereignty of the region.

Clearly, the all-enveloping context of the Kashmir dispute presents a series of significant obstacles to the development and implementation of any effective heritage programme. This does not, however, mean that progress cannot be made. The recent initiatives undertaken by INTACH, UNESCO and WMF noted above indicate the real urgency for raising awareness and resources for heritage conservation. However, as the following two sections illustrate, if a cultural heritage programme is to be developed which achieves 'higher order goals' to use Zetter's term, then it needs to be incorporated into the wider agendas of a humanitarian conflict-transformation effort.

Crafting stabilities

For the residents of Srinagar the violent period of the conflict is a continual reference point. Discussions on most matters veer to the situation pre-militancy as compared to post-militancy. It was – and is – a conflict that has affected all sections of society and physically impacted upon the built and the natural environment in various ways. This is apparent all around today: in the accelerated reclamation of the Dal Lake, in the bunkers and the sandbags on nearly every road, and even in the surge in construction activity in the suburbs – that ironically is fuelled by money made by some sections in the conflict. The 'old city' though has been the area most affected.

As the physical and ideological hub of the movement against the Indian state, it bears many scars from the years of violence. Most of the demonstrations and police action centred on this area, and many structures also suffered extensive damage from battles between militants and the police, and between different militant factions. A few prominent Sufi shrines were gutted, amidst conflicting allegations between the militants and the armed forces. However, even as the 'old city' was emerging as the focal point of the conflict, it was losing its vitality as the social and commercial centre of the valley.

A critical event here was the departure of Hindu residents in early 1990, many of whom fled because of the conflict. Perhaps most significantly, the departure of Kashmiri Pandits – a Hindu minority indigenous to the Kashmir valley and strongly in favour of Indian rule – altered the fabric of the city in various ways. After a spate of selected killings and deadly threats being issued by the Islamic militants, most Kashmiri Pandits abandoned their houses and fled en masse from the valley over the course of a few days. Many of them had occupied high positions in the bureaucracy and in educational institutions, and their social and cultural impact was always disproportionate to their numbers in the valley. They had a significant presence in Srinagar's old city and some of the most beautiful houses belonged to them. Many neighbourhoods have been strongly affected by the exodus of the

Pandits, and in various ways they have lost their original character and purpose, despite not having changed much physically. Officially, tenuous hopes are still held that the Pandits will return, and so in a sense any redevelopment is in abeyance. However, the Pandits are highly unlikely to ever return and they have begun selling their houses over the last couple of years. In many cases, their erstwhile Muslim neighbours, who need the space to accommodate their growing families and start new businesses, are buying the houses. To some the abandoned houses also represent a commercial opportunity, waiting to be exploited. In consonance with the needs of the new owners, many houses are being altered substantially, often beyond recognition.

The situation is complicated further by a deep ambivalence that characterizes many reactions to the flight of the Pandits. With most Muslim families in the city too having suffered deeply through the conflict, they may on the surface seem unbothered about the Pandits' plight. However, almost any discussion on the issue evokes a sense of sorrow – and even guilt at their helplessness to reassure their neighbours and friends, and prevent them from leaving at the time. There is nostalgia in Kashmir today of a time when different communities lived together harmoniously. The loss of the Hindus is bemoaned in various ways; it is a loss of a way of life as remembered. This also gets intertwined with a general sense of despair and sorrow in the valley, and is seen by the Kashmiris as an indication of troubled times. However, concurrently all the residents of the city also feel a need to move on, and to begin rebuilding their lives. The rows of abandoned, dilapidated Pandit houses, unlikely to be ever reoccupied by their owners, are a poignant sight, and to many in Srinagar the continuous reminder is also painful. Coupled with the shortage of housing space in the old city, this results in the desire to reclaim and possess these old houses. If these aspirations and rights for personal security are respected and duly considered, the challenges to conservation are many. Often as new owners take occupation of these properties structural changes are made for practical reorganization reasons. Such moves that create a rupture between the past and present represent a major obstacle for conservation.

Across the city, the Indian army has also occupied a significant number of historical structures over the last 16 years to accommodate the large number of troops in the valley. Throughout this period these structures have remained off limits for local residents. Among these are the many Mughal inns and other fortifications, including the prominent fort of Hari Parbat in the heart of Srinagar. The fort is perched on the top of a hill and commands a good view of the city, which makes it a strategic vantage point (Figure 15.3). As part of recent efforts at normalization, the army has just begun to cede control over the fort. Kashmiris have consistently resented the occupation of these structures, which for them are tangible embodiments of their rich past. There has also been little involvement of Kashmiris in even the

Figure 15.3 Hari Parbat fort, Srinagar (Tim Winter).

small efforts at conservation undertaken by the Indian government and its armed forces. The *Vienna Memorandum on Historic Urban Landscapes* is pertinent here as it advocates 'a vision on the city as a whole with forward-looking action on the part of decision-makers, and a dialogue with the other actors and stakeholders involved' (UNESCO 2005: 3). In essence the memorandum recommends replacing 'top-down' approaches to conservation with initiatives that foreground community consultation and a more open mode of governance. Such an approach seems particularly appropriate for developing heritage policy frameworks that attend to the layered socio-cultural histories of Srinagar. However, in a situation of continued conflict and tension, how can such a dialogue be fruitfully undertaken? With an ever-shifting political landscape and a multitude of voices, whose position should be privileged is a question that will need to be confronted in some way. Moreover, how can calls for restoration and preservation be made relevant to a population living in a conflict zone, struggling to lead a 'normal' life?

Despite such obstacles, the distinct cultural identity of Srinagar and its pivotal role within the history of the Kashmir Valley strongly point towards the importance of establishing a heritage discourse that captures the 'character' and 'life' of its urban environment: the elements which together constitute its distinct sense of place. As we have seen, however, Srinagar equally illustrates the significant challenges that arise when that sense of place is politically charged and associated with a violent conflict. Indeed, for many of

Srinagar's residents, it is an urban cultural landscape that has become intimately tied to their right to claim cultural and political sovereignty – a Kashmiri identity distinct from neighbouring India and Pakistan.

Negotiating regeneration and modernity

Given that this identity has become intimately linked to years of violent struggle, the dominant mood in the valley today is of gloom. It is the sadness that comes from the trauma of nearly two decades of violence, made worse by the realization that it has largely been futile. The Kashmiris have not gained any major political concession and are no closer to autonomy than they were in 1989 – and many of them hold the militants responsible, as much as the Indian and Pakistani governments for this mess. The need to move on now and rebuild their lives is thus constantly expressed. The consciousness of what it has 'cost' them is made more acute by the rapid economic development in India through precisely this period, a developmental curve that has physically and socially transformed many cities. There is a strong desire now to catch up, and go the way these cities have gone – with shopping malls, concrete houses and industries. The residents also aspire to the revival of certain trades and forms of commerce that gave the city's neighbourhoods their distinctive character. There is no desire to freeze the city as an architectural museum. The cultural identity of the Kashmir Valley captured in the urban landscape of Srinagar is inextricably bound up in its histories of business and commerce. The regeneration of the city's commercial infrastructure and the resultant modernization will thus lead to another set of challenges. If these aspirations and the right to economic security are to be respected, and thus approached as a 'place' inextricably tied to the dreams and hopes of residents, then any heritage policy will have to contend with these shifting needs.

It was noted earlier that since the beginning of the violence the city has been insulated from rapid economic development. As such it provides a rare example in the subcontinent of a pre-modern city that has not been overcome by concrete and steel. But with stability new conflicts arise, and old ones raise their head again. It is clear that while the violent conflict has impacted the city in various ways, it is not the only reason for the neglect of Srinagar's traditional architecture. Many of the issues around the conservation of Srinagar's 'old city' are not much different from those facing other old city centres across India, and precede the conflict by decades. Like elsewhere, the city's vernacular architecture was neglected in the years prior to the conflict. Many structures were allowed to go to ruin, in other cases they were rebuilt in a new style, and encroachments were not controlled. This has been the general story throughout India: there is lack of urban planning, and when people sell out or renovate their houses or shops, the aspiration is invariably towards the new – with concrete replacing wood and masonry. The strong desire to modernize leads to the old often being equated with 'poor' and 'backward'. The consciousness of heritage is also often missing, and the maintenance of old structures comes at considerable cost. Indeed, rebuilding houses using 'modern' construction materials such as brick and concrete is considerably less expensive (Figure 15.4). Modern materials have also become a metaphor for the modernization of the urban environment, and thus the economic recovery of its communities.

Moreover, there are logistical problems with materials not being available and skills in various crafts having been lost. Discussions with the owner of the Jalali Haveli, a Persian-style grand mansion located near Srinagar's old city, indicated that he is currently unable to secure the craftsmen capable of repairing the intricate woodwork of the windows. The decisions are not just difficult for individuals; governments too have tended to override calls for preservation. A notable instance here is the large stone-lined Nalla Mar Canal, which was distinctive for the arched bridges and the many fine, old houses lining its sides. In the 1970s, it was covered over with a road built on top. The bridges and most of the houses were demolished too. When discussing Srinagar's heritage today, many older residents lament its destruction. In this respect, we can see the 'conflict of progress versus preservation' was apparent in the city long before the political conflict turned violent (Langenbach 1982).

Figure 15.4 Housing with modern construction materials and techniques (Tim Winter).

Conclusion

Given the years of violence such issues and tensions receded into the background. However, with some semblance of 'normality' being restored, they are re-emerging with a stronger force. In essence the complex situation in Srinagar today is characterized by two distinct and divergent trends. On the one hand, there is a desire for maintaining the unique political and cultural identity of the city and the Kashmir Valley. As we have seen, however, there is also a widespread desire for economic and social mobility – for modernization and a sense of inclusion in the wealth and prosperity enjoyed elsewhere in India. The residential architecture of the 'old city' is enmeshed by these two desires. To fully appreciate such processes it is thus necessary to develop a cross-disciplinary approach that directly connects cultural heritage with other spheres of conflict transformation; an approach that enables heritage to contribute to the economic and political stabilities of conflict-affected communities, the reconstruction of their civic identities, poverty alleviation and the harmonization of community relations. The reconstruction of the urban environment, including domestic housing, can precipitate the revival of trust and dialogue within and across Srinagar's communities.

As Logan (2008: 439) states, 'local communities need to have a sense of "ownership" of their heritage; this reaffirms their worth as a community, their sense of going about things, their "culture"'. Indeed, in recalling the arguments made by Zetter and Barakat seen earlier, it is apparent that the city's residents must become the 'curators' of their environment, whereby a heritage consciousness emerges through initiatives that prioritize community-driven reconstruction.

Notes

1 For further details see: www.worldmonumentswatch.org, accessed on 20 November 2007.
2 For further details see: www.intach.org/architectural_heritage.asp, accessed on 20 November 2007.

References

Ascherson, N. (2007) 'Cultural Destruction by War, and its Impact on Group Identities,' in N. Stanley-Price (ed.) *Cultural Heritage in Postwar Recovery*, Rome: ICCROM.
Barakat, S. (2005a) 'After the Conflict: Reconstruction and Development in the Aftermath of War,' in S. Barakat (ed.) *After the Conflict: Reconstruction and Development in the Aftermath of War*, London: I. B. Taurus.
Barakat, S. (2005b) 'Post-war Reconstruction and Development: Coming of Age,' in S. Barakat (ed.) *After the Conflict: Reconstruction and Development in the Aftermath of War*. London: I. B. Taurus.

Beazley, O. (2007) 'A Paradox of Peace: the Hiroshima Peace Memorial (Genbaku Dome) as World Heritage,' in N. Schofield and W. Cocroft (eds) *A Fearsome Heritage: Diverse Legacies of the Cold War*, California: Left Coast Press.

Bevan, R. (2006) *The Destruction of Memory, Architecture at War*, London: Reaktion Books.

Chamberlain, K. (2005) *War and Cultural Heritage: an Analysis of the Hague Convention for the Protection of Cultural Property in the Event of Armed Conflict*, London: Institute of Art & Law.

Forty, A. and Küchler, S. (2001) *The Art of Forgetting*, Oxford: Berg.

Khan, M. I. (2007) *History of Srinagar 1846–1947: A Study in Socio-cultural Change*, Srinagar: Gulshan Books.

Kirshenblatt-Gimblett, B. (1998) *Destination Culture: Tourism, Museums and Heritage*, London: University of California Press.

Langenbach, R. (1982) 'India in Conflict: Urban Renewal Moves East,' *Preservation*, Vol. May/June: 46–51.

Langenbach, R. (2007) *Guidelines for Preserving the Earthquake-Resistant Traditional Construction of Kashmir*, Delhi: UNESCO.

Logan, W. (2008) 'Cultural Diversity, Heritage and Human Rights', in B. Graham and P. Howard (eds) *The Ashgate Research Companion to Heritage and Identity*, Aldershot: Ashgate, pp. 439–49.

Stanley-Price, N. (2007) 'The Thread of Continuity: Cultural Heritage in Postwar Recovery,' in N. Stanley-Price (ed.) *Cultural Heritage in Postwar Recovery*, Rome: ICCROM.

UNESCO (2005) *Vienna Memorandum on World Heritage and Contemporary Architecture – Managing the Historic Urban Landscape*, Paris.

Wijesuriya, G. (2007) 'The Restoration of the Temple of the Tooth Relic in Kandy: a Post-conflict Cultural Response to Loss of Identity,' in N. Stanley-Price (ed.) *Cultural Heritage in Postwar Recovery*, Rome: ICCROM.

Winter, T. (2007) *Post-Conflict Heritage, Postcolonial Tourism: Culture, Politics and Development at Angkor*, London: Routledge.

Zetter, R. (2005) 'Land, Housing and the Reconstruction of the Built Environment,' in S. Barakat (ed.) *After the Conflict: Reconstruction and Development in the Aftermath of War*, London: I. B. Taurus.

Zutshi, C. (2003) *Languages of Belonging: Islam, Regional Identity, and the Making of Kashmir*, Delhi: Permanent Black.

Index

eBooks – at www.eBookstore.tandf.co.uk

A library at your fingertips!

eBooks are electronic versions of printed books. You can store them on your PC/laptop or browse them online.

They have advantages for anyone needing rapid access to a wide variety of published, copyright information.

eBooks can help your research by enabling you to bookmark chapters, annotate text and use instant searches to find specific words or phrases. Several eBook files would fit on even a small laptop or PDA.

NEW: Save money by eSubscribing: cheap, online access to any eBook for as long as you need it.

Annual subscription packages

We now offer special low-cost bulk subscriptions to packages of eBooks in certain subject areas. These are available to libraries or to individuals.

For more information please contact webmaster.ebooks@tandf.co.uk

We're continually developing the eBook concept, so keep up to date by visiting the website.

www.eBookstore.tandf.co.uk

Related titles from Routledge

Places of Pain and Shame
William Logan and Keir Reeves

Places of Pain and Shame is a cross-cultural study of sites that represent painful and/or shameful episodes in a national or local community's history, and the ways that government agencies, heritage professionals and the communities themselves seek to remember, commemorate and conserve these cases – or, conversely, choose to forget them.

Such episodes and locations include: massacre and genocide sites, places related to prisoners of war, civil and political prisons, and places of 'benevolent' internment such as leper colonies and lunatic asylums. These sites bring shame upon us now for the cruelty and futility of the events that occurred within them and the ideologies they represented. They are however increasingly being regarded as 'heritage sites', a far cry from the view of heritage that prevailed a generation ago when we were almost entirely concerned with protecting the great and beautiful creations of the past, reflections of the creative genius of humanity rather than the reverse – the destructive and cruel side of history.

Why has this shift occurred, and what implications does it have for professionals practicing in the heritage field? In what ways is this a 'difficult' heritage to deal with? This volume brings together academics and practitioners to explore these questions, covering not only some of the practical matters, but also the theoretical and conceptual issues, and uses case studies of historic places, museums and memorials from around the globe, including the United States, Northern Ireland, Poland, South Africa, China, Japan, Taiwan, Cambodia, Indonesia, Timor and Australia.

Hb: 978-0-415-45449-0
Pb: 978-0-415-45450-6

Available at all good bookshops
For ordering and further information please visit:
www.routledge.com

Related titles from Routledge

Intangible Heritage
Edited by Laurajane Smith and Natsuko Akagawa

This volume examines the implications and consequences of the idea of 'intangible heritage' to current international academic and policy debates about the meaning and nature of cultural heritage and the management processes developed to protect it. It provides an accessible account of the different ways in which intangible cultural heritage has been defined and managed in both national and international contexts, and aims to facilitate international debate about the meaning, nature and value of not only intangible cultural heritage, but heritage more generally.

Intangible Heritage fills a significant gap in the heritage literature available and represents a significant cross section of ideas and practices associated with intangible cultural heritage. The authors brought together for this volume represent some of the key academics and practitioners working in the area, and discuss research and practices from a range of countries, including: Zimbabwe, Morocco, South Africa, Japan, Australia, United Kingdom, the Netherlands, USA, Brazil and Indonesia, and bring together a range of areas of expertise which include anthropology, law, heritage studies, archaeology, museum studies, folklore, architecture, Indigenous studies and history.

Hb: 978-0-415-47397-2
Pb: 978-0-415-47396-5

Available at all good bookshops
For ordering and further information please visit:
www.routledge.com